post impressions

a travel book for tragic intellectuals

hollis taylor

Published by Twisted Fiddle
P.O. Box 4666
Portland OR 97208-4666 USA

Thanks to all the voices who shared their recollections and reflections
with us. Additional thanks go to Penny Allen, Charlotte Cox, and
Elizabeth and Robert Lynch for supporting the project.

National Library of Australia Cataloguing-in-Publication Data:

Taylor, Hollis, 1951- .
Post impressions : a travel book for tragic intellectuals.

Bibliography.
ISBN 9780646471747 (pbk. + DVD).

1. Music - Australia. 2. Australia - Description and
travel. I. Rose, Jon, 1951- . II. Title.

919.404

Cover photograph: Twin Lakes, NSW by Jon Rose

Back photograph: Sand dune in the Strzelecki Desert, SA by Jon Rose

Additional photography and video: Jon Rose and Hollis Taylor

The bonus DVD is PAL coded.
Cross-platform media players are available, such as at
www.videolan.org/vlc/

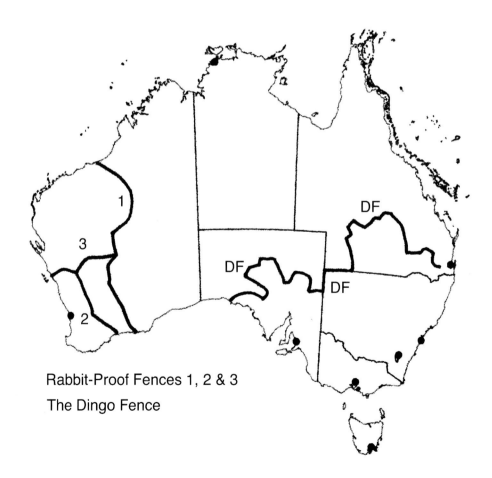

Rabbit-Proof Fences 1, 2 & 3

The Dingo Fence

T here's someone you should meet, KB told me in Paris. Jon Rose—

he's this wild virtuoso who plays the violin like nobody else, makes bizarre violins, invents stuff. He's Australian, but he lives in Berlin. This guy's all over the map, even founded his own violin *museum*—I mean he's Mr. Violin.

A violinist myself, I was intrigued. I wrote a letter asking to interview this Jon Rose for a music magazine. I took a November train and a warm coat. When he opened his Kreutzberg loft door, a shock of prematurely grey hair framing Cary Grant bone structure greeted me. He had factor. He also had the horned-rimmed glasses and the worn and wrinkled clothes of a tragic intellectual. I read it right in one glance and determined to resist it: *un coup de foudre.*

Would you like a coffee? he asked.

No, thanks, I only drink water or wine. Water will do.

There's plenty of wine. There are concerts here in this room, and there's always wine.

It's a little early … [I was distracted by the six violins hanging above the grand piano on the wall behind him: blue, white, green, and original in color, one had a sitar-like neck, another had double necks sharing a violin body, and yet another consisted of two violin bodies sharing a neck, Siamese twins of a sort.]

We settled on wine.

After six years in separate cities with separate lives, the two of us decided to travel together. We began with the obvious (to Jon): bowing fences, trading in the devil's box for the devil's rope.

I first saw Jon concoct a musical fence at a Berlin arts festival. Although indoors, his construction passed for a standard five-wire stock barrier, beginning with a barbed top strand, but the careful eye stopped at the second that was really five-in-one, a platform of closely strung wires forming a 75–foot long Hawaiian guitar. The lower three strands were again straightforward, the bottom wire sitting just an inch off the floor. Jon stamped on it with both feet as he moved along, giving new meaning to the term "walking bass." He bowed the fence and even violined it, meaning he ran an upside-down violin along the length of wire. Melody did not figure in his bold exploration of bare wire sounding out a broadband drone. Clearly an avant-garde activity, I thought.

Two years later in the outback of Western Australia, he mesmerized the local folks one Easter morning by bowing a rusty sheep station (ranch) fence. I began to reconsider this obsession of his— perhaps bowing fences is not so outlandish, and together we erected one in Paris for a techno and DJ crowd half our age that claimed it as their own. Who is the fence audience? I don't know what to think. Neither do my friends. Cajun fiddler Michael Doucet has convinced himself and others that my partner is named Bob Wire.

Are you hung up on Bob Wire? he emails.

Playing a fence is so out there! says Lana.

Yes, in fact the sound travels down the wires for hundreds of feet on straight stretches of a simple five-wire fence.

Hasn't bowing fences been overdone? Tim teases.

Jon began bowing fences in 1983 as an extension of his experimental instrument making. He puts it this way:

The wind is our universal musician and has been recognized as such for millennia. Twenty-five years ago I had an epiphany in outback New South Wales: if the wind could play a fence as an aeolian harp, then as a violinist armed with a bow I could also cause these gigantic structures to sing. Strings function in a similar way, whether the string is 20 inches, 20 feet, or 20 yards long. You could say that a string is a string is a string.

However, size does matter. Usually, a string is a trigger for a resonating chamber such as a violin. In a fence the string can be so long that it becomes the resonator as well as the trigger. What is happening at one end of a fence wire will often sound quite different to the sonic story at the other end.

Playing fences reveals a sound world that is embedded in the physical reality and the psyche of our culture. It's a language that speaks directly to us if we are prepared to listen.

Australia is full of collapsing and dysfunctional fences. Gravity gets its way in the end. Some fences just fall over and die; others are eaten by the saltpans in which they stand. Lonely fence posts, unattached, unstrung, dot the landscape.

FIRST FENCE TRIP.

At the moment, I'm trying to get to Australia. Travel rule number one: itineraries are mere wish lists. Like any improvisation, a voyage will find its own rhythm. All intentions, gestures, buffers, and rigor are futile—a fool's errand. Meet your fool, clinging to her strict itinerary, having uncharacteristically planned a trip without wiggle room.

After landing in Sydney within an hour of each other (me from Portland, Oregon and Jon from Amsterdam), we must immediately pick up the rented campervan and be off. First stop: The Adelaide Festival for his concert; then we'll continue on round the continent. Prone to road rage, he no longer drives. As chauffeur, I'll have two days to get him, rested, across the thousand miles from Sydney to Adelaide. It all needs to come together, and it should because I've thought and rethought of everything. Surely it's foolproof.

On the drive to the airport, I finger my beloved lists. A comprehensive and completed list is the best insurance policy, and it's free. I rely on lists to paper over the cracks of life's slippery destiny. I'll just make another check for my computer, wallet, ticket, passport, visa—Oh my God! oh no! oh noooooo! but *yes*, my Australian visa expired last week the expiration date right at the top it's three years from now but ohhh God! that's for my passport not for my visa look again it can't be what's it doing on the *top* line okay okay if I can just get to Australia maybe they will accept me the van is prepaid and Jon doesn't drive how could this happen his concert impossible to wait stateside four or five days for a new visa maybe if I can avoid early check-in at LAX yes I'll present myself at the gate for last minute boarding don't give them time to check my visa calm posture smile blonde—not a terrorist—yes it worked but now 14 hours of dread LAX to SYD who is the saint for lost causes if I could reach my mother she would pray on that direct red line of hers now finally Australian Immigration here we go smile again but not too brightly but no that was stupid to get in the woman's line they are always more efficient and rule-bound yes she'll check every detail of course she will.

Good morning.

G'day.

Naturally, it didn't work. She's sent me to wait outside this office with the illegal, the shady, the unwanted and uninvited, those with no return tickets and those with return tickets but no intention of returning. I see my bags circling down there, just steps away from this losers' lobby.

Je ne me souviens plus d'où je viens. I don't remember where I'm from—this is what my former French teacher Véronique trains her illegal third-world students to say when the French police want to repatriate them, but my accent and my American passport betray me. This phrase could be of better use to another of the detainees. I feel immediate camaraderie with them, all people of color, although my color is the palest shade of white I've ever been, my spirit a crumpled map of my fading trip.

Finally, it's determined to issue me a visa on the spot and fine the airline $5000 for letting me on the flight, in keeping with the age-old dictum "Punish the innocent." Forsaking my comrades with a twinge of guilt, I roll past the checkpoints to Jon. Time for a kiss but none for jet lag. We pick up the van and set off in the rain.

Kangaroos, emus, and parrots the unnatural color of cheap felt tip pens are quick to announce themselves. We stop at the side of the road after six hours of driving, across from the sign SHIRE OF BLAND. It's a misnomer. Our 360-degree view is anything but dull.

Both sides of J. M. W. Turner present themselves: the early, more literal landscape painter shows up in the astonishing detail of the tall gum trees I'm seeing as if I were suddenly given back my ten-year-old eyes (and the clean, crisp air of those days), each distant leaf outlined in silver by the crystalline light—all this set onto the later, impressionist Turner's power-of-light sky, a dozen shades of grey tinted with sunset colors, the whole panorama awash, a show. The mind delights in contrasts, the brain is hard-wired for opposites, and I am fully alive.

Tonight we dine alfresco. A bottle of Seppelt's Fleur de Lys *méthode champenoise* (marking Jon's fiftieth birthday the week before) accompanies avocado halves with olive oil, salt, and a dash of cayenne, then peanut butter and Vegemite sandwiches. Part gastronomes, part backpackers. I improvise a shower, and we fall asleep to the dense, pulsing presence of cicadas.

Eight hours later dawn is almost upon us. I intend to slip out for another alfresco event of a more personal nature but can't see well enough. Jon accompanies me with a flashlight only to find that our private roadside is actually a popular truck stop. Before we fell asleep, we noticed these benign space ships zooming by with their netherworld searchlights, but in our jet-lagged state we never heard a one pull in. Now in the 5:30 a.m. half light, we can make out at least eight parked trucks. I perform posthaste, with every hope that the truckers are still asleep, and then we make our getaway.

A thick mist impedes the daylight, as if dawn was announced but then failed to take center stage. The world is at 30 percent, receding from us no matter how I try to overtake it in the van. When the resolution achieves 100 percent, the wet red soil briefly dominates, but as the sun kicks in, drawing up the mist and searing all it touches, the shift is to bleached watercolor tints. I always figured rain made for a dull day, sun for a bright one. We're upside down here.

We drive past numerous pink salt beds, dry crystal "lakes" as they call them. Mirages, all. Who is the lighting designer for this continent? He's got crew everywhere fooling, tinkering, and rearranging, and he's throwing me off balance. With art I willingly suspend disbelief. In a masterly portrait, even as I marvel at the sheen of satin, the folds of silk, the delicacy of lace, or the depth of velvet, on approaching closely I expect the fabric to break up and be seen for what it always was, mere marks. Backing up, closing in—I can play this video again and again, this bewitching and disenchanting.

But when the sun has withdrawn all delicacy and my eyes clearly see a lake (a vision encouraged by the knowledge that the object in question is named "Lake _____")—it's not art but nature, so it must be real. I read that occasionally these lakes do fill with water, like today, but again and again we close in on nothing but a heat-hazed, light-laced, shimmering sea of disillusion. Small wonder that one salt lake is named after something that loomed larger in its discoverer's mind than his own name, Lake Disappointment.

It's only our second day, but already I tumble to the fact that gas stations are limited. I *must* stop each time. The needle sags lower than low as we cross the isolated Hay Plains in the heat of the day, arriving in Hay on fumes and a prayer to Asphalta who can find me parking places but is heretofore untested with gas stations.

Coming from the Pacific Northwest, I'm always surprised by a treeless landscape; it puts me on edge. Here the sky is so big, the land so flat, nothing with the possible exception of being at sea could compare. Oregon is with me often as I begin to explore this continent, providing comparisons and contrasts, bringing references of every sort. As we drive by these long fences, I remember guitarist Mason Williams quipping while our banjo player tuned onstage that the banjo is only one step above the barbed-wire fence on the evolutionary ladder. I smiled every time, not even bothering to figure how many steps above it my violin must be. It was just a joke. You couldn't coax a sound from a fence.

I'm not alone. People cannot imagine the sound, except Jon. For most of us, an object is an end in itself, an answer. For him, an object is something affixed with a question, and a well-formed question inevitably generates a burst of creativity from him. All the better if he can get a number of questions rubbing up against each other in a sea of ambiguity—his brain is a parallel processing machine *par excellence.* To uncover beauty in unexpected places, to tickle (some would say irritate) the borders of the imagination, to violate expectations—these are his inclinations.

Playing a fence proposes new ways of looking at things for the audience and for us. Although we have a few ideas from all the fences we have played, ones we have made and others we have come upon, fences differ sonically quite significantly from one another. Violins also have a range of sound quality, but not nearly that of their longer string cousins.

Cello and bass bows, both hair and stick, bring out the fence song and dance, although we've been known to employ found objects such as stones and bones. The acoustic sound of a fence varies, from scarcely audible to as loud as a violin. We rely on small contact microphones stuck into the wooden posts to amplify our efforts.

In bowing fences, accident, improvisation, and intuition take over. (This assumes 90 years of collective experience wielding bows.) Luck can surface, and we go to great efforts to encourage it. We play barbed-wire fences—the barbs add a jingle. We play electric fences that click click click. They also send a signal up your arm, which I reserve for Jon. We excite (the technical term for making a string vibrate) taut fences and slack ones, new and old.

We occasionally put percussion instruments to wooden fences, which can be difficult. Due to nonstop traffic noise, we rarely record in a city before midnight. Then, Jon will play these fences while I keep watch for aggravated residents or police. Imagine our parents reading the record cover: Jon Rose, fence; Hollis Taylor, midnight watch. It's not what our costly lessons or youthful talent promised.

We're here to play, record, and photograph every fence that takes our fancy, cartographers making a sonic map of the great fences of Australia.

Stop! Stop! Stop! Jon shouts.

We just passed some fence workers and turn around for a better view and a hopeful interview. The blokes assent, so Jon slips a few contact microphones into their fence-in-progress.

So can you just tell us what you're doing right now?
Well, I'm just tying a wire off on a five-wire fence.
When was the last time this was done?
When the fence was built, probably 80-odd year ago.

And that's about how long they last?

Yeah, I s'pose, roughly.

Do you figure out how many miles you're gonna do, or do you just buy a whole lot of materials and wait 'til it runs out?

Well, the blokes here want us to do 20 miles, that's how you work it out, by the distance, we done about a quarter mile so far today, about to start another quarter.

So you'd reckon on doing a half mile a day?

Uh, we can't quite roll it.

So there's three of you on it, you're a regular fence business, people just call you up?

Yeah, contractors.

You'll never run out of work?

Oh, there's plenty of them, it's just that people can't afford to do it nowadays.

What does this fence keep in or out?

Stock, mainly sheep country out here, this property is the biggest privately-owned property in the southern hemisphere, there's over 600 mile of boundary fencing alone, that's without internal fences.

Maybe you'd like these headphones to hear your fence better.

(The fence worker dons the headphones and begins tentatively: a casual flick, a cautious pluck, an inquiring tap. He pauses, and then he really goes for it. In fact, he's going nuts. He kicks it. He whacks it. He won't stop—it's a bravura performance. Ten minutes later, he looks up with a smile of sonic contentment.)

Now what are you doing?

This is the dropper.

So that's the vertical section. To put a dropper in takes you about …three seconds. So this is the sound of the dropper going in. [Metal striking metal, echoing and reverberating ad infinitum.] Excellent.

No worries.

Thanks a lot, guys.

Back on the road, I'm sizing up the range of sounds you can draw out of a five-wire fence; it staggers the mind. It can mimic most any instrument from any family: string, percussion, woodwind …even an avant-garde jazz trumpeter blowing burp-squeak-fart music to an audience of three in one of those alternative spaces. In turns ethereal and explosive, playful and plaintive, atmospheric and angular—the fence manages all this without electronic effects. An amplified acoustic fence can easily outplay a synthesizer going to town; this country cousin can pretend city ways. The sound hangs in the balance between nature and artifice.

We're not exactly "outback" by Australian standards but certainly "out there" in North American or European terms. At one point you reach a kind of radiophonic Bermuda Triangle: the strangest things start to happen on the car radio. While traveling this road in 1980, I heard ABC radio stations from three states competing for the same frequency on the dial, breaking into each other's broadcast one after the other. At one stage there were three guys trying to tell me what the time was, which was three different times, of course.

Soon, it's time to call it a day. We pull off the main road and head up a gravelly one. It's slow progress following a sign to the campgrounds at Crosbie Lake (lake meaning salt crystal mirage, Jon reminds me, for in my heat-induced state I had begun to envisage a cool dip before dinner). Agitated yellow jackets are also reacting to the heat when we stop. I move the van to another campsite, and then we venture out for a walk on the lake. Or are we on a pale pink moon? I take my first tentative steps. The salt lake is smooth but not too slick to walk on, solid but delicate. I worry I might leave footprints on its pristine crust. When I look up, I see kangaroos hopping and bounding in the hills around us.

> An unpainted shearing shed floating on its shadow in a paddock, moored to the homestead by the slack line of a fence. It almost goes without saying the land is laced with wire. The straight line is immediately sharply human.[1]

Adelaide! I've pulled it off. We check into our motel and set about exploring Queen Adelaide's namesake. Squeezed between mountain ranges and the sea, the well-planned colonial city is aligned in a rectangular grid pattern and counts five squares as the basis for its downtown. OR-der! Or-DER! It's an earnest place without a drop of convict blood, a triumph of the systematic and correct, an ideal place to raise a family, levy taxes, or conduct a census. Combine this shipshapedness with the early colonists' generous use of stone in their buildings and you have what, without being an architecture buff, I can best describe as the England-is-our-motherland style. It's all heritage charm. I wonder if this historic bearing also hints at a collective pretense, nostalgia, or insecurity in its founders. Is "home" still

---

[1] Bail, Murray (1998) *Eucalyptus*, Melbourne: Text Publishing, 91-92.

England? Does the crown still give courage? Does the prospect of a royal visit continue to validate and frame Adelaidian lives in some way? Perhaps we'll find out tomorrow when she arrives. We just saw a poster: Elizabeth II begins with a visit to the local Corgie dog club.

Jon turns in his Adelaide Festival performance, The Hyperstring Project. Violinist as one-man band sounds straightforward enough, but nothing he does is.[2] "Hyperstring pushes the envelope of musical expression through the use of MIDI controllers measuring the physicality of high-speed improvisation," reads the rave. "The subconscious intelligence of physical actions determines contrapuntal sonic events." You won't find yourself on hold as Hyperstring accompanies "Your call is important to us …"

From Adelaide we head to Port Augusta and the Flinders Ranges, Jon nixing my suggestion to visit the strangely named town of Coober Pedy. We drive through a paint box: first, Indian red soil, ultramarine South Sea, and summer blonde fields. Just out of Port Augusta primary colors cede to secondaries. The soil shocks in orange and pink while the mountains swell up in purple and blue-brown. In nature unlike my wardrobe, all greens work together. Speckled, textured …now cool greens and blues …no, the orange is back. Past light-enhancing silver tones and light-killing chalky ones. I see orange and cherry creamsicle colors, and in this heat I'm longing for its ice cream bar equivalent. Outlining, shapeshifting, color hijacking—the lighting crew's at it again.

I turn my attention to the grill, which protects the windshield and makes a good view of the road harder work than it should be. An assortment of dead insects worthy of a fly tyer's workbench is collecting. The splendor of the butterflies steals the show, but we also gather honeybees (I'm sorry) and yellow jackets (I'm not), dragonflies and mayflies of delicate transparent wings and filaments, and an assortment of severed legs and wings. It's a violent display of gaudy tinsel and glitter.

---

[2] An early experimental instrument of Jon's, the 19-String Violin, just had too many strings— hence he had to move on to fences. Begun as a violin on a frame, this instrument was bolted to a tripod and amplified in stereo, with strings going over, through, and around it much like a violin caught in a spider's web. In a perpetual state of experimentation, the instrument was the beneficiary of old cello strings, guitar strings, piano wire, any string or wire to hand. Jon stopped adding strings after the total reached 19.

How did you know to stop there?

In the same way that an abstract expressionist knows when a painting is cooked. I started with the idea of making the violin self-supporting. By putting it on a frame, my hands were freed up from any instrument support role, so I could move all over and around the instrument. When I took the instrument to London in 1980, someone thought it interesting enough to steal.

Image at http://www.jonroseweb.com/d_picts_19_str_violin.html.

For the moment, every 15 miles tosses upon the landscape an identical wheat silo, save that some preside over one-horse towns while others are the only show in town. Who minds these giant cylinders, these lonesome portions of geometry we whiz by?

Near Penong we come across a group of 17 windmills. It's a windmill convention, a theme park for—well, just for the likes of us, I suppose. Being studious tourists, we look for a clue to put it in perspective. Jon moves out to survey the sound potential, recording as he goes. The wind, the primary nutrient for the mills, is an irritant to the sensitive equipment. Eventually, he stuffs the microphones up his shirt. Each windmill has its own slurping soundprint.

The sun flickers and begins to close its treasure chest for the day. A few final gold coins flash, signaling their escape and suggesting ours, although we're still trying to figure out the windmills' purpose and why the choir of them when they usually perform solo. There's no sign of stock. The pumps feed a few pipes, which empty into several troughs. "As lonely as a nail on a post ..."[3] wrote D. H. Lawrence, but "snail" is also fitting. The sole inhabitants of the site are hundreds of snails, dead or alive we cannot tell, stuck to the remains of an ancient tongue-and-groove fence, its posts and laterals as thick as an Aussie bloke's torso. It's impossible to say what this endeavor is for.

Windmill at Penong

The morning tiptoes in, all pastel except parrots whose plumage shocks in the rich hues of satin evening gowns. This pageant is of little interest to Jon, who is well on his way to becoming a fence nerd. He is anticipating Yalata and our arrival at the Dingo Fence[4], about an hour away as near as he can tell.

[3] Lawrence, D.H. (1923/1960) Kangaroo, New York: The Viking Press, 102.
[4] It is believed that the dingo (*Canis lupus familiaris dingo*) is the ancestor of all dog breeds. Although not native to Australia, the dingo is variously estimated to have arrived between 3500 and 6000 years ago. The oldest dingo fossil has been carbon dated at 3450 years, the approximate time at which rock engravings of dingoes appear in Aboriginal art.

Whatever its origins, the dingo was a highly valued companion to the Aborigines. They took puppies from wild litters each breeding season. Dingoes lived, ate, and hunted with their human keepers; they served as bed warmers, camp cleaners, hunting companions, and guard dogs.

It's the world's longest man-made structure, he rattles off, traversing 3300 miles across three states, well more than twice as long as the Great Wall of China.

I've been slow to warm to it. This Fence doesn't figure on most maps, and when it does, it's a vague dotted line progressing in fits and starts as if the unsure hand of its cartographer had erased the displeasing bits, or as if some parts of it flow through prohibited areas under state censorship. It's downright un-American, this subtlety. Where are the T-shirts, the bragging billboards? Who will write its tourist text? If the Dingo Fence does not command a sign, a shop, or a TV screen, I won't believe a word of it.

As we roll over a grid, Jon shouts, Back up! Back up!

Something clicked in his brain: grid=fence. Yes, it's here, well before we expected it. We pull down a steep gravel embankment and get out for an inspection. Its six feet of wire mesh conclude with six inches of rabbit netting embedded in the ground. Warning signs hang from it: KEEP OUT, PERMISSION REQUIRED, DANGER: POISON (1080 poison is used along the Fence for lacing dingo baits). Jon never bothers obtaining permission. This will not even slow him down.

The Fence spans both sides of the highway, not so much interrupted by as continued by the unusual grid, a massive framework of widely spaced, narrow metal bars about 10 feet long. I can barely walk on it; clearly it's meant to stop something more agile and wily than cattle. When the heavy trucks roll over it, the grid rings out like a symphonic gong. Jon records every truck for 20 minutes and then performs a drum solo on the grid with sticks and brushes. Next, he plays the attached fence, which the grid amplifies as well. Farther down, we improvise a double bow solo on the dusty, barbed Fence proper.

First Grid at the Dog Fence

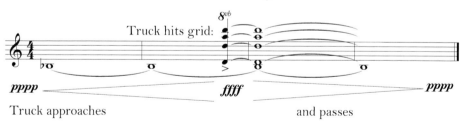

After recording, Jon wanders across the road and out of sight. On his return he reports coming upon some workers repairing a bulldozer.

They're laying down a fiber-optic cable linking Western Australia to the eastern half of the continent, so they're cutting under the Fence. You know this main road was only sealed in 1976; before that it was just a track,

Hmm. What else did they have to say?

Well, I asked one bloke if this was in fact the Dingo Fence, but he looked at my sandals and shorts and countered, "Haven't you ever heard of the death adder?" Evidently the place is crawling with them.

Right about now I realize how perfectly content I can be in the swelter of the campervan reading up on Dingo Fence history while Jon tramps around taking photos

In Queensland they call it the Barrier Fence, the New South Wales section is referred to as the Border Fence, and in South Australia they call it simply the Dog Fence. In its entirety, it is known as the Dingo Fence. The structure divides the eastern states from the deep outback, cutting and winding across most of the continent.

Over 100 years ago the Fence consisted of sections of perimeter fencing designed to thwart the invasion of the introduced rabbit. As with the Rabbit-Proof Fence in Western Australia, rabbits soon ate their way into South Australia and New South Wales. For Queensland, it was different. The Fence *did* stop the rabbits' northerly migration, and they perished in the millions against its barrier.

This "rabbit" fence was also successful in excluding kangaroos, emus, pigs, and brumbies (wild horses), but most significant for sheep farmers was the fence's ability to keep packs of dingoes outside their grazing properties. Efforts then turned to tailoring the fence as a dingo repellent. It was built at great cost to protect the richest sheep and cattle area west of the Dividing Range. When it does figure on a map, it's all zigging zags and bulging loops.

Maintaining the Fence is an expensive proposition but still considered a worthwhile one. Floods send debris against the Fence, which takes a toll. Even *repelled* animals can have a detrimental effect. Rabbits burrow under, weakening wooden posts and exposing the soil to erosion. Emus will pound along the fence line in their search for water, often crushing the bottom wire with their strong toes. Kangaroos moving at full speed can fail to see the mesh, punching holes as they crash into it. Wild pigs and dingoes rely on brute force, pushing, squeezing, and digging their way through.

Today I don't see a single animal at the Fence, but I do see Jon returning. It's time to push on. I survey the obstacles to getting the awkward van up onto the main road. It's a steep incline littered with potholes, big rocks, and loose gravel. Jon stands outside directing, encouraging, and when my confidence begins to fail, insisting. I make a run for it, and we're headed for the wilds now, dingo country.

The fence appears to be working. Within half an hour of departing the Dingo Fence, we see two dogs on their allowed side. The first is roadkill, while the second awaits roadkill for his afternoon meal. His coat is shiny and healthy, his frame lean but not skinny. With pointed ears and a white-tipped tail setting off his toasted golden-brown color, he's a live-wire dynamo. Back and forth along the road this "wild" dog taunts us with photo-ops; we snap away until we get an acceptable close-up.

As we continue, the terrain turns an increasingly desolate face to us. The stingy earth yields nothing but saltbush, bluebush, and the occasional patch of mallee scrub, our guidebook warns, but we find it more desolate than that. It's bare. *Formidable!* say the French to describe something extraordinary[5]—a soaring, expansive, or plunging terrain, say, or an intensely rich and colorful one. Being overwhelmed by the land's breadth and bounty is one thing, but being the tallest (by virtue of being the only) object in a desert is the most formidable. To say it is a dustbowl would imply some shape. There's no middle ground and barely a foreground. We see nothing but a flat stretch of parched earth, no visible means of support for even the occasional kangaroo roadkill. Still, in the desert struggle of sun versus life, some secret places must exist: a cave, a sinkhole … Clearly this land does not support narcissism. What do *you* think about me? It doesn't give a damn.

I press on, letting things add up in my mind. Words seem insignificant here, and the ambient noise of the van makes them not worth the effort. It's anathema to shout about something so subtle. Without the road, we'd have no bearings. Our drive through the unmediated and uncontainable unfolds in resolute uniformity. I'm grasping for hope, about to reinvent Monotheism. We've hit the Nullarbor Plain, an area four times the size of Belgium.

As recently as the 50s, this lonely track saw only a few vehicles per day. We don't see many more. Several are parked at The Nullarbor Roadhouse. Inhospitable though the terrain is, the local snakes appear to thrive. Oozing jars of faded, bloated coils line the gas station window.

I'll take a pickled jumbo to go, Jon quips as we walk by, and I shudder as if on command.

Next door, the cafe offers up meals served by an ex-pat British professor-type as waiter. He calls women, even strangers, "Dear." Under

---

[5] "Nature never indulges in exclamations—never says Ah! or alas! She is not of French descent," observed Henry D. Thoreau in his 1854 journal.

his spell, we can do no other than order fish & chips, although I embarrass Jon with my absolute need for ketchup—and not just a little.

Immediately outside of town, the road widens for several miles, accompanied by the sign R.F.D.S. With nothing better to do, we try to work it out. No idea.

A few miles later, Jon turns to me and shouts, Royal Flying Doctor Service!

Of course—it's their landing strip.

In the midst of the barren Nullarbor, signs announce the scenic lookouts of the Great Australian Bight, with eight roads to choose from. At Jon's urging, we take the second. To me it's just another dusty gravel track. I've never heard of the Bight and haven't an expectation in the world. A view of the ocean, I guess, just past the bleakest spot I've ever seen. I can't quite wrap my brain around it, and I've seen enough ocean views in my lifetime. I'm trying to make time on the main road.

I pile out dutifully. My first view is a close-up, a snake measuring several feet.

Don't worry about it. Look out there—it's straight to Antarctica, he encourages.

When I'm comfortable that I've put enough distance between me and serpent, I take it in. Or I try. What was from inland simply a parched plain becomes, when seen from land's end, a series of high, recessed cliffs scooped out of the coastline. This 125 miles of winding cliff face skirts a blue view, the sky and ocean hypnotizing in hues of Prussian, ultramarine, indigo, and cerulean. I sense these blues will be a measuring stick for years to come, archetypes of saturated color, and fix them on the blankest page of my memory.

As the landscape has grown harsher, so has the grill kill: big, hard black and ochre flying machines hit at regular intervals like golf balls without reverb. One is a Christmas beetle (*Anoplognathus pallidicollis*), which Jon tells me can bore through concrete. They stick and become part of our van. There are strict quarantine restrictions, but not so strict as to prevent our grill kill from coming on in, I note. At the South Australia/Western Australia border, as on the New South Wales/South Australia one, we give up all fruits and vegetables. Then we hit Eucla, population 45, which seems metropolitan after what we've been through. You could best describe it as a popular spot to …refuel.

We turn off on a dirt road, heading down toward the sea. EUCLA INTERNATIONAL AIRPORT says the tongue-in-cheek sign; all we see is a deteriorating shed. We've read about the 1877 telegraph repeater station, which was abandoned in 1929, and it sparked our interest. Set on finding our trophy, we park near the sea and trudge up and down white sand dunes until we spot some arching doorways and protruding chimneys. It's the station building all right, gradually succumbing to the dunes.

Back up on the main road, Jon plays and records the perimeter fence at the Telstra communications station despite, or perhaps because of, the Keep Out/Danger/High Voltage signs. Then, we're outta here—almost. The Eucla police must be test-driving a showroom demo with all those blinkers and lights flashing, not to mention the siren, or are they? There's no one around but us. Is Jon to be arrested for playing a fence this early in our trip? They can't be serious, but to be safe, I stop. The police take a look at our paperwork and send us on our way. I guess they just needed something to do with that new car, or maybe they saw a blonde in shades and wanted a closer look.

My eyes are hungry after their Nullarbor deprivation. Everything we encounter seems interesting beyond measure, including several more R.F.D.S. airstrips and kangaroo roadkill. At a gas station, I spot a dingo just up the road. I find even a solitary tree lit up with silver leaves worthy of a long look.

With so many big bugs on the grill, I suggest a mixed grill dinner. Jon plays along, offering to add them to his pasta dish. Instead, we pull out a sturdy German brown bread, a chunk of aged Romano, a round of Edith's goat cheese, and a cabernet from the house of Starvedog.

The kangaroo roadkill have become so frequent that we often have at least one in view. It's a war zone, and the winners are the wedge-tailed eagles *(Aquila audax)*. The largest of Australia's raptors, their wingspan can exceed six feet. We see one the size of a turkey standing by the road, then two in a tree waiting for us to pass so they can get back to dinner, and later three on roadkill. Once they've had their fill, they take flight only with difficulty.

From Caiguna to Balladonia, as if the view weren't bleak enough, the road sets course for a world-record 90–mile dead-straight stretch. The tedium is relieved coming into Balladonia where it's hopper season. Grasshoppers carpet the road and clog the air. I keep driving, crushing and killing as I go. We see a handful of small birds fluttering on the road, one pulling a dead or injured comrade. Then we encounter a billboard for the Eyre Bird Observatory, housed in a former telegraph station. A Haven for Twitchers, the sign says.

Let's check it out, I suggest.

We're here for fences, Jon reminds me, not feathers.

We now see so little traffic that whoever passes by gives us the high sign. Through the Dandus Nature Reserve, the palette is yellow and green trees with orange bark. Next we find orange-red soil, while the bark modulates within minutes from red-brown to whitish grey to olive green. Then stringy bark, smooth, or none at all. Into Norseman, we marvel at the crimson Mount Jimberlana.

It's not just colors that in my isolation and tedium are dominating. Songs, like other memories, reassert themselves from time to time. In fact, it's getting a bit much. All it takes to press the start button is the sight of a keyword like clouds: "I look at clouds from both sides now," hills: "are alive with the sound of music," or a sign for water: "cool, clear, water."

Waaaah-ter. The irritatingly catchy bits loop-the-loop in their truncated form, and I never even get through the whole tune.[6] Minimalist loops invented here, several decades too late. Every attempt to stop it is still that bit. Every attempt to at least run it through to the end of the tune is still only that bit. Every attempt to superimpose another preferable tune in its place is—it's just the jammed soundtrack to an inescapable bad dream. Wake up and press stop, my unconscious urges.

Read something to me.

Jon searches through the guidebook for the town of Norseman. A horse unwittingly made the first gold discovery here in the 1890s as it stumbled over a large nugget, he begins. Gold eventually gave way to quartz, and Norseman's reef is the richest in Australia …

After a brief lunch break, "On the Road Again" accompanies me through Salmon Gums where the local gum trees parade a fashionably pink bark, south to Esperance where—"I just can't wait"—two
immense
white, yellow, and rose
salt lakes straddle the road,
shockingly set against orange soil.
Their impossible beauty so overruns my faculties that no other sensory equipment remains intact enough to receive a tune.

W e stop for gas and a bit of local advice, knowing the Rabbit-Proof Fence is close. The local grocer is helpful if unimpressed by our mission and sketches a primitive map. We wind over back roads, up and down hills, now much further than he described—did we miss it, should we continue on or go back? Suddenly, there is the most glorious marker: RABBIT PROOF FENCE RD. We pull over to photo the sign, and as long as we're stopped, traipse around a bit. Several dingo skulls mounted on the post of an empty sheep corral are serving duty as death's-heads. A snake disputing the trail puts a kick in my step.

Back in the van, I try unsuccessfully to make the case to Jon that I wasn't *afraid* of the snake as such, but merely exercising a modicum of

---

[6] "Scientists call these ear worms, from the German *Ohrwurm*, or simply the stuck song syndrome," reports Daniel Levitin in *This Is Your Brain on Music*, (2006) New York: Dutton, 151.

circumspect vigilance. We head toward the sea on the Rabbit Proof Fence Road. Our contract with the campervan rental agency prohibits us from driving on unsealed surfaces. This one is nothing but, all gravel and corrugation, so I proceed cautiously. To proclaim it our manifest destiny to see this bit of fence would not skate with them. If we break down here, we bear the cost. Down to the wire …

After half an hour we see the Fence on our left doing double duty as a sheep barrier. As we set up to film and record, a stockman appears, acting like it's perfectly natural to be bowing an isolated fence in the outback heat. We want to trace it to the coast, we tell him, and he adds his local knowledge to our map. In all, we see three rabbits hopping at the bunny fence, wrong side.

No. 1 Rabbit-Proof Fence

Following a tedious corduroy of a drive, we stop in a primitive parking lot near the bay. The explorer Edward John Eyre, best remembered for his 1200-mile crossing of the Great Australian Bight and Nullarbor Plain in 1840–41, nearly died on this part of the rugged and unforgiving coastline known since then as Starvation Bay. Miraculously, a French whaling vessel rescued Eyre. Our time here is a bit more comfortable: a 1998 Jenke Barossa Cabernet served with roast pumpkin, sage, and Parmesan tagliatelle.

The next morning, we hike half an hour to Starvation Bay, and although the bay is obvious, the Fence is not. At last we find remnants of wire fencing, rusting metal posts still protruding from rocks, and a stone wall (marked by a plaque: Rabbit-Proof Fence 1901–2001) built straight into the sea. They really meant to stop those rabbits.[7]

---

[7] Wild grey rabbits *(Oryctolagus cuniculus)* were introduced by Thomas Austin of Geelong in 1859 for his hunting, and within 20 years Victoria was menaced. Work commenced on the Rabbit-Proof Fence. When it was completed in 1907, the Western Australia No. 1 Rabbit-Proof Fence was the longest unbroken line of fence in the world: 1139 miles from Starvation Boat Harbour on the south coast to a point near Cape Keraudren on the northwest coast.

The rabbits were eating their way west, and not even this great effort would stop the "grey blanket": as the 400 men worked, they could already see the rabbits on the wrong side of the fence, but being Anglo Saxons, they continued with their folly. (Nothing worked until the introduction of the *myxomatosis* virus in the twentieth century.)

From this remote and harsh bay on the Southern Ocean, the Fence stretches north across the continent to the Indian Ocean. For our photographic purposes, Jon undertakes a bit of reconstruction, dragging down ancient bits from the undergrowth of a hill some 50 yards away to the edge of the sea to connect them to the wall, a reënactment shall we say. After our shoot, he reburies them like any honorable fence-ologist. At water's edge, he records the extreme gurgles and splutters of a blowhole.

There's no way out for us but another wearisome drive down an unsealed washboard road. This time we choose the fork to Hopetoun, marked four-wheel-drive only, but two will have to do. And it does— just, alternating in texture between troublesome gravel and mud pie muck.

Once there, we spend the day making telephone calls. All told, there are eight legs of the Rabbit-Proof Fence. We want to see where the second one hits the ocean but definitely need a four-wheel-drive vehicle and a guide. The one ranger would gladly take us to Point Anne, but it's not his area. The ranger who could wants to go by the rules and have us buy a permit for $150. With a few more calls we locate Julianne Hill and arrange to meet her in Ravensthorpe at 6:30 the next morning to see her part of the Fence.

Because of the nocturnal habits of roos, I neither drive in the dark nor in the transitional twilight and dawn. This morning is an exception, and I'm watching for roo profiles on the narrow, winding road. The gum trees are thick here, and the chiaroscuro effect of light and shade makes me wary. But in life (and death, I imagine) it's never what you think, and just as I say I'm hoping not to hit a kangaroo, there's the small thud of a bird stunned by the grill.

Julianne's in a rush to begin her official day, so she loads us in her four-wheel-drive and off we head on a stock and mining road toward Carlingup ("water up there" in the Aboriginal language). An emu *(Dromaius novaehollandiae)* persistently runs alongside us.

They are a real danger, sometimes hitting a car, Julianne says [some might say us hitting them], and then hitting it again. They have a small head for a reason. [I notice she didn't once slow down for it.]

"Begun 1901, Completed 1907, Abandoned 1950," read the stats. To pass muster, the Fence was required to have posts 12 feet apart sunk one foot nine inches below, strainers every five chains, and netting dipped in coal tar to protect that portion below ground. The barb and plain wire were added later to make the Fence dingo- and fox-proof. It's currently known as the State Barrier Fence, but was previously known as the Rabbit-Proof Fence, the State Vermin Fence, and the Emu Fence and in these various transformations has reduced the encroachment of rabbits, wild dogs, emus, kangaroos, and other feral animals into pastoral areas.

A good source for both fact and local color is F. H. Broomhall's *The Longest Fence in the World: History of the No.1 Rabbit Proof Fence from its Beginning until Recent Times,* (1991) Victoria Park: Hesperian Press.

She brings us up to speed on this part of the Fence, the No. 1 Rabbit-Proof Fence's south leg. No longer for rabbits, it's being mended and rebuilt to repel emus and kangaroos who get caught in it and die; they can't be moved or rescued due to the strength of their back legs.

If you find them alive, you try to mercy-kill them with a hammer to the head, she explains.

The new Fence has moved from netting to larger squares and is no longer buried at the bottom. There's a wicked row of barb on top now, then a wire, and then the meshing. Like the Fence itself, those who worked on it had several names: fence runners, patrolmen, boundary riders, doggers. At their former camp we take stock of a makeshift waterworks: a hut with a steep, guttered roof for directing rainwater into barrels. Next to it is home-sweet-home, a galvanized iron hut locked in a cycle of wreckage and reassembly. Inside, a piece of piping dangles over a primitive fireplace, ready to receive a cooking pot (or billy, as it's called locally). A wire netting hammock hangs in the corner. A brown bottle with a scrap of attached wire is on the ground along with two former walls. A few rusty cans blend into the soil.[8] I have one friend who approaches all of life's challenges, big and small, with duct tape while another favors glue. Here wire served as both furniture and tool of choice, used in place of nails, string, and rope to hang, bind, and build. Man is not alone in this wisdom:

> Magpies are fond of wire, and why not? Wire nests last longer than nests made of sticks. Magpies search assiduously around barns and yards for good lengths of wire. One nest I know of was made from 243 strands with a total length of 100 metres. Cormorants have been known to use barbed wire.[9]

Jon positions Julianne in front of the hut, and while I take photos of the area, she tells her story.

My name is Julianne, and I work on the Rabbit-Proof Fence in Western Australia in the SW corner, my stretch of

---

[8] Whitefellas couldn't have taken over the outback without the tin can because they couldn't live off the land as they found it. In 1795 Napoleon offered a 12,000-franc prize for a method of preserving food for his armies. In 1810 a French confectioner, Nicolas Appert, won the prize for his work in sterlization methods. Meanwhile the same year in England, King George III awarded a patent to Englishman Peter Durand for a tin-plated iron can for food. Three years later the first commercial canning factory opened in England.

While the initial cans were so thick they had to be hammered open, as they got thinner a can opener was invented, and later a key-type opener for sardines came along. The climax for modern man was perhaps the 1935 appearance of the first beer in a can.

[9] Low, Tim (2003) *The New Nature*, Australia: Penguin Books, 11.

fence runs from Starvation Bay down on the coast up through to Hyden, we've been currently involved in replacing some of the Fence, we do about three percent each year on the whole length of the Fence, which is round about 730 miles, it finishes up on Zukdork Cliffs near Kalbarri, there are two legs inside that Fence, which were later put up after the rabbits had progressed through the first Fence, it's a bit of an ironic thing that you put the Fence up and the rabbits are already through it by the time it's finished.

We're standing right now next to Lindavila Doggers' Hut—say that when you're drunk—this is where they used to camp, they had camps every 25 or so miles along the Fence with water holes for the camels and horses.

One of the dangers of this end of the Fence was there were a lot of native 1080 gastrolovium poison plants that used to kill their camels and horses, for a while the Director of the Fence ordered the fence runners to ride on bicycles, which is a bit ludicrous when you think about it, they often had punctures, they shifted not long after that to four-wheel-drive vehicles, the practicalities of driving down the Fence on a bicycle always amused me.

The hut's a really rusty old building, one of our old doggers recently rebuilt it, they used to go out on six-month journeys from here to the coast, supplies for six months required a lot of pack animals and camels with drays, they were amazing people with a stamina I could only dream of.

The fair Julianne radiates energy and enthusiasm, proving you don't have to look like a mud fence to be a fence runner.

It was an all-bloke thing, I'm the first woman who has ever worked on the Fence, it would have been quite hard for women to be away for six months, it would have taken a very special breed of woman, and if they had family and children at home, that would have made it really tricky, at that time it was really frowned upon for a woman to run down the Fence with another guy.

A lot of them read books, and some of them didn't deal with the loneliness, as you've probably seen, there's suicides, there's murders, there's lonely graves—all this, about 60 miles up there's a little caged area off the Fence, nobody's ever been able to tell us what it is so we just assume it's an unnamed grave.

The Fence is an icon, I consider it to be a huge human achievement, and it's older than most of the buildings in this part of the world, a lot of it has been replaced, now it's into its second life, you can imagine being back there in those times, it's hard enough nowadays when you're here replacing fences, staying out here for a week or so at a time, having blisters and flies hovering around your face—to know what it was like for them for six months at a time and having to carry all this stuff and be so prepared.

You come through the Fence and think, I wonder what I'm gonna see today, what might I have to fix, and often there's dingo tracks or there's a kangaroo stuck in the Fence or there's emus piling up somewhere, there's always something different to look at.

A couple of years ago we drove up the Fence and there was this big break in the Fence with an airplane about 200 yards inside the Fence, we found out later that this guy had been crop dusting on a neighboring property, and he had taken off and had too full of a load to be able to miss the Fence so he ploughed right through it, the poor man, he must have been so scared—his plane was in bits and the Fence was wrecked.

People initially related to having a fence so they knew where the boundaries were, so they knew they were either inside the Fence or outside the Fence (if you were outside the Fence, then you were in no-man's-land), now the Fence is a really good aerial tool, it's a mapping device when you're flying ...there's still a sense of pride of ownership for people who are near it and on it, maybe not so much the southern end, but up north the people have a real pride—it's their Fence, you know.

> The fencer, a drifter like all his breed, had been pulled from the endless task of stringing taut wire between posts in the paddocks to repair the homestead's white pickets for the party.[10]

On the road from Lake King to Lake Grace, salt lakes keep popping up for miles, purest white to the left, almost khaki to the right. Then, an eggshell-blue lake insinuates itself against the crimson earth. Lakes alternate with deep violet bushes, then suddenly the bushes turn up *in* the salt lakes.

---

[10] McCullough, Colleen (1977/1978) *The Thorn Birds*, New York: Avon Books, 172.

Jon plays and records a fence past here, an electric one that shocks him. He likes the sound if not the feel, the steady snap-snap-snap of the current coursing through the wire.

But darling, it's powered by a 10-gallon drum of fermenting grapefruits, he enthuses.

Today we are looking for the third leg of the Rabbit-Proof Fence. We stop for photos of an ancient fence, likely the No. 3, where Jon observes that the wood has outlasted the metal. We pass another RABBIT PROOF FENCE ROAD sign before Dumbleyung, a place name ready made for a children's book. Jon records and shoots while I finish up *On the Beach*, Nevil Shute's best-selling novel about life in Australia after nuclear war. As the fallout drifts south, just a handful of people yet survive. Our subjects are in Melbourne, and the last days are near.

> "There'll be life in Melbourne long after we've gone…"
> "What life?" Peter asked.
> He grinned broadly. "The rabbit. That's the most resistant animal we know about …"
> The general pushed himself upright in his chair, his face suffused with anger. "You mean to say the rabbit's going to live longer than we do?"
> "That's right…"
> The general sank back in his chair. "After all we've done, and all we've spent fighting him—to know he's going to win out in the end!"[11]

Facing 50 days in this campervan, we've cut back to the basics of life (dinner will be a 1999 Robertson's Well Cabernet from Coonawarra with a Tex-Mex salad of borlotti beans, corn, avocado, and tomatoes, topped with cheese, black olives, and salsa), but even the basics we must fight for. We delay our meal for half an hour when the first few places we stop are overrun with biting ants. Jon gets fed up moving his hard-shelled "Big Yellow" suitcase in and out to make room for us at the table in the back of the campervan.

Here they come again. Put Big Yellow back inside.

We drive some more. The road narrows to one lane, forcing me to take my half down the middle. I don't slow down. If I'm going to make good time, I must accept the moments of panic when cars suddenly loom on the horizon surging toward us.

In Wubin we encounter a great flock of galahs *(Cacatua roseicapilla)* cutting an erratic pink route across the sky, wheeling in unison to grey, then pink, then grey. They land nearby, and their harsh "chirrink-chirrink" is a must-have for Jon. He tries to record them but fights the wind at every turn. He finally meets up with success in the women's public restroom, door propped open. Soon after, a woman

---

[11] Shute, Nevil (1957/1974) *On The Beach*, New York: Ballantine Books, 224-225.

approaches the door then steps aside, waiting patiently. Jon comes out wearing headphones and holding equipment, the ultimate nerd. The woman acts like this is perfectly normal.

Just after Wubin we stop to play The Trumpet Fence dividing end-of-summer wheat from bare red soil. We bow it until I notice two dead sheep nearby. The mood is squelched—plus I've lost an earring, my favorite. We comb the area for half an hour before it occurs to me that perhaps I had only put one on. I find its partner in the van.

A real gentleman will have no comment now, I suggest.

And he does not.

Trumpet Fence

A sign announces that truckers, "truckies" in Australian, can order a meal via their CB radio and have it ready when they hit Payne's Find Roadhouse, "in the golden heart of wildflower country." We were here last Easter for a nearby concert. The owner of the roadhouse, Tony, couldn't get away for it, and I'd heard he was disappointed. As we drove through afterwards, I walked in, fiddle in hand, and tossed off the "Cotton Patch Rag." Tony's jaw dropped. When he recovered, he gave me a book on the area's history.[12]

When we arrive this time, we tell the barwoman we'd like to see Tony.

He'll be back in a few, she says.

Jon orders a beer. Our barwoman looks dead poised over her coffee. We savor the air conditioning as we examine the antique equipment for tying horses to a lead mounted over the bar. The other walls are crowded with photos of people and their trucks. Our photo was taken last year, but we can't be bothered to look for it. With just a violin next to us instead of a semi-truck, we'd look wimpy. Here he is, all motion and talk: head rotating, knees flexed, feet set on springs. Tony welcomes us and begins holding forth, one hand on his stomach.

---

[12] Located 250 miles north of Perth, Payne's Find comprises a roadhouse and related outbuildings, a few palms, and several gas pumps, a three-pump sort of hesitation in the macadam, which widens enough to serve as an airstrip able to accommodate the Royal Flying Doctor Service. Although there was scattered pastoral settlement, when gold was discovered in 1911, a rush commenced. It collapsed and resurged several times, finally subsiding in the 50s.

We're rebuilding this place, it's gonna be big, goin' better all the time, I talk to the others in the area about tourism, but they don't understand, you gotta tell a story, it's nothin' without a story, there was this one kid walked into the bar with a sack of maybe a thousand gold nuggets worth 15 to 20 Australian dollars each, I immediately moved him to the corner table and talked business, I can handle it—my gold safe weighs three-quarter tons, I'm a switched-on guy ...

Indeed. His stories come fast and furious. He's hyperactive even in the heat, loaded with tales of deadly fights, suicides, and rock falls; bodies were laid out on a table in his cool cellar until the Perth undertaker could arrive. He claims to have a roo skeleton in place there now.

Let me drive you out to the Daffodil Gold Mine, he volunteers.

We assent and tank up on water. Of my own accord, I never walk in the noonday heat. My people are rain people for generations. Sunscreen, hat, long sleeves, more water. When we arrive, we're greeted by the only thing that will grow in this depleted soil, an overgrown garden of signs in their full flowering of negativity: NO VISITORS, POSITION CLOSED, DANGER: BLASTING NO ADMITTANCE, KEEP OUT, STOP, FOOT PROTECTION MUST BE WORN, HEAD PROTECTION MUST BE WORN, EAR PROTECTION MUST BE WORN, EYE PROTECTION MUST BE WORN, SEAT BELTS MUST BE WORN, PRIVATE ROAD, WARNING: ELECTRIC CABLES BURIED BELOW, GUARD DOGS ON PATROL, TRESPASSERS WILL BE PROSECUTED. Most signs *are* negative except those that want to sell something, and even those are suspect to Jon who spurns both rules and shopping. Neither a conformist nor a consumer he.

Holding himself above and beyond the jurisdiction of these signs, our Protector opens the gate without missing a word-beat of his banter and leads us in. We pass the makeshift office; there's no one working in this swelter. His dog dashes off to chase roos, looking for a romp and dinner, while Tony marches us down the road and into the open cut of the gold mine. With each descent into hell, it gets hotter. Round and round we go, hotter still, the earth modulating in color at succeeding depths: beginning nearly crimson, then red ochre—we stop periodically so I can rub soil samples onto a white page in my little spiral notebook—to burnt sienna.

God's own country, Tony marvels.

Dante's inferno, I'm beginning to feel, rubbing burnt umber and round again, down paler hot lighter flash of blood-red vessels back of eyes round rubbing in the white of sun flushed red-hot heartbeat jerk-shifts rhythms as ears hiss a high pitch round and ...

(Writer passes out.)

…round we circled above the parched expanse, hostages to the air pockets' chopping and changing whims, high over hallucinatory cinnabar and metallic green salt lakes trying to talk us down prematurely. It's been some years since anyone tried to get in here, worried our pilot out loud. The six-seater took a trial pass just a couple of yards above the primitive driveway about to do double duty as an airstrip. Our ground crew was tucked under an umbrella, sipping champagne with a proper ice bucket next to her. We circled again, and this time the pilot dropped the plane right on deck and parked it; then we helped him tie it down for the night.

That's how we met LJ, Our Lady of Bubbles, and her husband David at Wogarno Station in Western Australia's outback. Normally they run woolly-backs on these 152,000 acres of spectacular granite outcrops and breakaway country. It's the kind of place where they assign acres to a sheep rather than sheep to an acre (nothing so unusual in a country that figures two people per square kilometer). But on this Easter weekend they were hosts to our music festival, Violins in the Outback.

LJ tends a desert garden of people and animals. There's Jack, the seven-year-old blonde motorcycle kid of her close friend. He doesn't have a motorcycle; he *is* one. Wherever he needs to go, this kid rides. The dust and gravel fly under his bare feet as he paws in place, arms extended on imaginary handle bars, lips buzzing and spitting in a pivotal birth moment of the contemporary performance technique now known as The Extended Raspberry. Then he's off across the paddock. Although at these moments he is often the center of our attention, the others are used to the motorcycle him and don't seem to notice. He's not seeking attention—he inhabits another dimension. He will listen to you speak, you see him taking in your question, but since he *is* a motorcycle, he can only respond as above.

LJ is the local kangaroo equivalent of the Humane Society. She takes in orphaned joeys, raises them, and releases them back into the wild. She doesn't advertise this, and the expense is hers alone to bear. Sometimes she comes upon them; other times people drop them off, counting on her to dispense her love and care with largesse. She smiles, and you smile back. She offers you a glass of bubbles, and you accept. We can't say "no" to her.

Her husband David is away for a few more days. We meet him by eavesdropping as he talks to LJ on his remote radio. Click. Click.

Okay, we're out on the No. 1 Fence, just doing an inspection, heading north for the Sandstone-Meekathara run, over.

Yeah, a few little storms have gone through, but they haven't done any damage, it's cooled things off a bit, over.

Well, there was a coupla dog tracks padding along the fence, that's a bit of a concern for these guys on the east side, I would presume they'll come out and do something about it, I sent a message through to the secretary in Magnet, she's gonna contact them, over.

We've got another coupla days, we're going right up to the top end of the Fence, and we're doing a detailed survey for the MRVC so we've got another two nights out here before we'll be back, over.

When you get a chance, check the mills over on this side, over.

Yeah, we've got about five bundles of steel posts left and a heap of foot netting and we're just patching it up as we go, but I would expect that we would be able to get through to the top end of the Fence in the two, three days, so yeah, we've got plenty on board, over.

Yeah, well the alternative is not good, not having a fence, we'd be invaded by dingoes, and that's something we don't need here, we've got enough pests here now with rabbits and foxes, and we don't need dingoes chewing away at our sheep, over.

Well, that's good, absence makes the heart grow fonder, we'll talk again tomorrow night, cheers now. Click. Click.

Violins in the Outback was Jon's idea. For his part of the program, he took inspiration from visits to Chinese violin factories where he witnessed their peculiar style of violin mass production. They used a specially designed German steam press to stamp out 10 violins at a time, while every five seconds another machine haired and tightened up a bow in one go. Jon's response was a surreal fantasy, *The Violin Factory*, featuring actress, string orchestra (a sort of massed industrial string music), live sampling of the orchestra, the pounding rhythms of industrial process by percussion and samplers, and video counterpoint between Chinese violin factory workers and the string players.

People pulled up all day out of nowhere, and by that night under the moon, stars, and minimal set lighting, 700 people had amassed. The stage was built in front of the shearing shed, and perched on top of the sheep chute was a *Schreisprecher* Red Guard screaming anti-globalization slogans. Jon considered cutting the actress out of this performance for fear the locals might lower their heads, sprout horns, and charge the stage. However, he didn't lose his nerve, and much to our amazement, the pastoralists (ranchers) were walking around after the performance saying things like "Too right, yeah!" We participants were stunned. In celebration afterwards, LJ poured glasses of "cleansing bubbles" as a nightcap.

The next day began with Jon bowing some traditional Easter fence music. At about 7:00 a.m. tent flaps flung open and hung-over campers struggled out to the sound of amplified fence with broadband feedback. (Think Hendrix at Woodstock without the drugs.) The audience was both captive and captivated. At noon we drove about five miles cross-country where I played American fiddle tunes on Lizard Rock, an Aboriginal site.[13] Several hundred people crowded onto the ancient ironstone rock to hear my music. I marveled that they even found the place, let alone that they would brave the direct sun on this scorcher of a dog day.

After lunch, we searched for another remote site where sound artist Dr. Alan Lamb had set up an installation: long lengths of heavy-duty wire were stretched over boulders to collect sounds produced from the wind. We lingered until sunset, 300 strong, and I felt like a member of a tribe. Suddenly, the tribe was approached by a pickup truck with champagne in pails of ice and proper glasses—how does she do it?

It's been a year since we were at Wogarno. Usually, memory and anticipation act as a thinker's digest, paring things down to a manageable thought parcel, but here we can barely cope with all the looking back and forward. We sit down in the rambling kitchen to a glass of bubbles and begin to catch up on the news. LJ, who studied at the Cordon Bleu, has been doing a cooking show for ABC radio. David is preoccupied with the drought. Jack gets stars at school for going an entire week without making The Extended Raspberry motorcycle sound.

---

[13] The violin transmits a continuous message. The start and stop is arbitrary and not significant; we are inside the spell, we want to exist there. There is no such thing as traditional music; all genuinely orally transmitted folk music is contemporary. It must be created for the first time, as with the all the ancient traditions and their anthropomorphic recreations of the ancestors and creators of the universe. Music is not a vehicle of simulation. The actual universe, the birds, the rocks, the sky, the stars—everything has to be created afresh each time.

That's a hell of a gig. I hope they pay well.

Fiddling is like turning on the tap, not a trickle but a torrent. Fiddle tunes have more in common with minimalism and the circular breathing of the didgeridoo than with Dolly Parton (not that there is anything wrong with Dolly). Linear speed is critical. Although the cruising speed is high, the tune has to settle—too fast and you've lost it. The devil's gotta dance, so the feet have to have some traction with the ground; otherwise, there is no dance. With good fiddle playing, the Second Law of Thermodynamics is temporarily suspended.

For more, go to: http://www.jonroseweb.com/c_articles_fiddling.html.

Their neighbor Eva is visiting for the day, and I turn to ask her how she ended up here.

I'm originally from Brisbane, but I've been all over, I finished doing mackerel season, I went to Cockatoo Island, then I was in WA at the Mangrove Hotel as a cocktail waitress, I really didn't want to stay in hospitality so I did a computer search, it was meant to be six weeks cooking at Gary's, and here I am. Look in the bag behind you.

I glance at Eva's khaki pack hanging on the back of my chair, expecting nothing in particular. What I find gives me a start: the pack's cradling an upside-down joey (young kangaroo). Bounce is six months old. Later I find out through a perhaps indelicate question, although Eva seems comfortable enough, that the mother was shot for dog food. Her joey appeared old enough to make it, so they took her on.

We have our corner room-with-a-view again, complete with crisp white bed linen, fluffy pillows, and snowy towels. While Jon bones up on fence geography, I examine a copy of *Dangerous Snakes of Australia* cowritten by David's cousin, Peter Mirtschin.[14] There are 218 dangerously venomous snakes sidewinding their way around this continent. I search for the one I came upon at the southern part of the No. 1 Rabbit-Proof Fence. It looked similar to the photo of a venomless legless lizard. Relieved, I continue to thumb through and see it easily could have been a deadly brown or dugite, but that's just my mind working overtime. In contrast with American snakes, I read, "Australian snakes …cause minimal local damage but are strongly neurotoxic." To my surprise, David dismisses the idea of a legless lizard, believing it was indeed a venomous one. Suddenly, everyone feels a need to share with me an Aussie snake story.

I wander around vigilantly, collecting grass fishhooks on my socks, checking out the paddocks and fences, the equipment huts, and the shearers' quarters and trying not to let snakes-on-the-brain get the better of me. Macca, their Border collie pack leader, chaperones me everywhere. (Is he looking for a way to pass time, or am I, God forbid, a personality so lacking in self-confidence as to be sheepish?) When we return, Tillie and Cap, the other two dogs, succeed in roping me into a game that can take three forms and suddenly switches from one to another for no apparent reason: Kick the Ball, Stare at the Ball, and Stare at Marmalade, the moody cat on hormone replacement therapy.

---

[14] Mirtschin, Peter and Davis, Richard (1982) *Dangerous Snakes of Australia*, Adelaide: Rigby.

While trying to pick up the rules to Stare at the Cat, such as is this all that happens for an hour because I'm a good sport but I'm not an idiot, I hear a slow, rich, flute-toned bird call. It's like nothing I've ever encountered, coming from a sturdy little black-and-white bird with a robust bill. Its lonely song is answered in the distance—a duet of perfectly chosen notes.

It's the pied butcherbird *(Cracticus nigrogularis)*—they get their name from robbing other birds' nests of their eggs or hatchlings, explains Eva. They're experts in wedging prey into the forks of trees or impaling them on a broken branch. And they attack people's eyes, so some folks wear hats with eyes drawn on the back to confuse the birds, she warns.

It's hard for me to put this songster's name and savage reputation together with its angelic voice. I'm enchanted. I've fallen head-over-heels for a convict.

As we head back to the house, we discover a dead roo who has fallen into a narrow trench recently dug for a water line. Why couldn't she escape? We pry her out and take her to the bush for burial. LJ is distraught. She's sure it was not Amanda, her favorite, absolutely sure, yet doubts linger because she could not force herself to really take it in. Amanda doesn't show that evening, which is normal—she only comes a couple of times a week, but the distress shows in LJ's face. Should we disinter the corpse? It falls on David to do this, and he pronounces that it's not Amanda. Still, LJ worries.

I begin notating the irresistible songs of the pied butcherbirds as they exchange phrases across the range.[15] Transcribing calls from this feathered tribe has no downside. Their choice of notes, rhythms, and phrasing are all syncopated chimes, hip riffs, and blue notes. "Jazz birds," I call them, feeling they deserve a better spin than "butcher." As my collection of song snippets mounts, I conclude many would make good compositional seeds. I begin to imagine how I'll use their songs. Savage habits be damned—every war has its propagandist. Meet the new Vice President for Public Relations for the pied butcherbird. We'll

---

[15] It's a straightforward undertaking for me, since I have perfect pitch. Perhaps one in 10,000 people has this gift. My number came up. Sometimes called absolute pitch, it's the ability to recognize and name a musical tone without reference to any other note. When I began the piano at six, I always knew which note I was playing, even if I looked away. It was no different than conjuring up in my mind the color yellow or recalling a person's name—a simple memory task.

Scientists know that certain musical abilities are inherited, and certainly perfect pitch falls into this basket. I'm grateful for this gift, although I have had moments of panic, like singing in my grade school choir when the music we were reading was in one key but the teacher was playing it on the piano in another. I was stumped. And not everyone would enjoy knowing that a car horn was a D note, and the glasses we just clinked were an A-flat, and the lid put back on the metal garbage can was a low F.

just add bass and drums, change their name but keep the naughty image, and put them on a world tour. I think I can pull it off. I'll leave it to my people to iron out the minor details like baby bird skull smashing. They can't be any harder to manage than a rock band, just as long as my star doesn't get caught with warm flesh in his craw.

Antiphonal Pied Butcherbirds

LJ has arranged to take us to Gary and Eva's to see their section of the Rabbit-Proof Fence. We rise at five for an early go, but it's not to be. Before we get a hundred yards, we've got a flat. When we finally fix it, we pile in again for the hour-and-a-half drive to LJ's nearest neighbors.

Gary and Eva manage 20,000 feral goats on the 570,000 acres known as Narndee. I've learned that when reckoning geographical size, the country of Belgium is normally called into service as the measuring stick for bragging rights. Thirteen Narndees add up to one Belgium. However, Gary is neither printing his own money nor demanding a seat at the United Nations; he's busy managing his acreage and the local aerial baiting program to control the dingo population. Chunks of kangaroo injected with the poison 1080 are dropped by plane twice a year. The property owner goes up with Gary and the pilot to assist in navigation and to know where his own dogs can and cannot go. Once ingested, the poison speeds up the heart, setting dingoes on a frantic run until they collapse.

No animal should die like that, laments LJ.

At their homestead, Gary shows us a book on the area history. On this station in December 1931, "Mrs. Vogel, wife of C. H. Vogel on Narndee Station, was struck by lightning while riding her horse, leaving her four young children motherless.”

I think her stirrup touched the Fence, he says.

Eva shows us the large, black emu eggs in their walk-in refrigerator. As I'm cradling the waxy oval, I notice a kangaroo carcass hanging in the corner. Dog food, I imagine, maybe Bounce's mother.

Gary takes us in his LandCruiser for a tour of the property. We pass the two humps of Dromedary Hills. Thousands of camels *(Camelus dromedarius)* were imported into Australia beginning in 1840 to open up the arid areas of central and western Australia. The boundary riders employed camels for riding and as pack animals. A fence with a narrow opening encloses Dromedary Dam, the watering hole. Inside are three dead goats, including a tiny black kid right at the entrance who couldn't have lived more than a week before being trampled by the others on their way in for water. In death the kid continues to be trod on.

As we approach, the goats begin to run away, although age keeps one white nanny from getting up. A black-and-white one falls while running and stays collapsed for a good while before hobbling off. For seven years I kept dairy goats, each one named and precious and eager to see me. Here I'm confronted with the difference between a hobby farm and a going concern, between an animal husbandry that pampers individuals and one that runs the numbers. Each animal must pay its way and carry its load.

At first I think that tough decisions need to be made here, but perhaps not. More accurately, no decision needs to be made; no slackers are allowed. This indifferent land puts people like Gary and Eva (and David and LJ) under continuous pressure. I'm awed by the intensity of their everyday lives and surprised to find myself accepting in practice certain actions that I would not accept in theory.

After an hour and a half of driving, we come to a well, the high fence of a camel yard, and an old stone cabin. It's the Camel Station Homestead and just beyond is the still-maintained No. 1 Rabbit-Proof Fence. The fence gate looks like a doubled version of standard machine-made netting, but on close inspection we determine it was handmade from one wire. On a roll? How could something on such a large roll be threaded through such small holes?

Gary is as amazed as we are. He points out the Cobb & Co. twitch, a homemade clamp that twists. (We're real insiders now: I see that's 'n' old Cobb & Co. twist. Uh-huh.)

I can remember fiddling with them when you got a new fence, Gary says. You just go jooong, and they go for 10 seconds.

LJ is ready as ever. She's placed her battery-powered fridge in the back of Gary's vehicle; in it are chilled champagne flutes, strawberries, and bubbles. She thought this all through at five this morning. Of course, she actually thought of this long before then, since we are eight hours' drive from Perth, the world's most isolated city. We toast while Jon bows and records a five-wire fence. He returns for a quick glass of bubbles, then he and Gary head back to the cabin.

I'm Gary Scott, I've got country on both sides of the Fence, and I've also got a fair bit of my property just on one side of the Fence, farther north, and yeah, it feels a little bit different because all of a sudden you're stepping over this line and it's a little bit more remote or something, there's bad things out here—that's what this Fence is about, you can feel it as you go through the gate, you're sorta stepping into somewhere different, crossing over a fence can change your feeling, where it's actually not my lease and I'm outside the Fence, it really feels like you're in the middle of nowhere.

Nowadays, for us to put in a fence like the Rabbit-Proof Fence with the modern gear, you can put out probably 30 times as much fence as they did in the same time, this old stone-and-mud building was the major service center for the Fence in this area, quite a work of art actually, it's three rooms, the kitchen one end and lounge room the other end, a fireplace, the middle room would probably be the boss's quarters, I reckon, everyone else probably slept outside, it's a fairly dilapidated building now, unfortunately, the roof is mostly gone, and being put together with mud, once the roof goes the rain gets to the mud and consequently washes away, and she falls down.

In terms of the fence runners this was the best place to hang out.
Yeah, I s'pose.
Can you imagine what it would be like being here by yourself?
In a way, yes, I have spent time by myself at my homestead, and even with the modern equipment, telephones and what not, yeah, it gets very lonely, you have to be fairly friendly with yourself and be able to get along with yourself and—not recommended, it takes special people to be able to go for such periods by themselves or even with a handful of people.
Does it get quite cold in winter at night?
Wintertime here is *very* cold, it gets down to minus-5 here in the winter, and it would get up to 50 degrees, or 120-plus in the old Fahrenheit, just about every summer, one extreme to the other, very hot.
And now it's a kind of last halt for kangaroos, by looking …there's just hundreds of kangaroo bones in here.
It resembles a cave, and it's a lot cooler than being under a tree, so when they get weak and old, usually that's their last lay-down spot, it even makes it a little more eerie because you walk into what's left and all you see is death.
A place for dying.
And it looks the part too, you've got one window still hanging, that still swings …and death.

"Good fences make good neighbors," wrote Robert Frost, while Ralph Waldo Emerson felt at variance with a culture that was "essentially one of property, of fences, of exclusiveness." Friends of fences and dichotomy—which stories shall we sanction? One thing's for sure: fences try to deny a situation any greyness—either you have no right to be somewhere or every absolute right to do as you wish. A fence is a warning.

Like some wildlife, artists are edge-dwellers. They work on the fringe, the brink, and beyond, refusing to take boundaries at their fixed and unbreachable word, extravagantly wandering off paths and overstepping orderly lines. But stretching, crossing, or breaking barriers is one thing as metaphor and quite another when you're poking about the land, physically experiencing the fence as stranger, outsider, and potential troublemaker. A fence serves as a moral boundary post; forgive us our trespasses. When people approach us, we have mere seconds to decide whether to puff up or apologize. Today, for a change, we were inside, invited, guests. "Don't Fence Me In" runs its loop.

Just before we depart, we see a sky as big as the world, as if an encyclopedia were opened to the entry "Clouds," displaying every conceivable pattern. When we drive off Narndee, the horizon narrows and flattens to a movie's "The End." Later, it *is* the end, or so it seems. Just as I take over the wheel from LJ, the weather gods turn on us. We are blind-sided by concurrent storms named Rain, Hail, Dust (how can dust survive this water?), Wind, and Electrical. Bushes and branches join the mayhem, all swept sideways by the wind's henchmen set loose to scour the countryside. Then the lighting crew hits the switch, and the day goes dark except for the sheets and bolts of lightning. The thunder god roars his grudges in a brutish attempt to make us cower, but all I can do is laugh at his tantrum as I inch the car along.

David has set up a meeting for us with a neighbor who spent his life as a fence runner. A two-hour drive puts us at his doorstep where 50 years of rusting cars, cans, and other junk coexist among the chooks (chickens), all ringed by a solid wooden fence. Inside, we take our seats around a kitchen table with an old-fashioned oilcloth. Jon sets up microphones by the salt and pepper pots, but as soon as Ron starts to speak, we realize there's a recording challenge. His voice is quiet, and he punctuates every other sentence with an involuntary movement such as hitting the table with his elbow; in between he's sweeping the spotless table with his hands. His family sits around to watch the inquisition. I see the deep-felt respect they have for him—in their eyes he's an outback star. Ron is more than a match for the interview, with a fantastic delivery, pace, and sound. He presents as classic an outback image as a windmill or kangaroo. His voice articulates a life on the Fence.

This's Ron Moses talking about the No. 1 Rabbit Fence, I had some exciting times on it and some bad times, but the whole time on it I never had to walk home ...out there you haven't got much time to be lonely, you're busy all the time, you're cooking meals and you read a book and you go to bed and the next thing you know it's time to get up and start again, it's not a bad job in the winter time but it's not very good in the hot weather.

Mostly I was keeping rust off of the ground, and you have to put what they call foot netting to block the holes up, broken wires and general fencing troubles you get everywhere, sometimes you got a bush fire job, and you've got quite a lot to fix up there, then you get the floods and you get it washed away—there's always plenty to do, they'd let me stop when the Fence was in good condition so when I woke up in the morning I'd have to start work immediately, sometimes you might be in one place three or four days just doin' half a mile, it's a fence with quite a big story behind it if you want to follow it right through.

Heather, what did you feel when he was working on the Fence?

I didn't like him out there, there's snakes out there 'n' the car can break down.

How many days was he away at a time?

Usually about eight days, but when he started he was gone fourteen days.

Did you have any way communicating? Did you have a radio?

Not to start with. They bought him a two-way radio.

I never used it, they give me the nickname of Romeo Whiskey, I had to call Meekathara base, but I never ever used it the whole time, I still got it here.

Well, he could always get out of his difficulties, I know he's resourceful 'n' all that sort of thing, but you still worry a bit ...it's history, you're a little bit proud to keep it going, imagine how they worked with their camels and so on, when you started, you had about 400 miles to do.

Four hundred ten.

And then they started a No. 2 Fence—you did that too.

Thirty-two miles on that one, you get to know where the water is, where it's reliable, and where it's good water, a lot of time the rain fills the water holes up, that's the main thing to watch is the water situation, one night I had just got to the Fence and I didn't see nothin' but water and camped all night and you look out the window and all you can see is the lightning is continuous and what you see is just water everywhere and nothing else, and I woke up in the morning and there was 300 yards of fence down behind me so I thought well I can't move for a while so I've got something to do while I'm waiting for it to dry out, I started digging on that thing and I had about four or five days I think, it's a bit scary when you're out there by yourself.

If you drive down that stretch of fence now, do you think that's part of me, that's part of what I've done?

You know every bump in the road, you just about know every post, you do.

Remember that story you were telling us about one night when you were sittin' around the fire and you saw these little eyes in the bush, and you're sittin' there and you're lookin' and you're wonderin' what the hell's that and every time you moved they moved with ya?—it was a reflection from his glasses in the car, and he was thinkin' who's that in the bush.

What about dingoes?

I saw a few of those up at the top end and down at the bottom end, you don't see a lot, I haven't seen one for two or three years, you come across their tracks, most of them are on the outside of the Fence, one year, as far as you could see ahead there's just continuous emus, thousands and thousands, all half dead, you know, barely able to move, making their way down the Fence, looking for a way through.

> "Sometimes out here," I said, "I feel terribly lonely, and I say to myself that I'd gladly give a whole month's pay if I could stand for just one hour in Trafalgar Square, or outside the Mansion House, and watch all the people. Just stand and watch them all. Thousands and thousands of people in front of me, instead of one crow on a barbed wire fence."[16]

As we continue on to Mount Magnet, David explains that the town is the region's oldest surviving gold settlement. While it's a key service

---

[16] Lewis, Harold (1973) *Crow on a Barbed Wire Fence*, Sydney: Angus and Robertson, 108.

center for miners, tourists, and pastoralists (he and LJ pick up their mail, food, and champagne here), the local mine remains the focal point. It supports an otherwise fragile existence for the townspeople. Without it, most would leave.

A permanent film of mineral dust has settled on the place, an Emperor's coating as much concept as physical reality. A regular sprinkle of the stuff appears to bond Magneters to the town and to one another, producing a communal determination to hang on. Aerial wires with oilcans attached to them hover over the roads in and around the mine.

David, I'm good at lateral thinking but can't come up with any reason for such odd-looking constructs.

Fences in the sky.

Uh, what are they keeping in—or out?

The truckies do extremely long hours, and by the way, they're usually women, the mine prefers them because they're more careful, the blokes tend to drive like idiots, chucking wheelies 'n' that, anyway, sometimes the truckies drive off half-asleep after dumping a load and leave the back of the truck sticking up—that's courting danger as they can tip the whole thing over at the first corner, hitting the oil drums on the sky fences reminds them that the back of the truck is still waving in the wind, makes a hell of a racket when they strike a drum.

Farther down the track another enigma has installed itself across the land. The sun is set low in the sky, tucked behind a barbed-wire fence framing black, jagged modernist shapes. It's an incomplete jigsaw puzzle for admirers of de Kooning, the expressionist images both savage and unsettling. But as with most things in the Australian outback, artistic intention does not figure in; these are the arbitrary results of industrial process. The black shapes turn out to be the ripped remains of plastic bags blown onto the fence by a disinterested wind, trapped scraps in a cycle of fusion and disintegration.

As we continue our fence Odyssey further round the continent, we find the outback littered with snagged bags. It's the dream stuff of French art theory, this bag-and-barb coupling, where the ubiquitous artifact from the age of consumption meets its nemesis on the uncaring fences of Australia.

Well, since we're doing fences, let's check out the Mount Magnet racecourse. I'm the chairman of the course committee as it happens.

What might you expect of an outback racecourse—a few sticks in the ground, maybe? One tin shed to mark the spot? Think again. Australia is gambling mad. The settlement of a prison colony was founded on the risky wager of a desperate British government. Almost every aspect of the country's short history has been a gamble, from the various gold rushes to the hopes of every immigrant, from the traditions of the betting game Two-up to the Melbourne Cup, a horse race with the status of a national holiday. TV ads tout "bridalwear, racewear, eveningwear"; department stores carve out a "spring racing hats" section. There's even a town called Casino. Australia, the lucky country.[17]

When the citizens of Mount Magnet decided on a racecourse, it was serious. They may not have had millions of dollars to spend on plush fittings, but they had space and they had imagination. The course is the same size as that of Melbourne or Sydney and offers all the requisite facilities: clubhouse (David is here to water the immaculately mown lawn in front of it), members' enclosure, bookies' hut, men's showers, ladies' showers, and scratchboard.

The bets are still chalked up from the last meeting. And if you look over there, there are the holding pens. As for all the horses for courses, mostly they have to come up from Perth.

We walk around the stands and paddock, admiring the lines and curves of the neat white fences. Then I climb the starters' platform, which sways gently and begins to groan in the wind. Perched up here, I can take in miles of fences stretched out on the earth's powdered blood. I bring my eyes back to the courses for horses. And they're off!

One by one, the race takes shape: on the inside close to the fence, the pounding of a dozen horses' hooves, the incomprehensible voice coming over the tiny public address system, the primary colors of the jockeys' shirts, some fences are down, the roar of the crowd, the ecstatic shouts of the winners, fortunes made and lost, dollar bills changing with quick hands, the turned-down mouths of the losers, the smell of horse manure, the flies, always the flies.

A single crow breaks the spell, caw! aah!

When I look again, there's not a person or horse to be seen. I'm spooked and quickly descend the rickety platform steps.

Back at Wogarno, we're about to leave more than our hearts. David has helpfully taken out the van's grill kill; it's all scraped off and tidied up. I thank him, not having the heart to tell him it was a work-in-progress. We're halfway up the six-mile homestead road when he comes

---

[17] Horne, Donald (1964) *The Lucky Country*, Ringwood, Victoria: Penguin Books.

driving alongside us, Macca and Tillie standing sentinel in the back, waving Jon's boots.

Onward! Having found the southern end of the Rabbit-Proof Fence, Jon wants a go at the northern end. It doesn't figure on our maps but looms large in his imagination; he's gotta have it. Toward Mount Magnet we pass red anthills (termite mounds), some several feet high.

We spot more roo roadkill with eagles feasting on it and try for photos, but these jumbo jets manage to lift off at the last moment. Mount Magnet and Cue (once site of Western Australia's richest gold fields) get crossed off our list, followed by Meekathara (also a mining town), with its mournful Hits and Rumbles Fence.

Hits and Rumbles

A sign warns that it's 162 miles to the next services, further than we've yet pushed our fuel tank. We decide to slow down and go without air conditioning to get the best mileage. We're close to Mount Augustus, a large monolith, but birds, beaches, and boulders are not our theme, so I don't ask. A relaxing drive in the bush was never on Jon's agenda. We're travelers, not tourists, who have mounted a full-on cartographic mission. Perhaps pursuing fences sustains us as much as the gas.

I've tossed my accumulating cork collection. I don't want the irritation of corks dangling from my hat for fly relief any more than the darting flies. These Aussie flies *(Musca vetustissima)* are fast; they steal from mouths and eyes and noses. I'm fed up and determined to go for the protective elegance of a fly veil. LJ says I can even drink wine through the netting. She can say that, being a confirmed bubblesophile, but surely my preferred red wine would stain a veil.

Suddenly, it's so green Jon says the paints have been mixed wrong. Yes, yet another graphic design software overenhancement. In the space of 10 minutes, we've gone from an ashen desert to a startlingly English pastoral scene complete with grazing sheep. "Country Gardens" begins its loop, and though the green quickly cedes to aridity, the tune sticks.

Kumarina Roadhouse—let's say "not clean" for the ladies' latrine and leave it at that, except to mention the four frogs that swam for their life when I flushed and how close I had backed into them before noticing—next subject, please. From one moon to another, Jon reads to me that Broome has a spectacular ocean reflection on full moon evenings. That's good for several hours of "I See a Full Moon Risin'," until we pass through Newman, a company mining town—I had no idea such places still existed—and the Tennessee Ernie Ford song comes front and center, "I Owe My Soul to the Company Store." The song is passé, but the concept of a company town lives on.

We see more and more Aboriginal people, often three generations crammed into rusted-out vehicles. When they get out, barefoot with ill-matching clothes, to buy candy and soft drinks, I see the outer poverty and wonder what's going on inside, making every effort not to draw conclusions. I really don't know. "You take 16 tons, an' whadaya get, another day older and deeper in debt ..."

The words "lake" and "river" begin to take on their proper meanings as receptors and transmitters of water, unlike further south where lake meant salt crust and river meant dry bed. We spend the night in majestic hill country—I could be convinced we're in Kenya—watching a purple and red sunset become more and more striated. The sign describes the peak we are parked under simply as THE GOVERNOR. He rules.

We depart early, and from 5:30–6:30 a.m. it's actually cool. We drive with the windows down, savoring the chill. I don't spot a single kangaroo for miles and gradually replace my early morning straying-stock-and-wildlife watchfulness with anthill sightings. All the hills are giant red snowmen. Other folks have taken notice as well. One Frosty is painted with a white face, and another is fitted with a hat.

We're in the Pilbara, a region well covered in the tourist and eco-tourist tracts. I read in the guidebook that it's composed of the world's oldest rocks and offers a number of natural wonders in its 193,000-square-mile area (or 16½ Belgiums); then I close the book. We'll be pushing right on through. I don't want to know what I'm missing.

As we near Port Hedland, the grill kill is horribly beautiful: the gossamer wings of mayflies, dragonflies, lacewings, butterflies, and moths. The presence of verdant fields, sap-green chenille hills, and idyllic ponds belies the apparent absence of wildlife.

I'd like the concession for FLOODWAY signs; one prefaces each slight dip in this bone-dry highway. These signs seem to be crying wolf in such a sunburnt country. I won't have a bar of it. This is the main highway—how can it be subject to water across it at every depression? Jon tries to explain that the markedly variable rainfall brings extremes of drought and flood, but his information doesn't soak in; it sits on the surface and evaporates without effect.

We enter Port Hedland, palm trees swaying, as is a fence with a thick, wavy rope atop it, and continue on in search of a road that might lead to the top end of the Rabbit-Proof Fence. Our best guess is the remote Pardoo Station where John and Pam Leeds supplement their sheep income by taking in tourists. It's a well-organized place with even a little outbuilding for the sale of sundries, but in this, the off-season, we're the only ones around. There's been a recent cyclone, and much of the electricity has been on the fritz. Jon assists Pam in getting us some power and then interviews her husband John.

"Slow, hot, humid, flies," I note. I head for the showerhouse, after which I am prepared, based on a rigorous scientific sample of four, to assert that the Northern Territory toilet is a boon for the frog, although I haven't yet seen a postcard advertising this fact.

This homestead was the first in the northwest, built in the 1890s, Rabbit-Proof Fences don't come as something new to us, it had been around a fair while when we were kids, so yeah, the government was winding down the Fence at that point in time, I think the Fence did a damn good thing because as kids we used to love catching rabbits on the inside of the Fence, and they were supposed to be on the outside, and they used to be pretty good eating as well ...there's a grave right on the Pardoo side of the Fence, a casualty of the Fence, all's I know is that he's buried there, and he died constructing the Fence, it's a reasonable monument to the bloke, not just a stick in the ground, there's a little headstone there and a nice neat little fence around it, so somebody did the right thing by him anyway.

So the guy who worked on the Fence in life has got a fence around him in death.

Certainly, and you notice it, driving along what is left of the Fence in that area, we can't get there at the moment because of the amount of water that's lying around ...there's not much of the Fence left, the stone wall at Cape Keraudren is of course a big feature of it on the top end, I don't know that there's too many people that really care about the fact that it was there, but if you're talking about the actual Rabbit-Proof Fence, it was put there for a purpose, I don't think they ever achieved it, it became a huge white elephant, I suppose when you look back at the history of it—look at the construction of it—it's one helluva fence, on this top section here it was all done with steel, and it was steel angle iron, not the posts that we use today, and on the bottom, if you actually pull the post out, down about six inches above the bottom of the actual post there's a piece of flat metal plate welded on it, whether that was to stop them being pulled out of the ground or what I don't know, but these posts are only about 10 foot apart, it's one helluva thing, isn't it, it's almost a monument to the people who built it.

I remember clearing a cut line by hand with axes and burning out trees, today we can knock in a fence line or a road into a windmill in about a half an hour flat with the machinery we have, but I was brought up in that era where the last of things was done by hand, it was all crowbars, if you handed somebody a crowbar these days, they'd drop it on their foot straight away, we saw the end of that era, the Rabbit-Proof Fence that actually bounded one side of the property, it's the one that runs towards the coast near Kalberrie, I think it's the No. 3 Fence, I can remember going along that Fence even as kids and there were thousands and thousands of emus piled up on it because of a dry time, I think that the Fence maybe created more problems for other vermin than it ever did stop rabbits, to us it was just a beautiful construction, and as a boundary fence between two properties, the most wonderful fence you could ever own, because there's no way a sheep is ever gonna crawl through the Rabbit-Proof Fence.

> But sheep were so stupid they would blunder into a fence and stop
> three feet from an open gate, never see it.[18]

Okay, we have our marching orders: Cape Keraudren in the morning. Per Jon's suggestion, we kill mosquitoes in the van by lying in bed naked and letting them attack, then hitting the sting. It's the only sure way to find them in the dark, he insists, but I'm left with itchy welts.

We rise at 5:15 a.m. and head for the long dirt road that descends into the national park at Cape Keraudren. First thing when we turn off, a sign announces: BEWARE CROCODILES. It's 7:30 a.m. by the

---

[18] McCullough, Colleen: 252.

time we set out on foot. Even at this hour, it's sweltering. While Jon is keen as mustard, I can tell immediately that I will be a liability and turn back to wait for him in the van.

I set out past the croc sign on a dirt track, John drew a map of how to get to the top end of the Fence that seemed detailed enough at the time, but now that I'm here, it's hard to tell which is a road and which is a floodplain, I take a wrong turn and come over a set of sand dunes to find a fence, but it's the wrong fence on the wrong beach, just a dune-stabilizing fence to keep people out in order to rehabilitate the area.

Parked in full sun. All van windows and top vent open. No hint of breeze. Last full water bottle sent with Jon. I drain the empties, netting half a cup, which I relish. The water in our tank is not potable; I'd have to boil it. Can't imagine a hot cup of tea in this weather.

I take a guess and go left, looking for the wall that was the final marking point of the Rabbit-Proof Fence, I remember seeing a photo of this wall in a book, but that photo was a good 20 years old and the wall has crumbled severely, so it's hard to tell what has been a wall from just a pile of rocks, I figure it out but there is no fence connected to it any more, just sand dunes with very tall grass and a good chance of snakes or even crocs, by now my water's finished and with the severe heat and humidity, flies, and no hat, I'm beginning to feel quite shaky, having doubled my two-mile trip to four miles.

The sun frays the horizon with a hiss. Otherwise, there's not a hint of anyone or anything. If Jon doesn't come back by 10:30 a.m., I'm going to try to locate the ranger. He must be here somewhere. I'm not going to wait one moment past 10:30. But what if Jon returns just after that and I'm not here and he's about to collapse and I can't find the ranger and I've left Jon in the hot sun with no shade because he doesn't have a key and he's out of water and I'm out of water, wandering around looking for someone? I stop myself there and prepare to begin again. A hissssssss …

I decide to take a chance, I cut back across the dunes in the hope of finding the remains of the Fence and sure enough, standing up out of the dune is one very rusty, 100-year-old fence post, then I follow the line of it, finding bits of the Fence imbedded in the sand, and I realize I don't have much time before I will become totally dehydrated so I take as many photos as possible and follow the fence line, uncovering more and more as I make my way back until I see the floodplain again and know where I am.

Only mad dogs and Englishmen go out in the noonday sun, observes the Indian proverb. The mad dog returns at 10:30. It's then he lets me see his map: "$500 fee for towing ... Crocs ... Read warning sign before crossing to Mount Blaze ... This map not drawn to scale."

Why not? I demand of the hiss.

My passenger is still alive and directs me to head toward Alice Springs, via Broome and Katherine. Enough of this nibbling at the edges; we want a bite of the savory center. First stop, Pardoo Roadhouse, to buy water. We encounter a burnt field with checkerboard squares of black and red soil. Later, the Sandfire Roadhouse says yes to kitsch with a series of relocated, trophy-size termite hills set between palms along the road out. We pass another confusing palette: a stretch of bottle-green river flanked by sun-bleached wheat on one bank, while the other asserts Christmas-green weeds in red soil frosted white with salt. Haven't the lighting crew signed some sort of contract vis-à vis realism?

> There is no wind now but the wire of the paddock fence sings and a
> hiss is abroad in the weeds.[19]

Half an hour before Broome, we mount a hill to find that a lush pasture with dairy cattle has willed itself into existence. While my eyes insist we're in a cooler place and season, my skin knows better. We're here during the blameworthy Wet, and my deodorant is working right to the edge of its ability.

Situated at the top of Western Australia on the Indian Ocean, Broome is a pearl-diving town producing 85 percent of the world's finest pearls. Activity peaked in the early 1900s when 400 pearling luggers (small sailing ships) plied the coast. The introduction of plastic buttons had its impact, and today cultured pearls, Broome's specialty, have replaced mother-of-pearl. I've dropped hints about shopping for the perfect Jackie O three-strand to no avail. Pearls, interchangeable with amber and leather and opals and—each town has a theme to propose, but we have one for the whole country: Fences.[20]

---

[19] Winton, Tim (2001) *Dirt Music*, Sydney: Picador, 119.
[20] Have you heard about the Aboriginal leper fence near Broome? someone asks me later. I assume they were fenced *in*—well yes, and no. In the late 1920s leprosy infection among Aborigines increased sharply. They feared disease and the prospect of being removed from their environments and incarcerated in institutions. Then, in 1933 five lepers and a number of suspected lepers camped outside the native hospital fence at Derby. Officials feared that others would be attracted to the site. So some were fenced in, and others fenced out. Another name to add to Australia's role call of fences: The Leper.

Palm-lined streets, clean and sidewalked, confirm that tourist money has arrived. We half-heartedly set out for a drive to the port, which the guidebook does not mention—thus our intrigue, and the beach, which it describes as spectacular and obligatory at sunset during low tides when the moon reflects across the mudflats in a stairway-to-heaven effect. Reluctant tourists, we turn back after a few minutes before reaching either destination to instead photograph the irresistible cemetery with its small fence and Japanese-inscribed tombstones. Over 900 Japanese divers paid the highest price, having succumbed to the dreaded bends.

Jon telephones LJ to find out if her beloved kangaroo Amanda has shown up yet.

Yes!

We dine out for a change, choosing a Thai fusion outdoor cafe called Noodlefish IV.

Why IV? I ask.

We've just reopened in our fourth location, the waiter informs us. Since we are only open eight months out of the year, we often have to look for a new location when we restart. No one comes here the other four months due to the weather.

I nod in accordance, worn down by the heat and humidity.

You get used to the climate by never using the air conditioning, he suggests.

The sole patrons, we watch a storm make its way across the sky. We're hoping to add an Aboriginal person's voice to our interviews. Jon finds a guide listed in our book and calls him. Would he consider meeting us for an interview about fences? He sounds hesitant but does assent. I thought perhaps he would bring his mates with him given the quirky topic with strangers in a motel room, but he turns up alone. I pour red wine all around, and he begins.

My name is Stephen Baamba Albert, I've lived in every state in the country, this place is home here ...we never had fences, even though we knew our boundaries, our kind of boundaries were a certain kind of mountain or tree or river, and that told you where you were.

Were those boundaries in Aboriginal people's minds as strong as a fence?

Oh yes, oh yeah, you can find out where you are, there used to be a fence around Broome and because of the White Australia Policy within the pearling industry here, blacks could mix with whites or Asians, but if you lived in town by sunset you had to be inside town, inside the fence, and if you lived out of town you had to be outside of the fence before the sun went down and stay out, like for us Aboriginal people, if

44

you got picked up at nine o'clock at night, you'd get kept in the lockup, so there was a curfew ...the fence stopped us from going to our hunting places and that's really terrible, and when people are building round in town now, before they build a house, they put up a big fence, so you connect fences with the Europeans, a fence is like the beginning of being deprived of things.

It creates a fear inside you, it affects you physically?

It affects you physically, and you get annoyed, but it's always there, sometimes you feel like getting a wire cutter.

Like escaping from a prison, yeah. Did any members of your family work as stockmen on stations?

Oh, look—people worked as stockmen on stations.

What did they feel about it? They were working inside this person's land, but they could see that the borders of their land didn't coincide with what he thought the borders were of his land.

With the government policy you were told everything, it's only been since '67 that we've been able to get some rights back, in the early days when they were working on the fence line, they were good people, they were really proud when they built the fence, whether it be a wooden fence or the ones we have now, you could always jump over the fence if you wanted to or crawl through the fence, sometimes
you put traps in the fence, like if you saw a little trail where the kangaroos have been going through, you'd just put your little noose there and then you'd catch them in the fence, in some parts of central Australia when you couldn't get your kangaroo, and the rabbits took over, rabbit has become their natural diet now, so we adapted to fences, you know, keeping stock and whatever, like where I am from, when you see a fence line, well if you keep following it, it ends somewhere so if you're lost you can use that as a vantage point, but to put a fence up as a barrier from other people and that, mainly because it's a sense of insecurity.

You see how big this country is, if you're traveling by car and you're going through all these paddocks and all that, it's best to sit in back rather than in the front, 'cause if you're in the front you gotta keep on opening and shutting the gates, so if you're smart enough—usually in the city you always want to jump in the front seat—but in the bush here, you jump in the back seat ...like with some of our places, when we say we've got sacred spots or ceremonial places, people know where they are, and we say we don't have to fence it because you are told you aren't supposed to go there, the fear of going there and getting sick or getting killed about it is much more fearful than when you're fenced in, you know, one of the things that some of the people used to practice was, for punishment, they'd put you in the middle of the circle, and they'd just draw something, just a boundary, you get out of that boundary, you're in trouble, that's a fence, but a psychological one, the fear of stepping over is much worse than having a fence and jumping over a fence.

So in that respect, all human beings have this in common. There's the unknown and stepping into it or stepping away from it. The difference in culture is that European man decided to make it a physical barrier, whereas Aboriginal people have known how to make it a barrier without actually …

That's right, and you don't have to have that barrier because you already know, because you put up a fence and all of a sudden you gotta maintain it, you spend half your life maintaining the fence, and you go crazy over it, like you said, people have died trying to still keep the fence going.

We give Steve our hearty thanks and cab fare home. He has the soul of a poet, I say aloud to no one in particular. We haven't encountered anyone who could field our quirky, often abstract questions with such ease. And he's got me thinking about the management overload on humans since European settlement has been mucking about with the continent.[21]

> Each group through whose territory the [railway] line was passing saw its waters used up, the bushes destroyed for firewood and fence-posts—water-mallee and quandong and other useful shrubs—and the whole country turned to strange uses.[22]

I n tracing the multiple legs of the Rabbit-Proof Fence, we often don't encounter another vehicle for an hour or more. Inside the van, it's an oven. Sometimes I wear kitchen gloves to protect my hands from the overheated steering wheel. Our cracked cake of bow rosin resting on the dashboard has melted and been resurrected as a smooth round. Outside the van, it's the same oven. There's no respite.

---

[21] Seddon, George (1997) *Landprints: Reflections on Place and Landscape*, Cambridge: Cambridge University Press, 213. This extraordinary collection of essays examines our relationship to land, landscape, and place naming in Australia.
[22] Bates, Daisy (1936/2004) *My Natives and I*, Carlisle, Western Australia: Hesperian Press, 155.

What do you think it is today?

Hundred 'n' five, hundred 'n' ten, Jon reckons.

Any sense of joy or adventure has been baked or sweated out of me. Most nights we just pull off the road, make dinner, and fall asleep.

Today from Broome to Willare I keep seeing dirt bits on the road, then I notice they're pulsing. I slow down to confirm it's another grand hopper ball; sometimes for 30 seconds at a time I'm driving over them. I hold my breath like at the dentist's, trying to tune out what's going on, hoping for minimal damage. We get out to take a closer look at these yellow-green and green-yellow opportunists celebrating the good times. The hoppers are eating everything in sight with an audible group crunch. Perhaps this explains the small, like-colored butterflies starting to fill the grill.

The termite hills are changing. Small cones and stovepipe hat shapes continue, as do statuettes and figurines, but the color drifts from red to brown to beige, then the forms shift to bulbous and misbegotten, later redeeming themselves with more pleasing distortions resembling those of Gaudí. Jon posits that the hills are thin in response to the prevailing winds.[23]

Some days I wonder what we're doing driving around this ancient crust of a continent, sharing the highway with swerving road trains and other stressed drivers, setting up and breaking down daily like a rock band on tour without the roadie and crew, enduring endless cramped hours. It's a hot and sweaty trip with the constant threat of potholes, washaways, corrugations, wandering stock, wildlife, and floods, and with the price of gas (when we can find it at all) and that red bulldust that collects on our van and clings to our clothes and clogs our dreams and daydreams … The absolute unpredictability of even the main road keeps me on edge. The only good thing about an Australian

---

[23] He's close. Subsequently, we read that Australian compass termites *(Amitermes meridionalis)* have made these hills. They are a potential boon to lost travelers who know that the termites line up their mounds north-south as a strategy against the fierce sun of midday. Only the early-morning and late-afternoon sun hits the broad, flat surfaces of the mound. In addition to their efforts in giving directions and stage design, these termitaria provide shelter to birds, reptiles, and invertebrates.

Richard Braithwaite (1990, "More than a home for white ants," *Australian Natural History Journal,* 23: 306-313) recounts the wonders of termites:

"Termitaria are not the inert tombstones they appear to be. They are stationary cows. They are a vacuum cleaner removing the natural debris of the eocsystem. They are the pithead of a miniature mine that brings nutrients to the surface. They are an incubation chamber. They are a dependable larder to insectivores. They are a secure home to a wide range of vertebrates and invertebrates."

Not to mention their uses to humans pre-tennis courts: the mounds were a drugstore for Aboriginal people (the termitaria are rich in clay, which is used to cure stomache ailments). And of course these decomposers are luthiers, hollowing out branches for future didigeridoos.

highway is that it's named rather than numbered. What I would give for I-5, Portland to San Francisco, 10 hours of all-American driving.

The succeeding anthills evoke a five-and-dime shop's nativity scenes: Madonna and child, three wise men, choirs, pipe organs. We encounter four thick-limbed people leaning in together for a photo, straight out of Picasso or Henry Moore. It's time for a look and a touch. They're hard, the poor man's concrete (does the poor man have a tennis court?), but scratchable. One five-wire fence sends its wires right through an anthill. Jon's takes snapshots; I take notes.

Nicotine, we hear an elderly woman explain matter-of-factly on ABC talkback radio, is going out of fashion—like sunbathing, Christianity, and plastic bags.

The roads are elevated to minimize the effects of frequent flooding. We cross low bridges spanning muddy creeks, rivers, and lakes overspilling their bounds. Termite hills continue to evolve, and our imaginations are reacting like when you stare at clouds: there's a nude woman, Donald Duck, Buddha. The first of the boab trees seems an aberration, a wide vase with a tree placed in it instead of a flower, a grey Hofbrauhaus beer stein without the blue "H" logo. We ford water across the road, and suddenly the FLOODWAY signs seem relevant, making the many water mirages now a potential worry. People can get stuck for weeks, we've heard. Jon photos our grill kill, unlikely couplings of a pale yellow butterfly with a bright orange dragonfly, a pale blue butterfly with a emerald-green dragonfly, and opaque wings with translucent ones.

A series of one-lane bridges leads into Fitzroy Crossing, which began life as a watering hole for travelers stranded by floods at the river crossing. The roadhouse is still a hotspot—people gassing up, kids on bikes, and junk foodies collecting their score, while across the street a soccerfield and a basketball court complete the heart of town. Several Aboriginal girls of 10 or 11 charm us with their energy and curiosity, bright eyes and bright questions. (Later, we'll wish we'd queried them as much as they did us: Where are you from, where are you going, what are you doing, is this your van, are you married, where is your bed? Our unasked questions were about fences, of course.)

Just out of town we spot a NO ALCOHOL BEYOND FENCE sign, the frequent target and final resting place for numerous bottles and cans, and another sign warning about Murray River Encephalitis. Mosquito bites from Pardoo continue to surface on my arms and legs, and I trust the encephalitic region does not extend that far. Before Halls Creek, we come upon the results of a low-level fire, called a cold fire, which has burned out the grasses but left the trees untouched.

Later, Jon goes out onto nothing but red soil to catch a dramatic sunset behind a fence. While he snaps away, I watch the sun in the rearview mirror as it dissolves into cool yellows and violets. There's a click track of crickets keeping basic time while cicadas do four beats of an eggshell shaker, then pause seductively and repeat, and my blinker chimes in: "Sunset with Polyrhythms."

Our drive-by take on Halls Creek is that it's an intense place, with an accumulated energy neither positive nor negative but simply raw. Aboriginal adolescents are playing basketball. Alcohol appears to be absent. Still, we sense that if you struck a match, the whole lot might explode, that if you merely attempted to measure the charge, the pressure, it might all go wrong.

Just on the outskirts, we see a blue "P," and although it's getting late, we never camp that close to a town. We're accustomed to seeing a roadside rest area every 20 minutes so we'll wait. And wait. Tonight there's no place to pull off, and I'm forced to drive later than I should, slower and slower as I worry about the roos. And here they are; every five minutes one or two silhouettes can just be made out by the side of the road, and inevitably just as we pass them, a third makes a dash for it right in front of us.

Forgoing the Truckers Only area and the Parking on the wrong side of the road, which we saw too late (it's against our road religion to turn back), we finally spot a "P" marker 25 miles past Halls Creek. We turn off at what is normally a very short loop, but we go and go. Finally, we begin to take a huge dip, a FLOODWAY sign looms, and I see water over the road reflecting nothing but the black velvet of the night sky without the painted Elvis. We must be on the old, decaying highway. Across the water I spot another car, an aged Oldsmo-Buick gas hog, the sort with a trunk big enough for our two bodies. Its door spookily opens. Only a horror movie could propose an eerier sight. I cannot advance. Even if we could ford the stream in the black of night, there would be no point. Clearly, this other motorist is an axe murderer.

I back up the hilly, serpentining gravel track in the pitch dark, determined and motivated. We park at the spot where we initially turned in and feast: a bottle of 2000 Leaping Lizard Cabernet Sauvignon from the Margaret River and a pasta salad made earlier in the day. Then Jon has a radio moment, recording the bizarre sounds emitting from the radio, which will not really tune in. The no-see-'ems and barely-see-'ems always attempt an attack once we stop and open the windows. They're screened so it doesn't worry me much, but there do seem to be more than the usually small number of successful intruders. I make a close inspection, squeezing one of the black bugs between two fingernails. A flea! The bed is made in palest blue, and their black bodies bespeckle it. Fleas, hundreds of them, have overrun us. They must be coming in through the bottom of the sliding door even though it's closed; perhaps they're jumping from a recently dead animal.

First off, let's get out of here before more come on board, advises Jon.

He loads Big Yellow, I cork the wine, and we hit the road, struggling to come up with a plan, itching and slapping in the dark as we go.

Jon is convinced they prefer him to me, concluding in obviously imperfect Cartesian logic that my French perfume is a repellent. He sprays it liberally over the van floor as I count the waste. *Mon Dieu!* After an hour or so, with still no "P" in sight, we stop at a truckers' parking area, pull out the pieces of bedding one by one, and violently shake them in the pitch black, illuminated only by the headlights.

We get back inside, make the bed, and squish fleas for another 20 minutes. We attack the bed, the floor, the sink and kitchen counter, our own selves, and each other, mimicking a couple of monkeys grooming. Finally, we lie down fully clothed in the heat, having gotten everything in sight, and go blank as best we can for several hours.

The next shift arrives immediately and pesters us through the night. With the windows closed, we're sweltering. At 4:15 a.m. we give up and drive again.

I've got an idea, Jon says. When we get to the border, we just give ourselves up, tell them we're infested with fleas, and ask to be fumigated.

What if they give us a two-week quarantine instead? Not a good idea. Keep killing.

Before daylight we cross a creek. The road just dips, unaccompanied by a FLOODWAY sign or a fathometer to mark the height. None of my lists can deliver me from this moment, and we briefly descend into the underworld. I expect that a proper creek deserves a proper bridge, but then there's so much water and so few people.

I recall seeing a sign back at Halls Creek for the next town 100 miles down the road. I can't remember the name, but I'll know it when I hear it. Turkey Creek, Jon announces after studying the map. No, that's not it. He insists that it has to be; there's not another town for miles. We find it—them, actually; Turkey Creek has an Aboriginal name, Warmun, the one I'd seen the sign for. ("War-mun, wo wo wo wo oh oh mu u un, have you got cheating on your mind?") We stop at the first gas pump in Warmun amidst signs for NO ALCOHOL and NO PHOTOS, two of our themes rebuffed. A white woman with a poodle remarks how early we're up (5:30 a.m. by now), graciously tells us we are on community-only property, and suggests we drive another half mile to the Turkey Creek Roadhouse.

They'll open at six, she says.

Once there, we again shake everything out as we wait. I had worried today 500 fleas, tomorrow 5000, but so far so good. We just uncover a few. I cook up the tomatoes to get them through the afternoon quarantine at the Western Australia/Northern Territory border and make a final salad of forbiddens that we'll lunch on just before we cross. The gas station finally shows some signs of life, and we pull up to refuel. Boulders are interspersed with the gas pumps, both machine and nature brightly painted with regional birds, reptiles, and mammals.

W e continue through the Kimberley Mountain Range, its hills and mountains such a feast for the eyes that I'm finding it impossible to focus—red stacks of colliding geological strata, blue mountains, pale green velvet hills dotted with trees—Attention Deficit Disorder is courting me. Then I hit a bird.

This is a damn death machine, I fume.

Later, we see a few snakes and a number of goannas. These lizards are never in a rush to move, preferring instead to arrogantly flick their forked tongues as they soak up the heat of the road.

As we traverse the floodplains, Jon photographs a few more boab trees, our fascination with their swollen trunks continuing. One-lane bridges multiply; although some are quite long, they sit low to the ground, water lapping at their skirts. Jon enjoys a spiderfest at the Diversion Dam coming into Kununurra, composing a photo essay on the swollen-bellied black arachnids and their prey hanging on the bridge's fence. I stay in the van's cocoon, watching him climb the metal structure and dangle out for that perfect shot, trying to imagine the appeal, struggling with how to write the Death Orb eco-tourist text: "Get close to big black spiders of unknown temperament and venom on narrow metal bridge arching high over rushing water; share walkway-less platform with threatening trucks and other overheated, honking motorists; try not to slip."

We're about to leave the 83 Belgiums that are Western Australia for the Northern Territory, which comes in at a mere 16¼. The speed limit disappears, and my foot goes leaden.

North of the Ten Commandments, Jon warns. The worst road statistics in the developed world.

Out of Kununurra, we stop at the border and offer up our grapes, but they don't want them—they only collect from traffic going in the opposite direction. The genial ranger is amused at these two quarantine overachievers. While there, Jon photos a pied butcherbird with quite a repertoire, one who tilts back his head, opens his bill, and puffs out in song, a born performer who turns on for the camera. I grab my paper to notate his call.

Another jazz bird, I announce approvingly, the future poster bird for my ad campaign.

Pied Butcherbird

As we walk back to the van, I notice the grill kill suddenly come to life. Granted it's windy, but still I do a triple take, checking to see if any of these beating wings belong to a live insect I should rescue. It's a false alarm. When I look up, I see the wind surf its way through high grasses in the surrounding hills.

Today's 12 hours on the road again includes snakes, lizards, and vast mountain vistas. We spot a wavy fence at Glenarra Creek made from black plastic piping: the Tube Fence, we dub it. Coming into Katherine, we witness miles of termite hills reminiscent of penises, although there is one impressive battlefield replica—but perhaps that's the same thing.

Jon rewards my extended drive with a motel stay. I collapse in the room with a glass of 2000 Evans & Tate Shiraz/Cabernet/Merlot from the Margaret River, while Jon whips up a garlicky tomato-and-mushroom penne pasta with the only cheese at hand, a Margaret River blue. It's almost like dinner at the winery. I complete my revival with a swim midst palm trees, one of the great pool moments.

In the morning we head up to the Katherine Gorge. Carved by the Katherine River, it's really 13 gorges in one, each separated from the other by rapids. Although remote, the visitor center is of course touristy, meaning it doesn't suit us. On the balcony overlooking the river, we order a drink, trying to tune in the view as we tune out the piped-in rock 'n' roll. A tour boat is available. The motor noise, the other people, the flies, crocs, and snakes—we can't settle down here and instead charge back to town in search of a fly veil.

We hit the jackpot at a sporting goods store: my very own veil, although I'm disappointed with the hunter green color. I'd imagined Gothic black or bridal white. In any case, if I could just do something about my accent, I could perhaps pass as an Aussie. I'm trying. "Mobile" no longer rhymes with "noble" or "no deal": a cell phone is a "mobe-isle." I've quit ketchup in public places—it's a dead giveaway, Jon tells me. (While the odd restaurant does have it, if I can get myself to say "toMAHto sauce," the one glob coming from the tiny plastic container is just enough to frustrate me.[24] I desire an entire bottle delivered to my table, thank you, or none at all). I'm prepared to declare I remember the day I heard Gough Whitlam was sacked by the Queen of England's Governor General (25 years after other Australians first heard the news, but I *do* remember). Australia has the highest rate of skin cancer in the world (it's the national cancer), with 374,000 new cases last year. The bronzed and burnt locals have their precancerous skin afflictions attended to annually, but I am utterly without a tan. And I suppose the dark clothes would have to go if I were really going to try to pass myself off as a native daughter. I'm sorry I mentioned it. I'd rather wear black and look pale and interesting.

As I review my recent notes, I conclude that creeks have begun to tell a story in the last few days. There's the fauna: Emu, Camel, Dingo, Dingo Springs, Snake, Scorpion, Big Horse, Little Horse, Saddle, Yearling, Weaner; the landscape: Timber Pear Tree, Escarpment; and the struggles and follies of man in this environment: Telegraph, Quart Pot, Brandy Bottle, Skull, Mistaken, Disappointment, Lost, Chainman, and then Chinaman. This is welcome relief from the many Sandy Creeks and their ilk, the products of a lack of imagination or humor. There are no bad names, only bad namers.

Back in Katherine, I notice an Aboriginal woman lying on the bricks outside the post office, dead center atop the stairs, intentionally— she's not passed out but asleep. The small bag next to her is placed; there's nothing haphazard about her. It's her spot. Many miles later Jon wonders aloud if she is still sleeping soundly.

I remember hearing other Aboriginal people in the street. At first, their language seems squarely rhythmic as evidenced by the repeated syllables and triplet tonguings (and my bias that it would be so). A closer listen confuses as much as clarifies. The vowels are broad and flat, more complex than diphthongs—triphthongs at minimum. Sounds appear to be made far back in the throat, now in the nose, now from clicking tongues. I want to hear more.

Next to the Larramah Roadhouse, a sign touts buffalo and crocodile viewing. We find neither, although much ado is made at the overgrown crocodile cage. The warning reads: "Please do not throw anything into the pond or at the crocodiles, you may be required to go in and retrieve it!" Bushes and vines block our view, but we figure it's merely a scam to get folks to bring the kids and gas up here. The stuffed croc out front must be the very one that used to live in back.

At Newcastle Creek I make a U-turn to take in a bird sanctuary (unmarked and unofficial, unless you ask the winged ones). Cormorants, egrets, brolgas, storks, ibis, and ducks wade and paddle in integrated bliss. They're having a sewing bee, stitching and probing the water. It's

---

[24] Australia has invented a one-pinch, no-mess sauce experience.

prime birding without the entrance fees or crowds, and there's more than waterbirds below the bridge; there's the sinking old highway that is reverting back to nature, a macabre macadam.

Soon we see totem pole termite hills, white and pink ones burnt from bush fires and beginning to resemble a graveyard. There are so few cars passing in the outback that it's *de rigueur* to signal the other driver. I've begun a compendium of driver's salute variations: index, index and thumb, peace sign, thumb and little finger, four fingers, whole hand, whole arm. An index and middle finger salute came from the military passing us. Sometimes I'm up for it, but sometimes I find it a fake and burdensome event; I indicate without bothering to see if it's returned.

I suppose we salute one another to reassure ourselves that if adversity strikes, we're all family. It's a warm and fuzzy gesture tendered to suppress life's quiet desperation, like naming something after a place in England or introducing familiar flora and fauna or even raising a fence. Out of the car, fighting the flies, there's the national summertime salute: a quick flick of the wrist just in front of your face.

As I drive, hours and hours are at my disposal to figure it all out. For example, the Australian flora—ultimate conformists. I'm drafting a theory on herbaceous homogeneity based on my observation that all conspecifics match in size and color.

Already been done, Jon tells me.

Charles Darwin's younger cousin Francis Galton, who also discovered that human fingerprints are unique and founded the dubious field of eugenics, termed this "the regression to the mean," the mean in this case being the average ancestral type. He proposed that far from floras becoming freakier and freakier with each succeeding generation, they're trad; they want to be like grandma and grandpa. Galton believed the driving force in nature was the average.

As we sweep by in the van, the floras stick to their own clubs, making differences stand out as blocks of color. At the top of last night's screen, the canopies of large, grey-green trees were in total terminus agreement, while shrubs at the bottom ingeminated yellow-green. Our mid-screen highlight: middling trees in plagiarized purple, though not as deep in color as the glass of 2000 Taylor's McLaren Vale Cabernet we drank there.

Just before Tennant Creek we encounter a telegraph repeater station in ruins. It's the third one we've come upon in the Northern Territory, and we pile out to investigate. Several tall poles with ceramic insulators remain, plus a handful of deteriorating buildings and sheds. Nearby is a new favorite of mine, the grey Forked-Tree Fence, a horse fence with seven-foot-high tree skeletons for posts, all forming a V near the top. Lower down, two strands of barb are widely spaced, and where the third high strand might be expected, instead is a line of straight, fork-disabled timbers cradled between the V's, a wire substitute, a veritable trophy to unsustainability.

In town, the caravan park charges by the person, and I see why with the extended Aboriginal families in residence. It's a dreamtime-in-the-shower, slo-mo wait-in-line, what's-your-hurry kind of place. I'm always in a hurry on this drive. We're not spending the night, just stopping long enough to recharge our camera batteries, transfer digital images to our computer, and flip-flop to the shower. Then it's off to Alice Springs, having covered 4000 miles thus far. I'm a bit miffed about the indirectness of it all, actually, used to the American shopper's choice of routes crisscrossing the country at every angle. Here there's one road round and one road in. We're headed in.

We reach Alice by twilight and check into a trailer park, our second in one day. Our lights are on, our door is open, but there's not a bug in sight. How much do they spray? We ask, but they deny even a single squirt of bug juice.

At 27,000 inhabitants, it's the largest place we've been in weeks and reminds me of Bend, Oregon. This high desert town at the foot of the rugged MacDonnell Ranges was the main stopping point for the historic telegraph, which ran from Adelaide to Darwin. From there an underwater cable was extended across the sea to Java and on to London, thus connecting Australia to the rest of the world in 1872 by a single strand of fencing wire. The visionary in charge was Charles Todd, whose wife was Alice.

There were 12 repeater stations in the telegraphic lifeline; four survive. The other three are in ruins, but Alice's station is a proper museum. The restored stone structures were the first European buildings in Central Australia. In back, the camel yard comes complete with an arrogant, spitting beast. To reconstruct the milkyard, weathered posts have been gathered from a now-deceased four-foot fence and tilted against a square frame of rails. We are greeted by a bunch of aging, lounging chums all rounded up and leaning into a photo, a million stories there for the one who could decode them.

On our tour of the buildings, we come upon a piano that bumped up from Adelaide in 1870, making the final haul at rail's end on the back of a camel. (Consider the plight of the camel.) Two other uprights have also retired here. We pry them open and look inside, finding all three in various stages of distress. A small termite mound inside the Camel Piano crowds its inner workings, echoing the hump of the beast of burden that transported it.

Could we record on them? How is tomorrow morning? Great! We'll be back.

The simple harmonies of hymns realized on messed-up pianos could be useful to us in some future recording project, Jon says. Let's find a hymnal.

He relishes adding a fervent collision of the super-straight with the bent to our sound library. We stop at the closest Lutheran church and, trusting God and our ardent faces, the brethren send us away with a hymnal in hand.

Then Jon suggests a drive. I can feel he's up to something. Ten minutes out of town, he directs me down the innocuous Hatt Road. We come to an imposing sign: PINE GAP JOINT DEFENCE FACILITY **TURN AROUND NOW**. I've never heard of it.

Keep going, he says casually, banking on my ignorance.

I come to a full halt and stare at him.

That's fine for you to say, come out here with your guy friends some time and get arrested. I'm trying to immigrate. I'm outta here. As driver I prevail, and we do turn around now.

We don't get far. Jon stops us to record at a regiment of communication towers. I'm not heading into the tall grass to assist him—I've spotted a four-foot olive-green snake at the side of the road. I sit in the van trying to imagine what they do at Pine Gap, "Mission Impossible" theme music running in my head while my partner captures the superior sounds of the communications towers' perimeter fence. I turn to the guidebook, but information on Pine Gap is deliberately scanty.[25]

Jon figures he needs a telephone to complete this mission, so we check into a cheap motel at the south end of town. That's when we notice the Prince Charles and Princess Diana mail slots; they claim the royal couple actually stayed here. Forgive me, but it seems a bit downscale. Jon calls Pine Gap, but of course cannot get past the receptionist. He leaves a message with no particular hope of being called back.

I declare this evening a tourist one. Beware dinners with a title, in this case "The Drovers Blowout." We begin with cream of pumpkin soup with damper (an unleavened bread baked in ashes), then feast on steak, kangaroo fillet served with a red wine and mushroom sauce, emu medallion, and camel fillet served with plum sauce (all of which tasted like steak), plus an excellent crocodile *vol au vent* and a bit of grilled barramundi to stave off hunger. Three kinds of vegetables. Don't forget the apple pie. Quite an event for thin near-vegetarians. A crane is called to remove us from our table; we pay and take our leave, a cannonball embedded in each of our stomachs.

---

[25] Pine Gap was formally launched as a joint American/Australian "space research facility" in a 1966 treaty. Since then, it's been the target of numerous rumors and protests, including a recent march to the gate by the International Physicians for the Prevention of Nuclear War.

Jon tells me that it is the main communications center for the U.S. military in the southern hemisphere; the word on the street is that even the Australian prime minister needs permission from the Pentagon to visit Pine Gap.

A red-back spider *(Latrodectus hasselti)*, the deadlier cousin to the black widow spider, is lurking about the door to our hotel room, or perhaps we're the intruders. This spider bites two thousand surprised people a year; I don't intend to be one of them. If only I'd bought that "Keep Your Distance" insect vacuum: "Lets you quickly capture and dispose of insects at a comfortable distance without ever having to touch them." We make a fast if inelegant entrance.

The next morning at the telegraph station we begin on the yellowed, uneven keys of the Camel Piano. I choose classic hymns like "Onward Christian Soldiers" and "Abide With Me," which I pound out with the revived earnestness of my youth when I had to rally the congregation to song. The three pianos vary from detuned, to detuned and some keys don't sound, to detuned and many keys don't sound, that one bringing more percussion than pitch to the soundprint. Kerplunketty, Kerplunkettier, and Kerplunkettiest, this trio. And the tuning—it's quite a shock to my perfect pitch ears to read the hymns in one key and hear the music come out a haphazard six or seven semitones lower, akin to biting into an apple turnover and discovering it's really a meat pie.

Jon improvises on the worst two (the best in his view), choosing complexity over simplicity, motif over form, and chaos over order. He gives the farfetched pianos expiring in this obscure little room as thorough a going-over as a forensic physician expected to produce a report. It's just him and the tape recorder—the telegraph fallen silent, the choir disbanded, the audience a no-show save for the huge wasp worrying a corner of the room.

When I play a few more hymns, the stinging machine takes some dives at me, obviously attracted by the finesse of my clang-tinkle-thuds. Mr. Obsessive nods for me to buck up and continue recording. I look up pleadingly from the piano.

Just play, he barks.

And I do.

We attend The School of the Air to watch a class in session. The teacher talks into a microphone to her isolated outback students, their radio receivers powered by generators. Founded in 1951, the School covers an area of 386,000-square miles (or 1,000,000-plus-square km or easier still, 34 Belgiums). Today's lesson is on spiders, and I'm touched by the hesitant young voices piercing the hissing static. We've gone back in time, and yet we're *au courant*: our soloist for today is child soprano with distorted, modulating, phasing white and pink electronic noise, based on a surrealist text on an eight-legged predatory arachnid.

Next, we take a tour of the Royal Flying Doctor Service command post. Medicine, aviation, and radio came together in the 1928 establishment of the R.F.D.S., and it now covers an area larger than Western Europe (I'll get back to you on the Belgium stats). The sick and injured are attended to without charge from 20 bases, the R.F.D.S. doing 24,000 aerial evacuations annually. A doctor, nurse, and pilot man their flights, and they often land on gravel or dirt. Because the airstrips are not used continually, it is practice to test them by driving a motor vehicle over them before each landing. If a night landing is called for, everyone available gathers to shine car headlights on the airstrip.

On to the Olive Pink Botanical Gardens. The more I find out about this eccentric, the more I want to know.[26] We meet the current director of the Gardens, whose father knew Miss Pink. While his father was an inspector of noxious weeds in the Northern Territory, Miss Pink invited him for a memorable tour here. She conducted him along a row of planted river red gums, each of which had been named after someone. This was Miss Pink's way of expressing gratitude to those who did favors for her. She introduced him to the trees, but one tree was introduced with a stern voice.

I'm not watering him anymore. [He had fallen from favor.]

Stories about her continue to haunt the Central Australian landscape. A policeman in Alice once tried to arrest her for jaywalking.

She struck him with her parasol and shouted, Unhand me, you cad!

And he did.

She often appeared in court to monitor the treatment of Aboriginal people. One day as she stood up to deliver her protest, the judge instructed her to sit down or face contempt of court charges.

I am *very* contemptuous of this court, she insisted.

The judge fined her $30, which she refused to pay, preferring to go to jail. Within half an hour of hearing the news that the problematic Miss Pink would be locked up in his prison, the mortified town jailer arrived at the courthouse to pay the fine himself.

We hike around her Gardens, following a path up to a vista of vast plains, corrugated hills, and sawtooth mountains. A green and yellow-collared bird fills the air with its "tirrrit." Plains, hills, mountains, birds …that's all I know about what I'm looking at.

---

[26] I was able to consult Olive Pink's letters in the Elkin archives at the Fisher Library at the University of Sydney (with the assistance of Tim Robinson). ABC Radio's The Listening Room commissioned me to produce a radiophonic work on her life; *Shocking Pink* first aired on August 25, 2003.

Born in Hobart in 1884 to Quaker parents, Olive Pink died in Alice Springs in 1975, aged 91. An anthropologist who overcame her fear of spiders and snakes (this, of course, impresses me) to live for several years among Aboriginal people, Miss Pink anticipated many contemporary arguments concerning Aboriginal issues while sustaining a 40-year, one-woman campaign on behalf of the Warlpiri and Arrernte people. She opposed nuclear testing on Aboriginal lands and the establishment of the Pine Gap facility, although she insisted that the Aboriginal workers building the base were properly paid. Her prescience encompassed environmental matters as well, to which this Gardens is testament.

Naming—that lashing of new discoveries to the trusty rafts of the known by explorers, colonizers, scientists, theorists, and enthusiasts— eludes me. I'm out to sea, bereft of local knowledge and unable to name another thing or interpret how it all fits together. The Aborigines named as well, but their network of names served as a path to remembering rather than owning. They understood that mnemonic devices like melody, rhythm, rhyme, and pattern aid the memory.

Miss Pink's fieldwork hung in the balance between the two cultures. I'm drawn to her in part because she, too, was a list person, conscientiously scribbling down what others missed or bypassed. (Had I realized at age 18 that there was a profession where you could make lists for a living, I would have forsaken the violin and become an anthropologist.) One entry from Miss Pink's notebooks inventoried the practical lives of women, material absent in the journals of male explorers. I've reworked it with the Lutheran hymn "All Praise to Thee, My God, This Night" (aka "Tallis' Canon") as its mnemonic device.

a woman's possessions and requirements

HER DOMESTIC UTENSILS:
Two grinding stones, one flat, one small
Tied up in fi-ine vine, that's all.
Diggy diggy stick stick, poker, and
Four wooden vessels here on hand.

HER COSMETICS:
Red ochre decorates her face
And yellow sometimes takes its place
The grease from lizards looks just right
As does the larvae of termite.
FOR BABIES:
Her handkerchiefs are leaves and grass
The sandy soil dries baby's ass:
Her blanket is of paperbark.
The perambulator is a wooden scarp.

FOR PERSONAL USE:
As fabric clearly fur string's best:
Neckbands, headbands, a fur string chest
A fire stick, its embers hot
A handkerchief of grass, that's what.

Alice must be rich in naming. I incline my ear, squint, and concentrate, trying to tune into the vista's ecology. Of course, my efforts produce nothing but the same four words utterly resistant to nuance:

plains, hills, mountains, birds—not enough to even begin a rhyme.[27] I'm no better off than if I'd just driven by in an air-conditioned motor home with all the trimmings. No need to get out—we'll just pull off at this scenic overlook for 20 seconds; or if we decide to stay for lunch, we can always watch a bit of TV while the microwave heats our meal.

I try to imagine Olive Pink lecturing the Queen, who technically owns this land (although she prefers to live 14,000 miles away in her subsidized housing at Buckingham Palace), on how possession is an illusion, how the most one can attain, and the only reliable bit, is knowledge and wisdom. This approach has sustained the Aboriginal people here for millennia. It's a deep truism echoed by the indigenous peoples in my country as well, such as the observation attributed to Chief Joseph: "How can you own the land?"

I am a stranger in this land such as I have never been in any other place, a newcomer utterly without recommendation. At best, my knowledge is soft and eggheaded. I lack a sense of direction, knowledge of the flora and fauna, and even the most basic bush skills; worse, I'm one who fears them that bite, melts in the heat, and requires water in abundance. Should I live here for the rest of my days, I'd still be considered a blow-in.

---

[27] I don't know (until later) that I'm standing on a sacred hill, or that the small ridge in the middle distance is one of the first sites created by the caterpillar ancestors.

I don't know that the gregarious bird is one of Australia's most popular, the budgerigar (I've never even heard the word). Although they can exist without water for some time, these small bright green parrots *(Melopsittacus undulatus)* are highly nomadic and tend to follow the lush grass brought by rains. Then, budgies congregating in large numbers can put so much pressure on nesting sites that some will eventually have to settle for very low stumps or logs. (Later yet I discover that budgerigars are what we Americans call parakeets, but I didn't trust myself to make the connection in this kangaroo court of a place where everything is antithetic.)

And how am I to find a witchetty grub *(Endoxyla leucomochla)*? The larva of this large moth is prime bush tucker, creamy almond in flavor and high in protein, an Atkins-approved food source—who will suggest I look for the telltale piles of sawdust that the worms leave as they burrow into the lower limbs of a wichetty bush *(Acacia kempeana)*?

The Olive Pink Botanical Garden museum temporarily tranquilizes me by explaining how plants in the Central Australian arid zone deal with stress (such as an irregular supply of water, high heat and radiation loads, intermittent burning by natural or lit fires, soils low in vital nutrients, salt accumulation, grazing by indigenous or introduced herbivores). They cope just like people, by being Avoiders (existing during the most stressful times as dormant seeds or underground buds) or Tolerators (adapting).

I'm grateful for this expert information but tempted to concoct an antagonist, one who counters that perhaps this is just so much Eurocentrizing and anthropomorphizing—this isn't stress, this is how these plants exist. It seems these flora don't want a lot of water or a soil rich in nutrients. They're specialists. They would die in a pot in my house—*that* would be stressful.

This latecomer is trying to avoid the sins of the fathers. I don't want to own it, I want to get it, to escape my ignorant state and cobble together a story on Alice, on Australia, on Aborigines. I'm not a New Age natural; I don't trust that the information will come along when I need it. It's already late in my view, with my subconscious framing things hit-and-miss.

I'm forced to piece together my own guide, collecting information from every possible source: books, brochures, museums, the locals—but the big picture is not yet in place. I'm wondering, wandering. In my hunger for stories and concurrent skepticism of them, my mind begins to circle nineteen to the dozen. Once in motion, I can't regain my balance. I question the very nature of my thinking, desperate for grid and context.

I want to say I can adapt to the conditions set down by *terra australis*, but I secretly wish I could make some of them adapt to me. I'd upset the delicate balance in a heartbeat. I take back everything I said about the insecurity of Adelaidians past and present. Bring in the Royal Navy and set them onto the Todd River. Never mind that the river is normally dry. Something solid and known is what's called for, and even a waterless regatta will fit the bill in a town like Alice.[28]

It's true—The Henley-on-Todd aquatic festival is held each September, drawing the largest crowds of any Alice Springs event. A parody of the annual boating regatta between Oxford and Cambridge Universities on the Thames, the regatta has categories for sailing boats, doubles, racing eights, bathtubs, "Oxford tubs," yachts, and every other boat class, all bottomless so that the legs of the crew can run the sandy course. Canoes are paddled with sand shovels. I read of boats made of beer cans and bathtubs with sails, whole naval battles by "Vikings," "pirates" crewing battle boats on truck chassis, and high-pressure colored water cannons hurling flour bombs at their opponents. But if it rains and there is water in the river, the boat race has to be cancelled.

After the race, we'll have a bit of a hunt with all the Queen's horses and all the Queen's men, perhaps spread a picnic or host a formal ball. After all, England is still the template.

B ack in the motel room, our phone rings.

> Jon Rose, please.
> **Speaking.**
> Jon, my name's _____ _____.

---

[28] Shute, Nevil (1950/1991) *A Town Like Alice*, New York: Ballantine Books.

Thanks for getting back to me. So, did you get my message from yesterday?

I got a message about fences.

That's right.

Which organization are you from?

Well, I'm a freelance musician actually, but this is a project for ABC radio, and it's a nation-wide project, my partner and I are recording fences all over Australia, the famous ones like the Dog Fence and Rabbit Fence, and not-so-famous ones, so it's a huge sort of compilation of fences, and we're going to be making a piece for the Melbourne Festival with it, and we're going to build a fence in Queensland next year, and the whole town will play it, it's a massive project, and we're collecting famous fences, and Pine Gap's a famous fence, and we're wondering if we can get 15 minutes of recording.

Um, no, not really, we're a prohibited area.

I realize that, that's why I'm trying to get permission for it.

You can get some stock footage though, Jon, from Defense Public Affairs and Corporate Communications.

We don't want to film it, we want to record it, we use contact microphones and we put them on the fence, and sometimes the wind is strong enough to make the fence …I know straight off in the morning it sounds like a completely loopy thing but believe me musically it's very interesting.

Yeah.

And we either let the wind do its work or we use bows, we're both violinists, so it's not a visual documentation, we can make visual documentation, but we realize that might be a bit sensitive.

Well, there is stock footage that you can get from Public Affairs, now look in today's world, it's not appropriate to do this, we are a prohibited area and we control access to the place.

Right.

So I'm sorry I can't oblige you.

We have no political intent in this, you're very welcome to listen to the recording, it's just a musical project.

We have controlled approaches to our front gate, and we're obliged to do that under the laws that govern us, so yeah, I'm sorry I can't help you out.

And your official title is?

I'm the Deputy Chief of the Joint Defence Facility.

Well, ___, thank you anyway for getting back to me, and maybe we'll see each other at some stage.

Well, yeah, as I said I'd like to oblige you, but under the current circumstances.

When you say "current circumstances …"

The world situation—all of defense in Australia is under a state of alert.

Oh really, I didn't know that, [pretending ignorance] and that's due to?

Due to the war on terrorrrrrrism! [He articulates slowly and at maximum decibels.]

Listening back to the recording of the call—if it is legal to record a telephone call in Australia, and if it is not legal, then—thinking back to our memory of the call, can you blame the guy? Jon does sound over the top. But no wonder: one (unofficial, of course) website describes the Pine Gap facility as enclosed by a 50–mile security fence, a veritable Stradivarius of fine fence instruments awaiting our bows. I know Jon wanted this one badly.

Day and night, cars pass through the drive-up bottle shop just opposite our motel room. It's quite a succession of mostly Aboriginal people. We begin to imagine their stories, like the woman crying hysterically yesterday afternoon. Should we go blank or fill in the blanks? Some people hang out on the front lawn, joining the nearly continuous ad hoc picnic. We find the women can be as aggressive as the men. In town, we witnessed numerous fights, including a woman throwing ashes or garbage from a trashcan onto a man who proceeded to cower and strip to his underpants while she shouted him down. We see blank looks, drugged looks, limps and teeterings, clothes still as ragged as the first day decades ago that these people's ancestors were "given" (forced to wear) hand-me-downs by stationmasters.

Many of the Aboriginal people seem off to themselves, seeing and hearing in quite unimaginable ways, stunned, marching, disconnected, suddenly violent, as if we were invisible or something else was more clearly real. Their lines are broken. We saw a couple camping on Billy Goat Hill in the bus information kiosk. They were blissfully cooking and carrying on in their little bungalow, albeit one without walls. You might think their house had been relocated or land-grabbed, had become part of someone else's place, and they had been failed to be notified.

How are you? Jon asked. Do you live here? Do you like to come here?—trying to pose the correct questions.

It's our place, they said. We're just lookin' after it.

Grill Kill Three commences now, as we've lost Two to the well-meaning mechanic in Alice. All species may be equal in the eyes of God, but my human eyes play favorites, lining things up in the plus, minus, or neutral column (akin to the German *der*, *die*, and *das* for "the"). Our new collection begins sadly, with a dark-green dragonfly and another very red one. Iridescent golden rods support their window-paned wings, and set within each wing's glistening transparency, a single red pane asserts itself. Next, we add a dragonfly with the orange-red body of a thin, dried chili pepper. (The young are always anxious to grow up. That aquatic nymph lifestyle wasn't so bad, was it? Okay, always having to dodge those feeding fish, but flying seems so much more fraught with risk, and now look what I've done to you.) A yellow fluff of a moth recalling an old-fashioned peony comes on board, then a sleeker white one with black wingtips.

Five days of intensive driving are ahead of us, Alice to Winton. Again, we're running a one-lane road with a steep dirt shoulder, and nonstop hills hamper my view. On approaching each crest, I wonder if someone is pummeling toward us. We pass through the Devil's Marbles Conservation Reserve where huge spheres of granite boulders, understood by the Aboriginal peoples to have been laid by the Rainbow Serpent, are scattered about. Naturally, someone has built a fence through it all. Cables obnoxiously stretch *over* the "protected" rocks when they attempt to defy the fence's agenda. Smoke turns up at this devil's playground, then flames burn red and hungry in a tree right next to us. It's a bush fire, and we vamoose.

From Alice, we're retracing our steps north; after 300 miles we turn right just past Tennant Creek. I ask Jon how far it is, not really knowing if I mean that day or all the way to Brisbane.

Long—big long, he intones.

The wind, which has dogged us for hours, picks up, and the termite hills increase in size to half a dozen footballers leaning in a huddle. Later they thin out while keeping their width, a field of tombstones in shape, position, and number. Every day is a bad hair day for the stunted trees. Those dehydrated in fires contract into bulb-shaped baskets. Some bend at the waist, their distressed ballerina arms enclosing the bleakness of it all, most ending their life with their branches pointing in the same direction, like witnesses to a crime giving a final clue. Other trees appear caught in a last-ditch attempt to go two-dimensional rather than die outright. Past Barkly Station, the anthills resemble an orgy of people trying to keep each other safe and warm, although it stretches my imagination to think of it ever getting cool here.

Highway demarcation posts are quivering in the hot winds, and Jon is searching for the most a-tremble to star in a short movie. The road is littered with them, all snapped off and retired from the Highway Department, contributing in their final years as scraps of red and white color in an otherwise dull landscape. When we come upon one post vigorously shaking from ten to two o'clock, Jon struggles with the fierce wind, just as I have been for hours as driver. The camera is blown off the tripod but survives.

It was like being in a wind-blasted furnace, he says when he climbs back in, and the post made the unnerving sound of bones rattling-tling.

That's our highlight for hours, until the Barkly Highway leads us into Queensland where it doubles as Main Street for Camooweal. The town used to be the main dipping center for cattle crossing the state border. The landscape is one huge, green but treeless field for miles. I long for the vertical.[29]

When drivers see the sign UNFENCED ROAD AHEAD, it usually means time to ratchet up the powers of observation and try to avoid hitting animals who have not studied their highway code. In our case, however, it is time to relax a little, knowing that the fence watch can be downgraded and we can start taking in other aspects of the big outdoors. The eyes usually wander to the horizon, that land-and-sky schism where color theory is tested and tested again. But just as you've been lulled into a false sense of sit-back-and-accept-all-incoming-visions, there is a fence alert.

1. STOP! The shout should be loud and clear but not so the driver thinks a wheel has fallen off, thus upsetting her.

2. (This is actually #1, but nobody observing you would be able to figure this out except for a slight twitch of the nose, hence its position at #2.) In the space of two to three seconds, you run a sped-up movie, which takes you through all forms of fences that you have previously played and/or photographed. If the newly observed fence is considered quite generic, lacking any extramural qualities and anyway previously documented, restrain activating the STOP! response. If after scrolling through some 3000 images of fences and 20 hours of recordings, you consider that this fence will add to the experience that is Fence, activate STOP! code immediately. Failure to do this, which results in you shouting STOP! some five or even ten minutes after the fence event, causes the driver to slide into a bad mood for some hours, as turning around on unstable ground or reversing up a single-lane highway for a half-mile is potential cause for much anguish. This lady has an aversion to the past.

3. Some relief, as it is discovered that the fence looks like no other.

4. No time to waste, as it is mid-day and the temperature is about 120F.

5. Grab equipment. There are two options: one, take digital photographs and record audio to DAT or MD; two, the full Monty—all of the above plus the video camera, tripod, and toolbox.

---

[29] Carter, Paul (1987) *The Road to Botany Bay*, London: Faber and Faber, 286.

6. Open door, jump out of car, and swear at flies already awaiting you.

7. Walk quickly or run slowly to potential fence interest, checking ground for snakes.

8. Take photographs, then tap fence wires and posts for a quick sonic assessment. If response is good, yell at driver to come quick (as you are already overheated) and bring cello and bass bows.

9. While waiting for fence assistant to attend, find holes or splits in fence post in which to insert contact microphones. Set up video camera. Try possible shots. You are now completely covered in flies, and sweat is pouring down your face, covering your prescription sunglasses and making it impossible to see anything through the video viewfinder.

10. Inquire as to where your assistant has got to (yell again).

11. A squadron of flying, biting bugs has located your activities.

12. Assistant still not assisting, perhaps she didn't hear (yell still louder).

13. Consider musical strategies for fence: rhythmic potential, bottom end stuff, harmonic clusters, natural reverb—long or short and gated?

14. Assistant arrives looking unhappy, checks every step for snake attack but agrees to perform.

15. Press red button, produce performance or else.

16. Or else we do it again.

Across Blue Bush and Happy Creeks, fathometers posted to show flood levels bring on "How high's the water, sister, two feet high and risin' …" Although three days' drive from here towns called Longreach and Blackall threaten, the creek names now have a kinder tone. We encounter Bishop, Shakespeare, Wild Duck, Salmon, Plum Tree, and Fisher's Creeks.

Names aside, we're not totally won over by the area. Alice was the hottest city in the world for two days running, and we're still in the frying pan. I imagine that all my vitamins, creams, and first aid medications have deteriorated in the heat, like me. "Store below 85 Fahrenheit," they read; my body has a similar unwritten code. Last night, one half of the chapstick tube stuck to my lip when I pulled it away.

I do a double take at technologies two centuries apart: a windmill next to a fiber-optic telephone station, both in use. And there's another bit of technology at work here: radar. I'm stopped for speeding 118 in a 100 zone. I *never* speed, well almost. It's a single lane gravel road much of the way to Mount Isa. The cop counts on your total frustration by the time you get to the three miles of good, wide, sealed road, and he waits there like a fisherman lurking at the big hole. Fortunately, he lets me off, a sort of catch-and-release program with a barbless hook. No harm done.

Yes, Sir; thank you, Sir.

Since the track is one lane, dips with FLOODWAY signs pale in importance compared to CREST signs. I hold my breath near the top of each one, a captive on a carnival ride. Who's coming over the hill? Whenever, whoever, they will expect a greeting. There's been an evolution in my driver's salute, from knee-jerk to reluctant to withdrawn …then back to lonely eagerness and on to the current stretching out my hands from days of driving. They ache, and I need any break I can get from holding the wheel. Occasionally for relief, I even salute the spirits of last week's passing motorists.

The isolated Mount Isa is a mining town, not a tourist one; unlike, say, Broome, here in "The Isa" the only palm trees and the best gardens are at McDonald's. There *is* an unofficial tourist fence as you come into town, though, if you're that sort of person—and we are. Slender pieces of metal have been cut into the shapes of boomerangs, goannas, warriors with spears, and the like, then painted and mounted to compose a kitschy delight. Into and out of Mount Isa, we see lush hills and mountains in psychedelic greens.

I've finally figured how to drive in the sun. I tie on a kerchief across the lower half of my face, bandit-style.

"Desperado," Jon dubs me.

Yeah, the Eagles song—and isn't there a mention of fences in the lyrics? "Dessss-perado," I begin to sing, "Why don't you come to your senses, you've been out riding fences for so long …" I trail off as an act of mercy to Jon's ears, then revive and skip to the end: "Desperado, why don't you come to your senses, come down from your fences, open the gate." Nothing quite says it like rock 'n' roll.

Hours later, coming into Winton, we are taken hostage by the biggest sky possible (I'm learning that flat lands imply good skies.) Distant storm systems hold forth in every direction—there's one, and another, three, four, five, six, and seven, just in front of us and in our peripheral vision. Long purple-blue cords deliver the rain direct from the heavens to the ground, a punk-Rapunzel's hair let down. Jon turns to see more storm systems behind us. There's even a swatch of a thick but truncated rainbow. Behind the threatening clouds, white and grey-white ones go about their slower business. Sunbeams streaming heaven-to-ground match the rain cords in length and drama, the whole sky dripping in light and color. It's a gold-and-purple extravaganza scrolling straight from a religious calendar.

The rain has not cooled Winton, whose greater population is a mere 1800 although the shire claims to be "the size of Denmark" (translated from the Danish, that's 1.4 Belgiums, but even so, there's more sky than country). The remote town is the birthplace of both Qantas Airways and the song "Waltzing Matilda." The council wants to rev things up for the Queensland Biennale and is intrigued with our idea to design a musical fence for the town to play.

We spend our first Winton night at a caravan park where an obviously German couple speaks only English to one other (except when they fight). The other German in residence is a canine who corners me post-shower at the bathroom outbuilding. I hear him panting outside, it's already dark, and I'm the only one around. I call for Jon; I scream for Jon. He's gone deaf as a post. Perhaps this Hound of the Baskerville is merely curious about a hysterical camper. Finally his interest fatigues, he slinks off in the night, and I make my escape.

The next day we check into a motel. The TV commercials give us a plain-as-plain sense of place: sheep wormer, auto parts, water tanks, silos, and the night rodeo are the proffered products. Bob calls from the shire council to discuss our design for the Winton Fence and suggests we begin with a drive in Bladensburg National Park. He picks us up, and we head out of town, passing through the shade of river red gums and coolibahs up to a flat-topped mesa to view the vast plains of green (Mitchell) and red (Flinders) grasses.

My name's Bob Hoogland, I'm the Chief Executive Officer of Winton Shire Council, we're in Winton in outback Queensland, and we're on a jump-up looking out across the open expanses of grass downs towards the town of Winton, and it's a tremendous open view, I can see the remains of a lazy old fence made up of gidyea posts, gidyea's quite a hard timber, it's a local timber that we have a lot of here in quite thick forests in places, and so it was used a lot in those fences

These days because we're in a national park those fences are being taken down a lot, and the group that does that is actually the prisoners, who have teams out here that do that sort of voluntary work in the place, and that works very well for our communities too, there's still a few old people around who have fireplaces and wood stoves, and the guys come out and remove the fences, which is very good for the national park, and they use the timber for the people in town that need it, so the fences are still being very useful even when they've stopped being used as fences.[30]

---

[30] Wooden railings for firewood—that seems a bit rash. Fires and termites get their share. Can't a few be left for heritage? The colors and forms of timber stock fences are

That's called Scrammy, it's obviously been an outstation point where the guys who do the fencing and other property work with the stock used to camp when it was a working sheep station, and so you can see here where they have camped over a fair period of time and you can see the old drink bottles, so all those different kinds and colors of bottles and glasses and tins, the relics of a previous generation, are lying there, and it's quite interesting to see, there's a few places where you can see graves beside the road, and it speaks of a time when lives were shorter and life was a lot harder and distances were so much more because we didn't have cars, people were pretty much buried where they dropped.

Bob's enthusiasm for the land extends to bush poetry, and while we are perched on the jump-up (or plateau), he recites Banjo Patterson's "The Bush Christening." On our descent, a father and four adolescent emu chicks run like mad in front of us, feet kicking up dust just like in a Roadrunner cartoon. We follow the River Gum Route as Bob explains that anyone in Winton can put 25 head on the common land. Twice a year they muster them ("round 'em up" in 'merican), pairing the cows and calves; the owner can then sell them or resend them out. We pass the Shearers' Strike Memorial of 1894, marking the beginning of Australian unionism. In the course of our morning drive, over a hundred roos dart in and out of view.

Until two days ago, there'd been no rain here in over a year. Looking down, I see blue where I expect brown, barely aware that it's the sky reflected in the rainwater as it puddles in the hard claypans. It must be the lighting crew's own game board, ice blue puzzle pieces shockingly rolled out onto mudflats. The equally brown Bough Shed Hole is a boon to swimmers and crayfish, according to Bob. It's about six feet deep, and the top two are warm.

My wife didn't much like it at first, he says, coming from the coast as we did with the beaches 'n' that, but she'll swim in it now.

The next morning Bob the naturalist continues to hold forth. He points out a pair of brolgas, blue-grey figurines with bare heads and exaggerated beaks, their bodies stretched thin beyond reason, pure artifice, seemingly park statuary until they walk steadily away. No need to point out the roos who are again bounding everywhere.

Owls will eat a whole marsupial, he explains, then sit in a tree and vomit the fur and bones. If you come upon these rejected piles and look up, you might be rewarded with a view of the owl itself.

---

a picturesque record of Australia's pastoral history, plus they are habitat for invertebrates, reptiles, and fungi.

I learn that spinifex grass has volatile oils that make it good for starting a fire. He identifies spinifex pigeons, parasitic holly flowering red on an acacia tree, bloodwoods, gums, and a war zone of twisted gidyea trees that attest to the dry seasons when branches and roots search in all directions for water and nutrients (some do entire circles, and one we dub The Octopus). Mulga, with its characteristic curly red bark, lines dry creek beds.

We stop at Scrammy Gorge so he can show us the nine-foot, olive-backed pythons that eat a small kangaroo in the early morning, and then recline in the rocks to digest it. We find a snake *track*, but no more. I find myself unable to match his level of disappointment. I figure the pythons are still out cruising for their morning meal and make sure nothing I do resembles a hop or a bound.

We find a fence cable going through a white gum and try to work out which came first, tree or fence. Jon composes a photo essay of rusty corrugated iron fences against the sky—the classic outback colors of red-brown and blue.[31] He selects an automatic setting, improvising a camera position for every shot, 16 of them per frame.

We spend the afternoon considering sites for the Winton Fence. One electric fence gives Jon quite a jolt when he accidentally touches it. A vacant block next to our motel intrigues us; it faces out into the big Never-Never[32] where a permanent wind howls.

The wind could come in off the plains and set a fence going, Jon says. Why not make it a permanent structure?

Bob is enchanted with the idea.

I begin to formulate designs that will draw the site into the fence. My plan is based on the Fibonacci series, in which each new number is the sum of the two preceding numbers (1, 1, 2, 3, 5, 8, and so on). The beginning of the series is the beginning of a spiral. Then, where to put the spiraling fence posts—this should be measured exactly so that the

---

[31] Consider for a moment the ubiquitous corrugated iron. Where would Australia be without this invention, still the major material used in roofs on your average suburban home? It also features as a component in many pieces of fashionable public architecture. We, however, enthusiastically view it as a source of fencing. It's practical stuff. No beast or human can physically get through a slab of corri—most you can do is dent the thing and badly hurt yourself. In our photo archive, we have a selection of corri in various states of corrosion, having turned all colors of the rainbow and then some.

Then there's the sound. A composer like Stockhausen might have put a contact mic on a piece of corri rather than a gong if he had been an Aussie. It's a percussion instrument in a class all of its own—gong, ride cymbal, smash cymbal, high hat, bass drum, washboard, rattle—you name it. Efficient design, too—a whole heap of metal in a compressed format.

[32] Gunn, Mrs. A. (1908/1990) *We of the Never-Never*, Sydney: Arrow.

pitches correspond to the pure intervals of a scale in just intonation. The lateral tension would be quite severe, so they will need diagonal support and to be thoroughly bolted to a concrete base. It's awkward to describe, but the result will be extremely elegant yet functional.

Tonight's destination: the Rangelands with Bob and a couple from his office. We scramble over the 500 yards of cap rock on top, then climb between a rift, an over-our-heads split in the earth's surface just wide enough for us to pass through. Our eagle's-nest view is of all the great safari parks merged into one, although in our smokeless age, wires have replaced fires. At sunset, they pull snacks from the back of the LandCruiser and open a bottle of Brown Brothers Dolcetto, a red wine with a touch of sweetness and bubbles and an almost dusty palette. As the sun bids goodnight, the flies know it's time for them to go home too, although there's always a few who never attended finishing school.

> The stones and dust rose in a thick cloud from the whirling wheels and flying hoofs, and the posts of the wire fence on our left passed like magic as we went.[33]

The road atlas is our game board; Great Fences of Australia is our game. Jon's checking the rules to see when it ends. Do we fold when we run out of money? Perhaps we can collect fees from other players when they land on our fences. As we buzz through, most towns play a temptation card, like a hooker flashing a length of thigh or a scoop of melon. Longreach deals its Stockman's Hall of Fame, while Blackall hits us with the 1892 world record by Jacky Howe who hand-sheared 321 sheep in under eight hours, not to be broken until 1950—and then by a machine. Do we tarry? No dice! The rules say we press on in search of the end of the Dingo Fence.

While the lines and dots can be mapped, the multilayered stories to which they refer cannot be contained. We don't even try. For several days we've dwelled in 2-D, avoiding drive-by assumptions made from superficial encounters and instead waiting for something more to our taste.

We find the Dingo Barrier Fence 30 miles before Tambo, make a brief inspection, and again follow the road. I'm feeling numbed by the contrast between the then of Winton's teeming-with-life bush and the now of increased traffic and its inevitable result: the only roos we see are roadkill. The eagles are surviving, though; we saw over 20 of them jockeying for position on one fatality. Death in its various stages

---

[33] Franklin, Miles (1901/2001) *My Brilliant Career*, Sydney: HarperCollins, 102.

surrounds us, from fresh roadkill to skeletal remains and everything in between

Coming into Tambo, a long, black row of birds on a power line burns into our memory—so long, so black. But looking back at the photo, there are neither so many nor are they so dark. Perhaps we remember them vividly, however incorrectly, because they stayed and stayed no matter how close we got, while everything else has been fleeing us for weeks. I'm taken aback, but I try to follow the logic: I can't trust my notes because I can't trust my memory because I can't trust how I took it in to begin with. (It would appear that details of the original memory trace have suffered degradation during committal or retrieval, or was I just pruning?) Like the birds of whatever number and color they might have been, today's creeks appear amicable: Packsaddle, Christmas, Galah, Windmill, Black Boy, Wet Rocky followed by Dry Rocky, and Home.

The red dust at our camp is inches thick, and then once again we hit the road where heat, humidity, and tedium confound and collapse time. My consciousness unravels into thinner and thinner strands, strains, or is it trains of thought? I can't find the word, the picture, or the notion, am unable to tell if my mind is lagging behind or has drifted too far ahead. Afraid that if I tug on the wrong thought, I'll come unstrung altogether, I try to match the region's simplicity. Be grateful for the least event, I insist, like the alternation of stopping and starting, of day and night. But that won't do; I'm sick of the landscape having its way with me. I'm going to imprint my vision and desires onto this wasteland.

I decide to make the roadkill into something more interesting and begin by seeing them as other animals, even inventing exotic ones as a bad joke—An anteater!—knowing that Jon will insist everything is a kangaroo in mock censoriousness. Finally, in a rare move that strikes at the very heart of our road religion, I stop the van and back up to see the most giant lizard ever, no joke, I'm sure this time. Whoops!—just another roo skeleton.

In Miles ("and Miles and Miles and Miles") we see so many eagles on roadkill that we wonder if they will some day lose their ability to hunt and depend on the road to sustain them. Just out of town, we pull off at another Dingo Fence grid. We hear an incredibly loud insect but can't spot it. For a rare moment, fences be damned, Jon rushes out with the recorder to capture the insect's soundprint. The boisterous tone comes and goes as the mimetic insect apparently responds to passing trucks. We speculate that he hears them as one of his own, only bigger. When the trucks stop for the day, the insect falls silent.

Could insects lose their interest and ability to sound for survival, their sense of place and purpose?[34] We linger, listening, sole participants at a Dinner at the Wild Dog Fence gourmet event (a bottle of 1999 Tim Adams "The Fergus" from the Clare Valley accompanies spicy Mexican rice, refried beans, and a corn, tomato, and avocado salad).

The publican at the Jandiwae Hotel sends us to Robinson & Co., Seed Merchants. We're still looking for the end of the Dingo Fence. Tom Robinson chews on a straw. After 74 years of living here, he doesn't know where the end of the Fence is. He remembers it being erected in the 50s. Send me a telegram if you find it, he mutters. We don't find it, despite every effort, so we go back with a personally delivered telegram: Can we interview you for a local take? STOP.

He flatly refuses, so we head out on a different road and approach a pastoralist to ask him about the end. It begins to rain and blow, so I jump in the back with Big Yellow to make room for our interviewee and his answer. Jon turns on the recorder, and off they go.

I'm John Coleman, I own country in the Jindiwae East area, and it's not far from this property where the Dingo Barrier Fence actually finishes, the Fence itself on this particular end does get maintained by professional barrier men, possibly once every 12 months, the chap who looks after it actually lives in Injune ...the Dingo Fence finishes on some black-soil country between Bell and Jimbour, from then on it's virtually open country for quite some distance, from this property here as you head towards Bell you'll cross the Dingo Barrier Fence, it's virtually only a mile or two farther on.

His middle-aged son arrives on a horse mid-way through the interview, surprised to see his father sitting in a stranger's van, but rides on after assuring himself that Father is not a kidnap victim.

The dogs on the eastern side of the Fence give them a few more problems over there, I understand, I can remember going to school about four miles from the home and nothing to be just riding along and see a half a dozen dingoes or so just tootling through the paddocks, they'd just stand and look at ya, if you're brought up with dogs, you just don't take any notice of them, if we've lost a few tiles 'n' that

---

[34] Later, we hear on the radio that a Dutch scientist is studying the differences in dialects between city and country birds. He has perhaps witnessed the first step in the evolution process, called speciation: some city birds have shifted their call's frequency upwards so as to be heard over traffic noise.

(Hmmm, tiles …tiles …I reverse the cassette, he clearly says "tiles," I check the Australian dictionary, it must be a technical term—nothing, reverse and relisten: tiles, I say it out loud, tiles, TAILS!)

if we've lost a few tails 'n' that, then you know the dogs have got bad, I've seen them take cows, the calves, they start flanking them and grab them by the end of the tail, by the throat, they get them down and knock them up.

We take his directions, "virtually only a mile or so farther on." Not! We log eight tedious miles on wicked gravel, dodging interminable potholes, before turning around.

But here's a lucky break: the postman. Surely he can tell us where the Dingo Fence ends. At Jimmy McGuire's, he reckons, and gives us a set of complicated instructions that I carefully repeat back to him.

We begin with the road to Bell, stopping at a bare, black field abutting a Nordic blonde one awaiting harvest. I assume we've stumbled on an end-of-summer burn.

Black-soil country, Jon reminds me.

I grapple with the concept and its graphic realization, that the soil peeking out from under the pale, unharvested field is as dark as midnight. Jon gets out to take some photos, but it begins to rain again. He dashes back in and rolls down the window to capture the sounds instead of the view. A contact microphone feeding back from a nearby fence adds its slowly modulating soprano to the alto of the rain, while the bawling cattle inhabit the bass register. "Screaming Feedback with Unsettled Cows" is Jon's opus, performed on black soil with black clouds and a strange, silvery light.

It's a spooky zone, Jon says.

Does the Dingo Fence end at Jimmy McGuire's? We can't find either.

We hail a couple pulling out of a long driveway. While sympathetic to our question, they're unsure and argue where the end might be, explaining in the process that they used to own this place before selling it to their daughter and son-in-law.

What's up? It's the world's longest manmade object, we want to lecture these locals, it ends right on your property or thereabouts, but neither you nor anyone else can pinpoint where. Our impatience and disbelief are fed by the fact that none of the people who have worked on this land for years, those whose families have been here for generations, are able to give clear directions or accurately estimate distance. Is it an unwitting conspiracy of incompetence? How can they own the land when they have yet to fully take it in? Is something going on here that they can't talk about? It's a fence; it ends. Or is it a conundrum that circles back around on itself?

Screaming Feedback with Unsettled Cows: End of the Dog Fence?

The prospect of dissolution is before us, but we won't give up. We run every back road we come upon. Jon directs us through a gate. The road is paved, and since there's no KEEP OUT sign, I feel I must comply. Then, we stumble onto something unusual. It isn't on our map, or perhaps we're just confused about our whereabouts. It's a sort of camping theme park, or was. A plastic box hanging at the entrance still holds a few weathered brochures explaining that an explosive store was located here during WWII, but its 20 concrete underground bunkers have been converted into motel units, the grounds landscaped, and picnic tables strategically placed. From here all we can see is the perimeter fence from the Army days—a high, solid, grim structure.

Of course, Jon intends to disregard the NO TRESPASSING sign we come upon, while I intend to follow it to the letter of the law. I park and watch him slip through the gate and disappear along the gravel track. Nothing to do but wait. The quiet and ensuing darkness are partners in crime. About half an hour later he returns and hands me a flyer.

What's this?

Just read.

I start the engine, turn on the inside light, and relock the doors.

---

4 sale
The Tin Dog Hotel with "FenceWorld" theme park facilities!!
View 2 die for, you can see Wallabys jumpin
Needs some work. Got atmos…

Gaming lisence currently under revu but you can still bet with the all nite "wots in the tin".

Centrelink[35] booth <u>on premises</u>, take away fish and chip ect and all in one building with footie on bloody great plasma tele.

No tyre kickers please!

You wrote this and were just waiting to give it to me.

No, I swear.

Come on, I don't believe you. Don't *do* this to me. This place gives me the creeps, like we've slipped off the map or something.

I'm suddenly aware that my anxiety has tagged every pore on my body with a sweat droplet; it's like being onstage and suddenly spotting a famous person in the audience.

Let's get out of here.

Once again it's time to turn around now. I make a few miscalculations exiting the maze, but as usual Jon has an unerring sense of direction. While I drive, I have him read me the FenceWorld blurb again. Clever, but I'm not fooled. Jon likes to imagine these little stories; he relishes tampering with history, embellishing the mundane and the lackluster. Like Mark Twain, he has a democratic view of fact and fiction. He's not one of those with simple answers, a simplifier, a simplistifier, who reduce and limit and straighten.

I prefer to stick to facts. It doesn't stack up, I'm thinking just as a white bus loaded with soldiers passes us headed in the opposite direction. I thought the scene was a wrap, but like the end of the Dingo

---

[35] Centrelink is the Australian government's welfare and social services division.

Fence, the conclusion of this episode eludes me, resistant to logic and lists. Is the place a cover? Were the locals keeping something from us? Even if we're onto a half-truth, which half?[36]

The day's search results are mixed. We give up and head to Brisbane. Sheet and bolt lightning shock the sky pink as we descend a mountain during punishing rain; the wind seems intent on expunging the landscape. Though civilization is an unwelcome change for us, we stop at the side of the freeway and sleep soundly in the roar of the traffic and glare of the lights. The woman in full siesta mode at the Katherine post office—perhaps we're on to her secret.

At Brisbane, we turn north toward the Sunshine Coast, passing sorghum and hops fields and Ma and Pa vegetable stands. Just over Murdering Creek, we find quite a cast of characters holding forth at the Noosa River Caravan Park: a loner in his van, an extended family with extended gear, various motor homes, and nine guys with two gals in three dome tents. After setting up their tents, the nine-plus-two immediately head off to the bar. We focus our attention on the family with a canoe atop their four-wheel-drive, a trailer with push-outs in all directions, and a monster canvas tent with extensions circa 1963.

Dad gets out to unpack his car. His kids scatter. He must, with Mum's help, erect his tent. His brother-in-law assembled a simple dome tent next door and departed until the collateral damage could be completed. Dad is overweight and sweating, his hand on his brow. His tent, unfortunately, did not come with an instruction manual. Dad is male, Dad is intelligent, Dad has a job, Dad is a gear-junkie—he can solve the problem.

But half an hour later, the tent's still limp. His children return to watch. Everyone in the park is watching, but he can't get it up. He needs

---

[36] Two years later, while searching for pied butcherbirds several hours south of here, I come upon a sign: DINGO FENCE. The town of Yelarbon, not having a big pineapple, a big mango, a big banana, or a big prawn, has seized upon "The End of the Dingo Fence," plaque and all. There it is, next to the Spinifex Café.

However, not content with "Proudly Rural: Where the Bunya Pine grows and the Condamine flows," Wambo Shire currently offers a different "end." Their website describes the northern end of the Dingo Fence as follows:

"From Jandowae, head south toward Dalby; proceed 10 miles, turn left into Lyndley Connection Road OR from Jimbour, head north towards Jandowae, proceed 4.3 miles, turn right into Lyndley Connection Road; then 1.4 miles turn left into Lyndley Lane; then .9 miles turn right into Fletchers Road. The Dingo Barrier Fence begins its journey to the Great Australian Bight (some 3300 miles away) at the corner post of the four fences to your right.

"The fence has just been restored for the first 2.3 miles along Fletchers Road. When you cross the next gird, the fence is on your left. A little further, the older part begins. Follow Fletchers Road to a 'T' intersection (Jimbour-Cooranga North Road) and turn left (100 yards) to see an example of a 'dog gate' and 'road grid.' Turning right at the 'T' will bring you back to Jimbour."

time alone. He lets the dogs out, and they run off with the kids, Mum in pursuit. More fooling around, but the tent is not erected. Brother-in-law returns with a light attached to his forehead to cook a one-pot dinner for his family. It's twilight, but Dad and Mum have yet to put it together. We're watching: still no tent erection and now dark. His unfed children pick up their helter-skelter pace. Dad lights his lantern. Wait, we might have a partial erection. The tent pole is up, the canvas is spread. Things are definitely progressing. But now look—Dad's applying himself to erecting the *dining* tent and screen. And we're all watching.

Perched above the sea, Noosa Heads National Park marks the most northerly point of the Sunshine Coast …B-b-bonk!

Goannas *(Aranus gouldii)* are posted at the entrance; brush-turkeys *(Alectura lathami)* tamely wander the place, their black fantail, yellow throat, and red head making a pleasant contribution to the landscape; the laughing kookaburra *(Dacelo novaeguineae)* obligingly sits in a gum tree; and the koala bear *(Phascolarctos cinereus)* bottoms can just be made out high, high, high up. Okay, we saw them—mark them all off the list.

B-bonk-bonk!

What *is* that? Minimalist bluegrass, well I never …

It's the Northern banjo frog *(Limnodynastes terraereginae)* living up to its musical name, Jon explains. When enough frogs are calling, each with a slightly different pitch, the chorus sounds like a plucked banjo.

We wander about, taking in a string of bays, then choose a return loop through an explosion of trees on one of their prescribed paths. It's not common for the do-it-yourself likes of us, but there are benefits: this living museum is well interpreted with discrete plaques of eco-information along the way. I learn that the huge root buttresses help trees obtain oxygen from the air by protruding from their trunks. We knock on them. Wonderfully, resoundingly hollow—we should have brought the recording gear.

We encounter monstrous brush box trees with bulbous roots and creepers, one vine over a hundred feet, suggesting a jungle swing à la Tarzan. Epiphytes such as elkhorn ferns, crows nest ferns, and staghorn ferns have attached themselves to trees, producing food from sunlight, rotting leaves, and organic stuff that falls into their basket of leaves. It's a dense landscape. While the desert lacks middle ground, the thicket of rain forest is all foreground. It's in your face, breaking design rules big time. I flail about, dizzied by this massive shift in perspective.

Noosa is a sophisticated and well-done tourist town, which as elitists we can appreciate, although we're not able to take much advantage of it. Our budget and inclination strictly limit our tourism to fences. Still, a plate of potato wedges with sour cream, bacon, cheese, and sweet chili sauce washed down with a glass of 1999 Tatachilla McLaren Vale Cabernet for lunch before departing does seem requisite, for scientific purposes. Pelicans line the bridge on the way out of town, as if assigned to community service there by the Noosa Heads Chamber of Commerce.

North through Bundaberg, a humid sugar cane and rum town, we catch sight of a sugar cane factory. It takes me back to the summer I spent in the Dominican Republic. These factories, at least in the third world, are dangerous places to work. Death and injury most often visit via a vicious steam burn. "Drinkin' rum and Coca-Cola" is a pleasant island song and pastime, but I'll stick to wine. No one ever got hurt trampling grapes.

We continue on to 1770, a beach town commemorating the date of Captain Cook's first landing in Australia. We decide to camp two nights at the 1770 marina parking lot. A full day off   unheard of! We're tourists, no fence expected and no fence found.

Not exactly, says Jon, proud to never be caught taking a vacation day. It is the Great *Barrier* Reef.

At 1240 miles long, it's the largest living structure on earth, a maze of 3000 or so individual reefs and 900 islands. We boat out to the closest island, Lady Musgrave, to inspect nature's fence. A reef surrounds the coral cay. I've only seen these tropical colors washing across the pages of a pricey picture book. We're really here, so let's jump in. Although I'm a good swimmer, "snorkel" is a word that suits my nose about as much as the tube and mask. We manage to float around nonetheless and ogle the vivid seascape. It's a feminine place, all lace and ribbons, fluttering fans and fringe.

Lady Musgrave Island serves as a green sea turtle *(Chelonia mydas)* nesting site (we see them swimming from our glass-bottomed boat) as well as a major seabird nesting spot. The protected black noddies *(Anous minutus)* sit low in the trees, thousands of them, and return our looks. They are so without enemies that the concept of fear has been drained from their DNA, or perhaps fauna in the wild are not inherently afraid of man until trained otherwise. We've definitely come upon an untrained mob. Meanwhile, there's an intense smell of guano overfertilizing the soil.

You can't spit and not hit shit, sums up our captain.

Old salts, like the Irish, have a way with words.

Eco-camping is permitted, but no one lives here. They've kept it primitive; it's not Marine World, thank God—or in this case Neptune, Oceanus, and Triton accompanied in the foam by shell-trumpets, sea-nymphs, and water sprites.

It's difficult to imagine Brisbane as a former dumping ground for convicts. Seven bridges span a proper river and await admiration from any number of lush hills. Early builders attempted to replicate Europe but no longer. While luxuriating in its superb Mediterranean climate, Brisbane keeps one foot in its British past and another in its American future.

Downtown along the river I come across an open-air swimming pool designed to resemble an ocean beach. Dubbed "Kodak Beach" by the locals, it's a minute, manmade moment: white sands, tropical lagoon, palm trees, big rocks, brochure blue water and green grass, bright flowers, and tanned lifeguards. In fact, the entire riverside park is cleverly designed, one theme flowing into another. Everything Queensland has to offer is yours in a ten-minute stroll (except the punishing treadmill dubbed "everlasting staircase" by those convicts chained to it; I can locate neither the early nineteenth-century ruin nor the amusement park replica—perhaps the staircase is now in a local gym).

Whether this abbreviated tourist stretch is a triumph of the ancient principles of Feng Shui or modern industrial design or just a whitewash of the convict past, I know not. Someone has studied well and knows how we work, knows we humans prefer the simulacrum to the tedium of reality. I may work this way, but I rail against it. Comfort, beauty, and insurance appeal to me, this mock beach is inviting, but something inside me resists it. It's a clever forgery straight from the convict days.

(Even so, I notice on my promenade that I've finally let my snake guard down.)

Our final night here is spent in the recording studio, in this case at the extended picket fence surrounding the yard of a suburban home. I keep midnight watch on the corner as Jon raucously rattles the side of the fence with a drumstick. RA-ta-TA-ta-RA-ta-TA-ta. Jon takes care to be particularly thorough tonight, applying drumsticks and brushes on not just the wooden fence but also its metal bracings and even the adjoining shrubs.

I'm panicky, worried about the residents, the police even, and must hold up the proceedings at one point while some drunken revelers head home. As they walk by, we just stand there. They heard the noise, they see our recording gear hanging from us. They're not convinced when we play dumb, but they must figure it's too weird to ask, "What are you doing?" Instead, they look at us like we're strange animals, which we are.

When the house light goes on, we take our leave briskly and stealthily.

Picket Fence

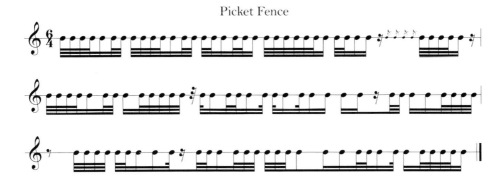

Headed south the following day, we notice a fence covered in hides and take the next freeway exit to investigate. They've got many a natural and dyed skin flopping in the wind. We learn that most animal hides in Australia are fence-marked via barbs. The unmarked ones get exported.

> The miseries of hunger made the bird willing to eat raw flesh, since it could get no other food, and it began to pick remnants of meat from sheep-skins hung out on the fences to dry.[37]

Jon warns me of the concrete hell that is Surfers' Paradise as we close in on it, but we manage quite a fine time here at the World Championship Spoon, Bones, Washboard, Lagerphone, Bottles, and You-Name-It Competition, organized by Tommy Campion.

Tommy, this do-it-yourself, localized, and personal music that we have here—how did you get in to it?

I was raised in a children's home until I was 16, and they used to bring in bands to entertain the kids, like entertaining the troops in Viet Nam, there'd be always a spoon player, a harmonica player, and a piano-accordion, something like that, and I probably used to sit there and think when are they going to finish so we can all have a fight, but obviously it stayed there and years later, I'm a photographer by trade, I had to photograph the Spoon Championships in Surfers'

---

[37] Twain, Mark (1897/2006) *The Wayward Tourist,* Melbourne: Melbourne University Press, 180-181.

Paradise 19 years ago, and I actually thought oh I'll have a go, and I entered it and got right up at the top, second or third.

So that's the last time it happened here, 19 years ago? You've revived something …

Yeah, but completely different, we've got 15 other instruments, which is quite amazing.

What are the criteria? Why no trombone?

I've traveled a lot in the bush, and I'd see these people sittin' underneath a tree with a harmonica or a couple of stockmen [cowboys] around a fire with sticks and bones, and I thought there's gotta be millions of them around here, so one night I got out of bed at 2:00 a.m. and got on my computer, which I barely know how to work, and I sat there for two days typing out the proposal, in 48 hours I had it up with Variety Club—the proceeds go to a worldwide charity.

So you were brought up in a kids' home, and now you're helping other kids.

Yeah, that's what's happening, but I think basically that the day I helped this little lady across the street and pinched her handbag I was destined to do something good.

How do you see your festival in this world of electronic music? Are you fighting a trend?

I am strong enough to carry this on and try to get the word through that you can play music with a set of spoons and you can have beautiful music with just about anything, and I am determined to fight on.

Liz Dall, Spoons: I was brought up out west, if somebody pulled out a guitar, somebody else would have a comb or go raid the kitchen, no one taught me to play spoons, I just picked 'em up and played 'em, one day I was assigned a set of motorcycle handles—that was interesting, my family are country folk, Australian since the first fleet.

Alex Tronza, Bottles: I went to Moscow Conservatorium, I play classical clarinet and saxophone, also trumpet, flute, and keyboard, I was principal clarinet in State Symphony for 15 years, then 20 years I was musical director on cruise ship, that's where I met my Australian wife, we were married in 1994 and she didn't want to live in Russia, you understand, so I came here, a few years ago I started to put melody on unusual instrument, I have six songs, a Russian medley, "Hava Nagila," "Jingle Bells," "Carnival in Venice," and a medley of "Grenada" and "Waltzing Matilda," but this is just relax, you understand?

His case consists of 16 bottles forming a chromatic scale of just over an octave. The liquor labels are covered over with photos of Nicole Kidman, Harry Potter, and ice cream in keeping with his school concert activities. I ask to smell the contents of one.

Ukrainian vodka! Sometimes in show for adults, I fill one bottle a little over and pretend to tune it, then pour shot for two guys who help me set up, still no good tuning, then shot for myself, good, then we clink glasses, *prost!* and I begin.

Peter Morley, Lagerphone: I'm a financial planner, the lagerphone[38] is a traditional bush rhythm instrument, bottle

---

[38] It is unclear if the lagerphone originated with the introduction of Crown Seal beer bottle tops in 1905 or morphed into existence as far back as the music halls of the 1840s. Sheer lack of interest by Australia's official cultural commentators means we will probably never know.

It seems to me that the lagerphone's precursor, the bumbass, occupies some interesting musicological middle ground, as its sonic function exists halfway between a string instrument (generally used as a pitch generator) and a percussion instrument (mostly used as a rhythm and noise generator). Indeed, the way in which a bumbass is traditionally played (with a serrated or notched stick used as a double bass bow) points to an area of music making that became the happy hunting ground for many extended instrumental techniques in the 20th century. The bumbass can be considered as a precursor to the whole story of serialism, which would eventually demand an integrated world for rhythm, timbre, and dynamics as well as pitch in both structure and instrumental realization.

The bumbass is basically a stick, a string, and some kind of resonator in the form of a pig's bladder, a gourd, a small drum, or a tin. A simpler string instrument there is not. Any number of bells, whistles, gongs, rattles, and cymbals can be added to this basic format. Technically, the bumbass requires independent dexterity. High levels of rhythmic counterpoint can be achieved with circular and bouncing bowing in the right hand while also bouncing the body of the instrument on the floor with the left hand.

Tradition dictates a wild carving be worked at the top of the pole; this figurehead literally or metaphorically pokes his tongue out at ordered society and its rulers. The bumbass comes to us from a long line of God's sidemen, men (for they were) with serious protagonistic clout that included the king's fool or jester, the jongleur, the anti-religious Feast of Fools, gothic gargoyles, and images of the devil himself.

The lagerphone got a raw deal. Unlike the bumbass, lagerphones come without any visual titillation. Drink hard and play hard without distraction seemed to be the modus operandi. Want more rattling bottle tops? Then drink more beer.

tops nailed to a hoe handle, I had to drink quite a lot to get the bottle tops, when you want to retune the lagerphone, you just drink a few more beers; this wooden whacker has one side with closely-spaced triple notches for "dee-dle-lee dah's," and the other side has wider-spaced single notches for a staccato effect.

Spike King, Lagerphone, Tin Dog, and Spoons: I made this lagerphone myself from an old farm artifact, no one knows when the lagerphone originated, but certainly when the shearers were rained in they did bush music and poetry, Australia is losing its heritage, people sit and watch TV—I don't, I go to pubs, knock around the bush, pick up ideas, I learned piano-accordion as a kid, three years ago I began to do heritage things—yarns, poetry, different voices, I also play the tin dog, which settlers had 130 years ago to muster sheep, they'd just pick a tin dog off the fence and rattle it like hell, once the sheep got used to it and just stared at them, they'd have to make even more noise, this one is made from No. 8 wire and flour tins, seven-pound syrup tins work fine too or plum jam tins, you just need four or five of them but this one has ten, and the smaller one I call "the pup," I once worked on a place where I was not allowed to use the tin dog, they said the only thing sillier than a tin dog is the person using it, but other properties I could show you their tin dog hanging on a fence.

The full day of music was a welcome respite, although I cringed at the back-up tracks. Most of these bush musicians played along with synthesizer versions of American tunes. It's a dilemma for Australians, with so little music of their own. (Of course, there's the pied butcherbird, but the campaign's not ready.)

Pied Butcherbird

For more, go to http://www.jonroseweb.com/c_articles_bumbass.html.

Since most Australian music has been borrowed from Europe and America (even the melody "Waltzing Matilda" comes from an old Scottish air), there's no local source material to rework/overwork. In theory, there is the wealth of the Aboriginal heritage, but not that much remains; it's fallen into the shadows of the Never-Never. What does remain is not readily available. With the disruption of traditional forms of music, artists often reinterpret the traditional by guesswork instead of working from an original, a sort of invented remembrance. Songs and songlines are everywhere, if we could just untangle them. Perhaps someday, Australian bush musicians will write their own tunes or play without the prerecorded stuff. They're good enough.

We've added almost 10,000 miles to the odometer since we began. The signs, traffic, towns, people, lights, shop windows—it's all coming too fast now.

Nime? the woman asks as Jon checks us in at the Lismore Caravan Park.

I'm sorry?

Nime?

[Jon's thinking, *What* number nine?] I don't understand, he says.

Nime! What's your nime?

Oh!—Jon Rose.

We come upon an isolated graveyard with a picket fence and have a go at it: a clicking duo on the run with wooden drumsticks, no midnight watch required. Nevertheless, it's not ideal. The sound suffers due to the constant traffic, plus there's the WATCH FOR ATTACKING BIRDS sign, complete with a lengthy warning about the resident magpie-larks *(Grallina cyanoleuca)* who are reputed to regularly attack people here. (Obviously, these are the cousin-culprits who give my angelic pied butcherbirds a bad reputation.) True to form, Jon won't let up until we give the recording our best effort; the entire time I'm expecting Alfred Hitchcock to release the birds on us.

Further down the highway, the Ugly Fence presents itself, a gruesome collection of boards, metal scraps, window frames, doors— you name it, all nailed together, with intermittent squares painted landlord green. *Mondrian Moments* is my first reaction. Jon marches right up to take a photograph.

What you want? I hear shouted from around the side. Then she appears: a short, slight woman with a scarf wrapped around her head.

Your fence, I answer.

Why? It's ugly!

(I think about trying to explain that I see various references to Kandinsky and Klee but realize she would throw something at me, so I limit myself.) I think your fence is very beautiful.

No, it's not—it's bloody ugly, looks like an Abo's humpy, she counters

I can see that convergence is unlikely in our conversation, so I don't risk taking a photograph of her.

We come upon the Giant Yellow Fence, a wall of wood with no neighbors or traffic noise. The midnight watchwoman and all-around fence nerd handler is able relax in the van and leave it all to him. Next, we stop by the side of the road, and he's onto metal fences that ring like bells. I'm onto the little red-browed finches *(Neochmia temporalis)*, which zip around unaware of gravity's normal constraints. Each impossible second of their cinematic choreography is robbed of a few frames.

Captain Cook named Byron Bay after the poet's grandfather, John Byron, who was commander of the HMS Dolphin. Much later, the town saw a brief period as a hippie haven, but the beach and surrounding countryside is too fabulous to leave to that ilk. Byron Bay has evolved from hippie to rich-hippie (the Rolling Stones still hang out here when they're in the country) to clearly ex-hippie—"international," meaning that beach condos now reign as king and queen of this tourist destination. Of course, we do not go to the beach, although I gawk at it approvingly from the plastic fence above it. Jon grabs the gear for a recording.

On a *plastic* fence, I balk.

Our long, slow bows conjure up beginning trombone students at half-speed. The deep buzzing vibration is inaudible to the nearby teenagers preening and parading on the first day of their holiday.

The Pacific Highway cuts agreeably (for car and driver, though perhaps not for nature's other residents) through a forest. The trees are in a gold rush to the sun. Would-be koala saviors have hoisted a banner protesting a proposed tree harvest. We take a side road and decide to record the Forest Fence that is Overhead Bridge, a primitive structure high above (as its straightforward name implies) a pair of train tracks. The infrequent drivers-by drop their car speed to a crawl for a goose-necking look at what we're up to. Quite simply, we're bouncing bass bows on thick fence wires in the classic question-and-answer form popular from Mozart to "Dueling Banjos."

We stop for the night at a lonely interchange just a minute off the highway. There are no road signs, so we count on a quiet night without much traffic. There's a picnic table and room to park a couple of cars, although we mentally make claim to the whole space.

A car pulls up and turns off its lights. What! This is an outrage—how will I manage my makeshift shower? And Big Yellow—is he safe out there? Hold tight, here's another car. A bucket is carried from one vehicle and discretely emptied into the backseat of the second, then returned. Engines restart, lights come on, and both cars drive off, leaving us to reclaim our privacy in the night.

Forest Fence

Over Double Crossing Creek and into Coff's Harbour, we spot the Go Bananas Motel. Bananas are the local crop and tourist theme. We tourists are considered too dull to notice or appreciate the acres of verdant plantations flourishing in the surrounding hills—thus the need for Banana World, an overblown fruit stand with "the world's largest banana." We take a drive-by glance. It's not so big; there's just no competition, and for good reason. Welcome to vandalism posing as boosterism. Meant to enhance Coff's Harbour, the concrete lump diminishes it instead.

Jon's avoided photographing, and I've avoided writing about, the omnipresent attempts, sometimes garish, sometimes awkward and homely, to distinguish one Australian town from another.[39] As expressions of communal identity, whether based on something real or contrived, these concrete and fiberglass monstrosities perhaps began innocently enough, but we see them as blights on the land, cheap clichés called in to disguise the absence of ideas. (We aren't alone—I hear the Big Orange has a bad rep: the Big Lemon.) This failure of content, now so frequent in the world, finds our fuses short. Don't get me wrong—we like bananas: raw, split, flambéed, cream-pied, or deep-fried with peanut butter on white à la Elvis. In color, red, yellow, or chocolate-covered will do; in function, edible, laughable, or provocative all pass muster. In our first-degree earnestness, we just want our fruit with a point of view.

No comment, says the Big Banana.

In my reading on this area, I come upon stories of dolphins driving fish toward wading Aborigines. Once speared, some of the good-sized fish would be rewarded to the dolphins in a triumph of cooperative

---

[39] Robin Boyd in his 1960 classic *The Australian Ugliness* (Melbourne: Cheshire) proposes that Australian design is loaded with "featurism"—the feature serving neither an aesthetic nor a functional purpose. Instead, its *raison d'être* is to set apart.

hunting. It's an engaging story from an enchanting place. But like a convict, Coff's Harbour is instead known for the worst thing it ever did: reduce its essence to a concrete banana. I step on the gas pedal, preferring to stop at a little roadside stand: seven bananas and four avocados for three bucks.

J on's on the track of a Nambucca Heads woman who plays gumleaf.

She wasn't at the Surfers Paradise World Championships, but he's heard she's world-class. We stop at a gas station, where the attendant reports that she and her husband have moved to nearby Macksville. We get her phone number and address out of the book and, once there, try to call her but can't get through. Jon suggests we simply drive to her house. We park in front, walk up, and knock on the door, unknown and unannounced.

Hello, are you Roseina Boston?
Come in! Come in! and call me Auntie Rose.
She's all hugs and kisses. I'm taken aback. I feel absolutely white, even as I'm being made to feel no particular color or clan but human. We could be the tax man or worse. We explain our interest in her music and off she goes, as if she were expecting us.
Can you tell us how you got started on the gumleaf?
I was born under a lantana bush on Stewart Island in the Nambucca Valley in 1935, I'm filled with happy memories from that time, my mother taught me how to fish, dig for worms, catch seaworms, and swim, and then at night my mother, uncles, and aunties would gather all the children around the campfire for a night of yarning and telling stories, I was so fascinated by the gumleaf sounds that my uncles made that by the age of eight I had begun to master it, playing "Happy Birthday" and other short songs, and today I'm the only Aboriginal woman who plays the gumleaf, everybody knows me—that's how you could find me, and my grandfather's brother Uncle George Possum Davis was well-known for his Burnt Bridge Gumleaf Band in the late 1800s to the early 1900s, and here, this photo is a 1933 gumleaf band in procession.
How did these bands get formed?
People good at anything get together and wanna make music, that was the thing with the squeeze box and the gumleaves and the clap-sticks and the boomerang music sticks.

Was the 1920s Aboriginal gumleaf music vaudeville music, like the white gumleaf players were doing, or was it traditional music?

It was traditional, carryin' on from the younger days when they used to pick the leaves just walkin' in the bush and imitatin' the sounds of birds, that's what I was told, and it just grew, the sound is similar to a violin but different again, it's got a sound of its own, I've got one here in this glass of water, I keep 'em wet to keep 'em flexible, it took my husband Harry 18 years to get a sound out of it, when I do the schools and talk about our culture, I always take my gumleaf and show 'em how to do it, you put your hand there and you can feel it, it's sealed off all between the lips, you're not blowin' it, you just give a little toot.[40]

A gumleaf band marched across Sydney Harbour Bridge for the opening in 1925—I wonder what they played then, "Farmer's Daughter" was a great hit, and country music, they loved country music, I love that and hymns, and they always get Harry and I to play the national anthem for schools and events.

So it's a musical instrument and you can play whatever you like on it.

It is, you only have to get the knack and control, it's so magical in a way, when I walk through the bush playin' my gumleaf, just pickin' a leaf and playin', all the birds come around me, I love it.

Tell me about your paintings.

That's Starfish Dreaming over there, that's my first painting, it was Christmas time 1993, my husband Harry and I had kept a bait shop going for seven years, catching seaworms, and we picked up a lot of things on the beach, starfish, seahorses, dead pipe fishes—I'm a mad collector of things like that, I was sittin' at home once and didn't know what to do with myself, so I got this piece of masonite and slapped some white paint on it, then it just sorta come to me,

---

[40] Auntie Rose demonstrates a number of bird calls on nature's simple green reed aerophone; kookaburra, parrot, willy wagtail, whipbird, and hawk all sound like the real thing, as near as we can tell. The gumleaf is high-pitched and incredibly loud, and Jon grabs his recorder to turn it down. We can feel the vibrations moving through the air. Then, Aunty Rose runs through a number of popular tunes and hymns, her intonation spot on. She's accompanied by the howling of her little dog Minn.

Later, Jon adds them to the Australia Ad Lib interactive archive at http://www.abc.net.au/arts/adlib, where he has assembled the wild, the weird, and the vernacular of Australian music. A video of Roseina playing gumleaf backed by a seven-piece band at the Melbourne International Arts Festival in 2005 can be found at http://www.jonroseweb.com/f_projects_pannikin.html

it's beautiful, that was my childhood days of growin' up in Nambucca, playing around the rocks with the seaweed and little fishes come pickin' your toes and all the seashells around ya, and the jellyfish come driftin' past ya, starfishes in the water there, that's just our lifestyle, and the giant mystical dreamtime starfish who hypnotizes everything and paints them all these pretty colors, and when they wake up they're all painted up for the celebration of baby Jesus at Christmas time, that was the story told to me. It's beau-ti-ful!

That painting up there really happened back in 1985, down near Taree, we was bean pickin', Harry had a dream one Sunday night and I had a dream the same night, Harry dreamt about helpin' yowies in the mountain, yowies are our mountain people, we've got little ones and big ones, and they've been seen, people go campin' and dig holes and chuck their tins, and this yowie had cut his leg, and Harry helped him, and the yowie was askin' Harry in signs, "What you lookin' for?" and Harry pulled a little bit of gold out of his pocket and showed it to him, then Harry ripped his shirt and bandaged the yowie and fed him on berries for a week, and when that was over he took Harry into the mountains, and yowies was comin' out of the bush, little children yowies and adults, it was beautiful, he told them what Harry was lookin' for, and the men went away and come back with armfuls of gold and put it down at Harry's feet, and his dream ended.

The same night I dreamt about walkin' along a river on soft, green velvety grass, and all these old Aboriginal women were doin' the washin' and cookin' the feed, and the kids was all swimmin' in the water, it looked so beautiful, and when I was gettin' close to them I looked out at the water and could see a big mob o' sharks, so I started to run to tell the kids, Get outta the water, sharks comin' up the river! and the kids was all scatterin', but some were divin' and swimmin' and weren't takin' any notice, and when the sharks got level with the women, they turned into dolphins, and they said, "It's all right, they're our brothers and sisters," and when they got to the bridge a youth dove down and come up cuddlin' a dolphin like that, and my dream ended.

Dreams are very significant in Aboriginal culture, I said to Harry we gotta go tell someone about our dreams, so we go in to Kempsey to see this old Aboriginal fellow, and we told him, then he said, "You make yourself a cuppa," and he went in the other room, and five or ten minutes later he come out and said, "I've gotta take you down there—you're being called by the old fellahs," we had no money, we only had our bean pickin' money, pension was comin' up that week, we had a Holden [Australia's own generic Ford], soon as we got our pension we picked him up, and as we was goin' down to this place, it was gettin' late, we got there just as the sun was setting just behind that big black cloud the shape of a dingo's head over the mountain on the left, and in the other corner you see two dolphin-shaped clouds floating towards it, it was so beautiful, and we went to see that old fellah, they called him The Mountain Man, Bob's in his eighties, and when we went in he said, "I knew you was comin'," just like that, and then he said, "They're tryin' to kick me off this place, I've been here since I was a teenager," (this millionaire fellah from Queensland bought the property off Ike Livermore who Bob worked for for years, and they was movin' old Bob off the place, but the old fellahs told him not to leave there, he's the keeper of that area, so he was very upset), "Come on," we said, "We're goin' to Port Macquarie," we took him to see Mr. Livermore, "Well, Bob," he said, "They can't move you, you go back there and live, we made a three-way handshake that you're not supposed to be moved from there"; and we went back—he's still there today, and the man of the mountain is a yowie who Harry was helpin' through the dream.

"Don't kill any black snakes," Bob said, the place was crawlin' with 'em, I painted those black snakes next to the kids who are playin' with the spears 'n' boomerangs 'n' swimmin' in the river there, people used to travel for miles by foot, they called that place The Racecourse, tucker [bush food] was there, the kangaroo and goannas, the fish, and black snakes everywhere, and those skulls—there's a cave there, I walked up and stood on that round, flat rock, those pyramid rocks are taller than this house, and I'm lookin' straight across at the Skull Cave where they used to bury the old important chiefs, and Bob asked, "Was there a hawk there?" and I said, "Yep, he's always watching over people," that's why I put the eyes under his wings, and see the crown up in the center—that represents God our Creator who created all things, very spiritual our ancestors were, they wouldn't have survived in this land for 45,000 years or more without Him, powerful things happened to me there, the birds—I come down from that mountain and was walkin' around the creek, I was on me own, all these birds were circlin' like they was tryin' to coax me up the other mountain, that mountain where I come from was the women's mountain and where the birds were tryin' to coax me was the man's mountain, something was in me tellin' me, "Stay on the track, Stay on the track." I'm on me own in the bush, and I just kept goin', I stepped over a big carpet snake, it was very hot so when I got to Harry I sat in the water and this big giant black snake swam around me like that, powerful stuff, it was beautiful, our culture calls through dreams to help people, so many religions in the world today and only one God, our culture is very strong and it's very powerful.

On occasion we have played fences in public places, and a small crowd has gathered. The fence without amplification is quiet, so what folks first notice is two people going like crazy with bass bows on a fence. This presence of musicians/absence of sound shifts as they close in and begin to pick up something—but is it from a submerged memory that can be reeled in or from the shadow of a dream just the other side of memory? The real and imagined duck and bob until, closer still, a thin but vibrant euphony emerges. Kirra Beach saw one such spur-of-the-moment concert for the closest dozen. We stood in the sand along the sidewalk promenade, our backs to the South Pacific, and bowed a thick wire fence. "Played real good for free" goes the song.[41]

---

[41] While Jon finds it an obvious continuation of his work to play a fence, for me it's a departure. I will never feel as free on the violin as I do on a fence. When I bow a fence, there is no expectation, no history of expensive lessons and years of practice, no right and wrong way. Hold the bow this way, make this sound—no! It's just me being variously a child, a scientist, a rummager, a search party, and a scrutineer—just me looking to discover the secrets of each fence each day. I don't know what I might do because I don't know what the fence might do. Its wide range of moods, timbres, and pitches depend on weather, time of day, tautness, wire thickness, and age. Once I size up a fence, I still can't count on it. Fences are prone to downright orneriness. We've had a great-sounding outback fence become unplayable in the space of a few minutes. There's a certain charm in their unpredictability as long as you aren't onstage.

The invention of steel cable in the nineteenth century gave the fence its present distance-warping ability and signaled the end of the hunter-gatherer way of life. Whilst in Australia decaying fences attempt to keep out marauding dingoes and plagues of rabbits from settled white man's land, they far more persuasively mark off the furthest edge of the national consciousness. The outback fence, that iconic divider and protector, is a metaphor for the duality with which the human mind analyzes and copes with situations.

Most animals mark out their territory in one way or another; man's way is with fences. Fences incarnate the exploration, competition, control, and exploitation of resources, ancient struggles known as Man versus Nature and Man versus Man. At the same time, fences also mark the *close* physical association of man with his environment and fellow man, the notion of belonging to lands and cultures and political systems. The fence is now used to protect the natural world from man's excesses.

Kew, Pacific Highway, New South Wales. It's 5:30 a.m., and I'm wide-awake. I slip out of the van, leaving Hollis to sleep, and can just make out a gas station across the street. I walk over and see that it's open, so I go in and ask the guy if he sells coffee.

Are you American?

No.

Well, then you can have a cup of tea.

So he sells me the tea and comes straight on with it.

Do you have an open mind? [Even at that hour of the morning, I think it is comparatively open.] I've got something to show you, he says and gets out some boxes.

We've stepped into the Twilight Zone. In this conspiracy theorist's files are newspaper stories about strange goings-on—extraterrestrials, space ships, military bases—and then we come to his current obsession: 9/11. He shows me letters he has written to government officials around the world demanding the truth about the airplane that supposedly crashed into the Pentagon.

This is the hole it shoulda made, he points, versus the small hole it *did* make. And why was no wreckage found? It's because that crash never happened—they just blew up a bit of the Pentagon to increase the attack vibe.

Halfway through my cup of tea, with my toes finally warming up, I admit, yes, indeed, not a sign of airplane wreckage.

He asks what I am doing at his petrol station at 5:30 in the morning. I answer we are circumnavigating the continent of Australia bowing its fences. He accepts my confession, but clearly I've become part of a new conspiracy theory he's working on. He doesn't ask me if I want another cuppa.

We've rented the campervan for 50 days; it's due back tonight. To linger is not our modus operandi, but for once we feel like it.

Let's take a ferry out to Dangar Island, suggests Jon. I'll show you where I used to live.

Some landowners still prefer the watering hole to the fence as a leash on their wandering cattle. There are people who sing the lasting qualities of a live wattle fence. Whatever your view of fences, they seem unstoppable; they are everywhere. Fences are by far the most visible artifacts on the continent.

Fence music encapsulates the vastness of the place in music of distance, boundaries, and borders. This, however, is not the songlines, or even the white fella's ironic version of it, but the unexpected and elegiac music of the Australian land sounding its recent history, a celebration of the pioneer spirit and a requiem mass for an environmental disaster. Fence construction has inadvertently given us a means of expressing musically, with a direct physical connection, the whole range of intense emotion tied up with the ownership of the land, from the outback to the backyard.

In the 70s and early 80s, I lived on Dangar Island, a chaotic rock with dozens of little holiday houses. This Sydney backwater was a poor man's paradise. These days, it's got a damn great tourist marina on the mainland that offers guided tours of the quaint island natives. I hear the illegal house I built out of stone, glass, and wood has been pulled down. I wonder if I can find the ruins.

In the days when I built my homemade castle, few people bothered to survey, and there were no fences by which to judge borders. (To this day, the island remains relatively fence-free due to the rocky terrain and vegetation.) I eyeballed my land and figured where I should build the house, as simple as that, without the aid of a surveyor. I figured exact measurement unnecessary, as I wasn't going to erect a fence or build to the edge of my property.

Unfortunately, I built half of my house on someone else's land, only discovering the oversight five years later when someone next door had his block surveyed, allowing everyone adjacent to find where their blocks began and ended. The notion of private property is a rock-solid belief system in Australia; great public works take a distant second. Everybody aspires to his little piece of heaven-on-earth. That someone could accidentally build part of his house on someone else's property stretched all credulity. My house and I had crossed the boundaries of suburban morality. This would not have been such a disaster if the house had been a lightly made wooden structure, but the stones and huge rocks made it unmovable. It was one of my least successful improvisations.

The solution was simple, or so I thought. I would buy that little bit of land off the neighbor. Every six months I ventured over to Alex's house to negotiate. Alex was a fisherman. Life had not been kind to him, and he spent much of his time drunk as a newt. I would sit with him as he plied himself (and me) with beer after beer. I'd point out that he would only be selling a tiny part of his block to me, a part he never thought he owned anyway (he had built his chook run well away from the recently discovered border). Yes, he knew that, but it didn't make any difference. Land was something you could buy but, spiritually speaking, you could never sell, he would say. He considered the extra land as a heaven-sent blessing and therefore something not to be traded. The result of these meetings was always the same: Alex would say that my house would have to come down but all in good time, plus I'd nurse a dreadful hangover the following day.

Jon clearly has always had an issue with borders. We hike around the now-upscale island and find the land and remains of his house, which looks like a nineteenth-century English folly, those mock-Gothic ruins built in gardens and parks to give a feeling of antiquity. He points out the beach where he anchored his dingy and tells tales of stormy midnight river crossings returning home after gigs. This boat also featured in one of the many homemade instruments he built while living here: his Tromba Marina[42] (or trumpet marine). Jon's take on this ancient instrument was attached to the side of his boat and had six sympathetic strings. The main playing string was a double bass A string.

I used a metal drainpipe, an excellent resonator. The sound was transformed depending on how much water filled the tube. Contrary to scientific opinion, there is a sonic difference to the pipe being half full as opposed to half empty. The locals used to think I had some weird, state-of-the-art gizmo that attracted the fish. While out playing on the river, I would often notice fishermen's boats closing in, hoping to profit from my mysterious aquatic machine.

The inventors/developers of the tromba marina uncovered a sonic problem similar to that of the twentieth-century electric guitar. Both instruments generate very pure, grainless sound. Superb as the natural harmonics of the tromba marina were, the musicians wanted more grain for their bow, just as the guitarists wanted, and still do, pedals to dirty up their squeaky clean sound. The solution was either to join a crusade or fit a drumming bridge to the tromba marina.

The drumming bridge is a beaut piece of instrumental engineering. Observe the asymmetrical bridge with one foot supporting the string on the front plate but the other foot going through the sound hole and not quite reaching the back plate. The result? A serious buzzing, throbbing, drumming sound. Sorted. Then the name arrived that was short on description, although I suspect the medieval imagination dealt with "the sound of a drowning trumpet" with more ease than it handled a virgin birth.

Stroppy rainbow lorikeets *(Trichoglossus haematodus)* flash by as we wait for the return ferry. Once across the Hawkesbury River, we drive an hour south and over the Harbour Bridge into Sydney, having logged 10,000 miles circumnavigating Australia in 50 days.

---

[42] Image at http://www.jonroseweb.com/d_picts_tromba_mariner.html

color plates

photographs by jon rose and hollis taylor

> The color plates have been arranged to read as a visual essay; consequently, they are not in chronological or geographical order. The states and territories are abbreviated as WA (Western Australia), NSW (New South Wales), SA (South Australia), NT (Northern Territory), and QLD (Queensland).

1. RABBIT-PROOF FENCE ROAD sign, WA.
2. The southern end of the Rabbit-Proof Fence at Starvation Bay, WA.
3. The last standing Rabbit-Proof Fence post at Starvation Bay, WA.
4. Ex-post at Starvation Bay, WA.
5. Jon interviewing Julianne Hill at a Rabbit-Proof Fence runner's hut, WA.
6. Ex-fence runner Ron Moses at home near Mount Magnet, WA.
7. The northern end of the Rabbit-Proof Fence (crocodile country) at Cape Keraudren, WA.
8. More remains at Cape Keraudren, WA.
9. Hallucogenic colors at the Waka Claypan, NSW.
10. Waka Claypan, NSW.
11. Jon bowing at Wubin, WA.
12. *Pas de Deux*.
13. Track fence of the Old Ghan, SA.
14. Flooded fence, NT.
15. Fence graveyard.
16. Tent Post Fence.
17. Windblown fence post, WA.
18. Shattered fence post on salt lake, WA.
19. Lateral spider webs blowing in the wind, Oodnadatta Track, Coober Pedy, SA.
20. Fungus Fence, Noosa Heads, QLD.

21. Jon bowing at the Dead Sheep Fence, Milparinka, NSW.

22. Snail-encrusted fence post near Penong, NSW.

23. Dead dingo at Dingo Fence, Birdsville Track, SA.

24. Goanna near the Rabbit-Proof Fence, Narndee, WA.

25. Sunset at Snowtown, SA.

26. Sunset at the Dingo Fence, Lake Frome, SA.

27. Horse fence post.

28. Parrot fence post.

29. Adam and Eve.

30. Eastern brown snake at Sturt National Park, NSW.

31. Salt lake at Snowtown, SA.

32. Salt lake at Snowtown, SA.

33. One-legged fence post at Snowtown, SA.

34. Collapsed spider fence tangle at Snowtown, SA.

35. Milparinka, NSW.

36. Fence wire, Wogarno Station, WA.

37. Near Broken Hill, NSW.

38. Milparinka, NSW.

39. Lateral fence at Milparinka, NSW.

40. Cut-off fence posts, Milparinka, NSW.

41. Lateral wood fence, Sturt National Park, NSW.

42. Lateral stone fence, Sturt National Park, NSW.

43. Color photo of a lateral wood fence near Wentworth, NSW.

44. Another color photo near Wentworth, NSW.

45. A fence post hollowed out by termites.

46. A color photo of a salt-encrusted post.

47. A classic corrugated iron fence, Winton, QLD.

48. A net fence, QLD.

49. Hardwood stock fence, Alice Springs Telegraph Station, NT.

50. Tire fence.

51. Ubiquitous sunset with barbed wire.

52. Cow and fence, New England, NSW.

53. The Dingo Fence crosses a property fence, QLD.

54. A fence goes through a termite hill, Katherine, NT.

55. Misty (a fence at Hay Plains, NSW).

56. Golden Mean Fence, near Broken Hill, NSW.

RABBIT PROOF FENCE RD
17
24 DUMBLEYUNG KUKERIN
WAGIN LAKE GRACE 55
5 MOULYINNING

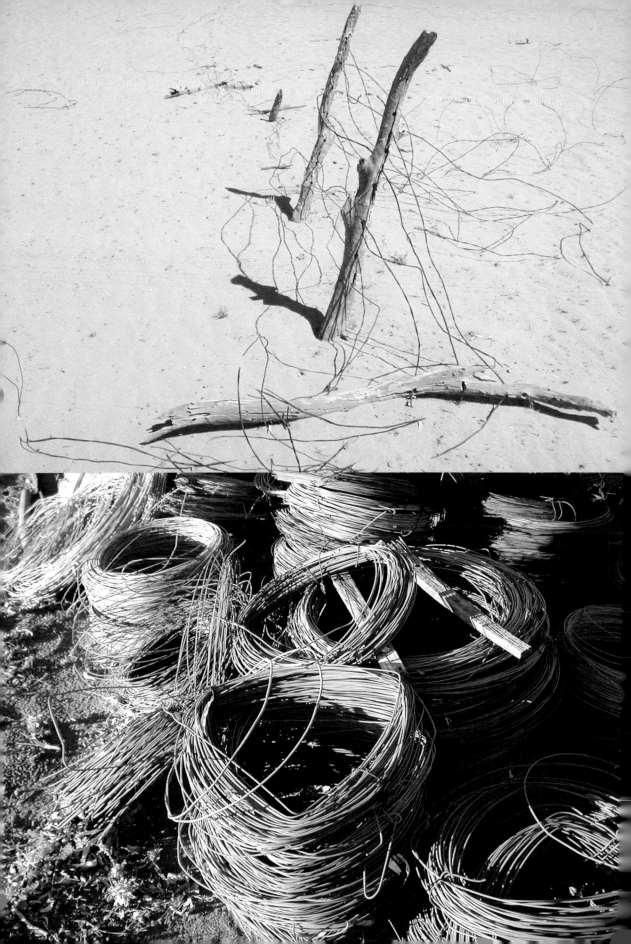

PLEASE DO
NOT DRIVE
ON FENCE
ROAD

DINGO BARRIER
FENCE

PENALTY FOR LEAVING
GATE OPEN £200

J. BREBNER
SUPERINTENDENT OF STOCK ROUTES

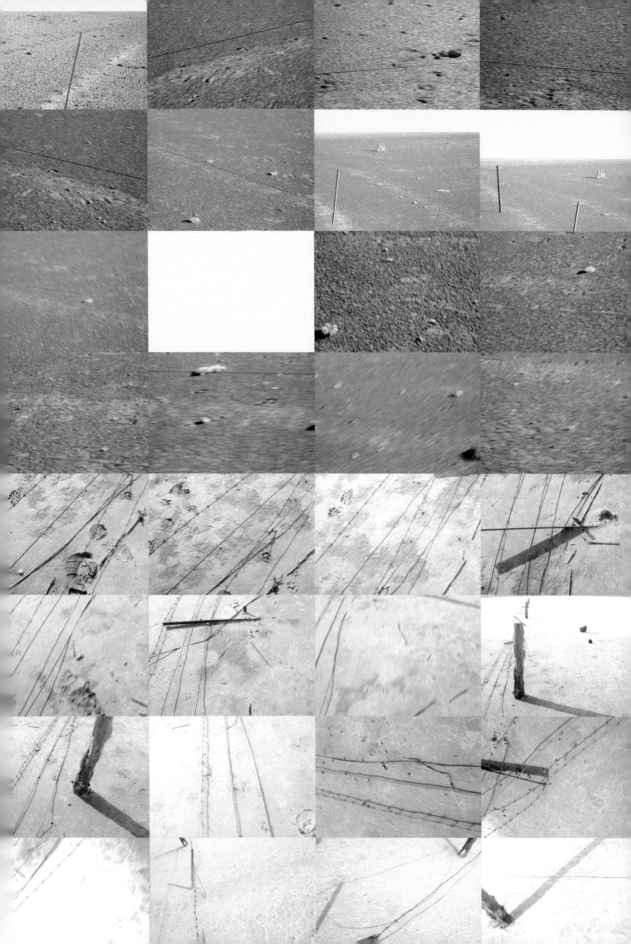

W e've got our own fence. The Melba, we call her. She's a sixty–
foot five-wire with stringy bark posts that we've installed at the
Victorian Arts Centre. Strung with piano wire, a high-carbon steel that
produces a better quality sound than regular fence wire, and played with
bass and cello bows and drumsticks, she's a star at the Melbourne
International Arts Festival. The Melba is such a diva that she has her
own barbed-wire fence running in front of her as protection from the
audience. And to protect the audience from the barbs, someone has been
hired to spend two days twisting fake barbs onto the plain wire. In all,
Bowing Fences will see 60 performances, plus we've installed various
slide shows of our round-the-continent fence photographs and covered
the gallery walls with prints on paper of our favorites. Our audio
interviews and recordings run when we're not performing: My name is
Julianne, and I work on the Rabbit-Proof Fence in Western Australia in
the SW corner ...

The reaction we get from the press and the 10,000 who flock to
hear The Melba is enthusiastic. People volunteer their own fence
stories.

As a child, I sometimes helped out putting up fences and was
always fascinated by the sounds you could get from taut plain wire
running through a steel post—the way to test if the wire was stretched
tight enough was by tapping it with a pair of pliers, though I never tried
playing it with a bow, reflects Vicki Powys, a wildlife recordist.

In my childhood, after Dad had prepared the roo stew, recounts
pianist Norma Geddes, I used the sinews from the kangaroo's tail to
"bow" the fences around the homestead.

Back in the 1950's my father Jack and my uncle Clary had some
bananas, photographer Allan Chawner reminisces. The patch was across
a deep creek crossing, and they had set up a flying fox to get the fruit
boxes out. It ran for about 500 yards (it seemed much further to me at
the time) and was made from old fencing wire. I remember how it
resonated if I struck the wire. The sound would be visible as a wave
running up and back to the shed. It was wonderfully strange, like a
ringing, wiping echo as it traced back and forth. It is one of the
strongest memories of my childhood.

But one stockman can't be fooled. That wouldn't hold back no
steer o' mine, I overhear him hurrumphing.

The pastoralist is more than made up for by the two wide-eyed
Goth teenagers in heavy makeup, black clothes, and belly button rings,
who approach us after a performance, their fingers held up to form
quotation marks, and breathe, Other!

143

Back in Sydney, beach fences keep me and the state occupied. New South Wales has 125 miles of shark fencing safeguarding 49 beaches. My barrier of choice is the shark fence at Nielson's Beach, which protects us swimmers with its indestructible (one hopes) red netting. A battalion of skyscrapers camped across the harbor awaits the floating inspection of swimmers who strike out to the furthest reaches of the shark fence.

Then, there's Our Lady of the Fence Post at Coogee Beach. It's big news in the papers and on the radio. The optical effect caused by the sun shining on a white fence rail is interpreted by the faithful as an appearance by the Madonna. Visiting a sacred site is a time-honored pastime, and all manner of folks flock to the daily afternoon apparition at this low, neighborly fence. Some sit atop a slope, a natural amphitheater overlooking the fence and the beach well below it.

The faithful arrive early to set the stage, reading holy tracts, praying, doing their bead thing, and whispering their stories to strangers. Then the merely curious begin to straggle in. They're here for a vision, not a message. They accumulate lower on the grass slope, standing where the view is best. True believers don't really need to see, I guess. After all, the Bible tells us that faith is the belief in things *unseen*. As the time grows near and the multitudes swell, the least faithful appear, barely-clothed philistines wandering up from the beach.

It's a laid-back group, which fails to explain why one weekend someone painted the fence black and deposited a toilet bowl next to it. The following weekend the fence was pushed down the cliff. The city fathers, bless 'em, have put it back up, and here we are.

By 3:15 p.m. the veiled Madonna wrapped in white robes makes her timid entrance doubling as a zigzagging fence post, head bowed and hands slightly outstretched. The devout begin a Hail Mary, while the doubting Thomases squint, crane their necks, and point their fingers at the interplay of shadow and light, interpreting the chiaroscuro as their levels of faith allow. As the afternoon moves on, Our Lady turns slightly, opens her arms, lifts her head, and some say her white robe takes on a blue tinge. As an outdoorswoman and fencist, I cannot disapprove of this revision of the holy equation: Mother, Sun, and Holy Post.

The launderette owner and initial Mary's Witness ("I just looked up at the fence one day, and there she was.") claims no particular interpretation. She's not religious, but as the skeptics harass her for making money—she sells a video, $10 postcards, and $50 T-shirts—and the death threats roll in, she's moving more in that direction, speaking of love as the beadsmen gather, if she speaks at all. She's posted a sign that she and her employees have clothes to clean, so don't disturb them with questions. Unless, one assumes, to ask how much is that T-shirt in the window?

After we stare for a while, the crowd thins out. No one is walking up the hill on her knees, no one shouted anything or fainted, a prophesier failed to emerge amongst us. Did we see the light of Our Lady or the shadow of a doubt? Come have a look for yourself, and don't forget your zinc cream.

Jon is restless. The song of the Dingo Fence is ringing in his ears, a modern-day siren luring him back to the rigors and dangers of the outback. He surfs the net and pores over maps, speaking of places no one's heard of, remote stations and isolated roadhouses, ghost towns even. I hear him on the phone trying to convince strangers that we are serious musicians who play fences. It's only a matter of time before he hatches a grandiose plan: to see the Fence in a number of new places and drive along it when possible. Of course it's not *ever* possible—it's a private track, but he sets about getting permission from the district manager.

Len is the manager of the Dog Fence south from Cameron's Corner. I ring him up from Sydney to say that we are coming and would he mind talking to us about his part of the Fence. His voice is dry, as if sand has permanently lodged in his throat. It's a voice of resignation.

I ask him about the current conditions there in the midst of a ten-year drought. A man of few words, Len paints a picture of "bloody hell." It's a report from the front line trenches. The enemy is not the dingo but the desert. It cannot be restrained. When a wind blows in from the west, sand piles up against the Fence, pushes it over, and buries it. His men are flat out making quick repairs and then rushing on to the next crisis point. It sounds like a last-ditch stand.

How long can they last?

Well, it's touch and go, but we'll make it providing the drought breaks, Len vows. That's forecast to happen within the next month.

And if it doesn't? [He doesn't give an answer.]

Look, I don't have time to give an interview when you get here. You have my permission to drive down this part of the Fence, yes, but I can't spare any of my fencerunners if you get into difficulties. Sorry, I'd like to be more helpful, but this is really not the time.

He hangs up. I feel like I got some grains of sand caught in my throat, too. This is heavy frontier stuff, and we are unproven lightweights.

Second Fence Trip

For this part of our sonic mapping we choose a Toyota LandCruiser, a four-wheel-drive vehicle that, unlike the campervan, the rental company allows to be driven on unsealed roads. I read the contract carefully, knowing that while the large print giveth, the small print taketh away. Travel on the Oodnadatta and Birdsville Tracks is not permitted without special dispensation, which I ask for and receive, provided the tracks are legally open. It's a converted vehicle with sink, fridge, and upper and lower beds. We remove the lower one, a padded place to sit during the day—we won't have time for that. We'll need easy access to our gear in the storage bins below it.

Why must men and women fight when packing? She has purchased 10 large collapsible water containers capable of seeing them through a worst-case scenario. He does not want them in the way.

Fill one or two for now, he directs; we can get water as we go.

In the middle of a drought! she shouts.

She can see them stranded in the outback under a relentless sun, desperate from dehydration, four tires shredded, without hope of being found. I may have to cry, she thinks, and then she just does, her face buried in her hands. She cannot leave without her water. Pity the man that should ask this of her.

Water loaded, we take the Great Western Highway over the Blue Mountains toward Molong. Within two hours of departure, we've escaped our urban routine and are exhilarated to be on the fence trail again. By day's end, as the road carves a low path between hills, the sky remains lit while the earth plunges into darkness like a photographer's negative. Exquisitely detailed black tree cutouts top black hills, backlit by a pastel sky. From green and bulky to dark and flat, one by one the trees shift from nature to symbol, from arbor to arborescent.

The next morning echoes this paper doll panorama of trees, tombstones, and windmills. Into Wellington, galahs congregate on every utility wire for blocks. The town's inviting and appealing, with good bone structure, unlike several we've just wheeled through which appear ill-conceived from the start, where the feel, the approach, the lay of the land are all wrong. They have hilly bits where they should be flat and vice versa. There's no logical or obvious center, no natural vista or bit worth landscaping. These towns were neither planned nor did they organically unfold. They're do-it-yourself that should never have been done. Symmetry, balance, and a strong center are always intriguing in man's viewfinders, but you'd struggle to find a single decent spot to frame in these failed scraps of topography.

It doesn't stop there. No positive energy can seem to be harnessed. A quick glance tells you that you can't get your mind or heart round this type of wear-you-down town that breeds acrimony and bitter disputes over boundaries and spouses, that breaks finances and families. A permanent and quarrelsome gracelessness has taken hold. When the fed-up finally leave (eager auctioneers at their doorstep), they shoot holes in the town WELCOME sign. Even the meek are compelled in retreat to subtract their numbers from the population with a permanent marker pen.

We approach a chocolate river over which ragged strands of mist are insinuating themselves in white, not grey, fluffy spun sugar hanging in the air waiting to tempt a passing child. As we cross the one bridge, just to our right I glimpse another: a high, slender, latticed gingerbread bridge. I promised myself to take up space on this trip, to stop when inspired and fully absorb the moment. I have *carte blanche* to leave the straight, change direction, or circle back. But on reflection, I'm content with the briefest encounter here. If I go back, the bridge will be ordinary, with a beginning, an end, and a purpose. Memory did a quick fix. It remains for me a magical structure, a real-life study for an Escher drawing, my Once-Upon-a-Time Bridge.

Near Trangie, a field is clothed in a light beige polyester leisure suit, an unnatural tint insisting it is true to life. While our passion is fences, color and light continually make a play for our attention. Topsy-turvy is our daily lot.

West toward Cobar, we spot Luke and Dave taking their final rest behind an ugly barrier fence of five-foot high mesh wire, the kind of thing you might keep a wild dog behind. Two white crosses roost on top in memorial, and in front is set a third cross inscribed "Luke and Dave 20–7–91." A few artificial flowers hang as wreaths (one just a bare wire circle now) and several more are stuck in the ground. Jon says the only worse memorial would be an abandoned fridge. A mile later we see one and fantasize a pilgrimage where people bring their dead fridges here, a Princess Di sort of thing. "Fence of Dead Fridges" they'll dub it.

We find a seven-wire fence that we bow and film, and later we drive along a five-wire fence set in red earth, Jon shooting short movies on the go while sitting (precariously to my way of thinking) on the hood. We look forward to our evening at Poopelloe Lake. Past Cobar and just shy of Wilcannia, it's big on the map. The only question is whether it's a salt lake or a freshwater one. In either case, it's a perfect place for our sunsetter glass of wine. We search and search. It does *not* exist. We should be able to see it from the highway, but there is no road of even an insignificant nature leading to it, no driveway or track, no signpost missing its sign—zip. On the map but not on the ground, it forces us to search for another pull-off.

We continue until 100 miles before Broken Hill where we spot a truckers' rest area. We're still in time to catch the sunset with a full moon rising. Jon photographs *Moon with Barbed Wire,* his doomed masterpiece, barbs stretched across a blue sky dissolving to violet with a silver-white moon pasted in it, knowing in advance that the camera will document this dramatic shift of sky colors as grey and more grey. Inky clouds poke along, gradually collecting at the sun.

The fence is being excited by the wind; we hear a strong A-flat ringing out. We linger, sipping our 1999 Wirra Wirra Church Block and listening to the fence. It shifts midsong from string to percussion family, turning in an admirable high-hat drum performance. Dinner is couscous salad with curried chickpeas, baby beets, and feta cheese, and we take it outside so as not to miss a thing. We keep turning 180 degrees—sunset, moonrise. The fence dies right as Jon decides to record it but returns the next morning ringing out a D-flat.

We don't get far before a five-wire fence catches our eyes and wins our ears with its aeolian keenings. The wind whips up a chill, and I grab my coat.

You can't wear that, Jon directs.

Apparently, my costume is the wrong look for our resident filmmaker. I have to settle for a T-shirt and skirt, black boots, and fly veil over my khaki hat, but not without complaining—it's winter.

He sticks two contact microphones under a couple of fence wires, giving the already super-charged wind a surging voice. The aeolian sounds become my string pad, my karaoke support group, and I solo over the top. I have no feeling in my freezing fingers save a low ache.

I begin by playing long, slow notes that don't really get going until I lift the bow off the wire. Later, little rhythms arrive and depart. Violin harmonics are vanishing and thin, while a fence's have presence. An ideal instrument, I'm thinking. I see but don't feel that my finger is cut. Between takes, I dive into my coat for warmth, resting the bows on desiccated cowpies. The fly veil becomes more and more necessary as the morning progresses.

A danger of youth or travel is to come ill-timed upon something. Piecing things together bit by bit normally suffices, but occasionally, well before you can absorb the context, you're suddenly given not a cautious homeopathic dose but body and soul. If only we'd known—but seeing requires an apprenticeship we've not fully served. As far as we look, it's flat flat: red soil domed by a blue sky. The colors are exaggerated. The shift from brochure 2-D to far-and-wide 3-D is from ahhh to ah-hah. In Heisenberg's physics, we alter a phenomenon by the very act of our gaze. No longer land, it's now landscape. We get it, or we get that there's more than we can fully grasp.

Who am I? Thoughts well up then collapse. The advent of cell phones has perhaps eliminated the need for such a question and the existential angst that accompanies it. These days, we've moved on to the locative case. *Where* are you? suffices.

Hawker: Aeolian Fence, Bowed Fence, and Flies

Aeolian fences are sounding nonstop the entire length of the Mitchell and Barrier Highways. Very little old, rusty, slack stuff remains. The new, taut wires just go off in the wind. Jon suggests there could be a 24-hour fence radio station, similar to television's fireplace channel or Innsbruck's camera pointed at the oft-cloudy mountaintop. Our lonely blue planet is ringing and vibrating as it spins.

Pythagoras held that music affords us a glimpse into a world we cannot otherwise know. Early Chinese mystics had their Wu-Li masters *dance* physics rather than explain it. Albert Einstein felt that the mysterious is the fundamental emotion that stands at the cradle of true art and true science, and our current crop of physicists agree these ancients were on to something. In their search for the Theory of Everything (the result, hopefully, to be a concise set of formulas silk-screened on a T-shirt), physicists grapple with how gravity, which governs the universe in its large aspects, and quantum theory, which governs it in its small aspects, fit together.

One promising explanation is String Theory, which claims that all matter is composed of tiny strings or loops vibrating in a space that has many more dimensions than the three we think we live in. And now two bent manipulators of sound are positing a new equation, Fence Theory, which claims that when the boundaries between nature and culture break out in song, fences rebalance pockets of negative energy

149

created by their very presence. Transforming something ugly in both desire and design into something beautiful has cosmic value, these theorists insist.

To my irritation, a billboard announces that Broken Hill is in a Fruit Fly Exclusion Zone. Why can't it just be another Tidy Town? We aren't even leaving the state of New South Wales, and they want us to turn over all sorts of fresh produce that I've been squirreling away. We stop at the designated disposal bin three miles before town—leave your fruit or pay a huge fine if you're checked is the gist of their welcome message.

We stay half an hour, taking in their garbage bin view, cooking up tomatoes and red peppers for tonight's pasta sauce, eating an apple, squeezing some orange juice, and then we dispiritedly toss the rest. A waste. The flow of travelers coming through and offering their fruit to us rather than the bin remains steady. You could eat your fill of handouts. I make a mental note that should we become down and out, we camp here. Later our compliant approach is rewarded when earnest civil servants pull us over to inspect the vehicle.

Broken Hill's Line of Lode once stretched nearly five miles, making it the largest deposit of silver, lead, and zinc in the world. German-born boundary rider Charles Rasp happened upon this vein in 1883, thinking he had merely discovered tin. Rasp's luck transmuted into Broken Hill Proprietary Company (BHP), Australia's largest company—quite a step up from dogger to digger.

These days, a number of mine tours compete for your tourist dollar. It's hard to miss one of them. A giant slagheap interrupts downtown or, to put their spin on it, offers a "mining streetscape." Sitting atop this eyesore is the opening to Delprat's Mine, the original BHP site. Their underground tour guarantees "Complete safety in accordance with the Mine Inspection Act." We pass since we can see no bowable fence up there.

Silver City is its nickname, and the namegivers didn't stop there. Minerals, heavy metals, and semiprecious gems serve as street names in the downtown core. Imagine giving instructions to your home: We're on Garnet between Cobalt and Beryl. But even the romance of names like Crystal and Argent can't really get going, gridlocked as they are between industrial by-products and downright poisons.

A quick check reveals the hazards of living on:

Mercury St—Even in very small quantities, mercury is a poison more toxic than lead or arsenic. The vapors are readily absorbed through the lungs and rapidly transported to all organs of the body where it can cause harm; health problems may occur much later in a very insidious way.

Gypsum St—EPA has opposed using gypsum in roadbeds and construction projects because radon gas could pose a danger in the future if homes are built over those areas.

Mica St—Mica is a "non-fibrous silicate" akin to asbestos.

Bromide St—Methyl bromide will soon be banned, not because it's toxic—and it's very toxic—but because it attacks the ozone layer.

Silica St—Respiratory diseases may be aggravated by exposure to respirable crystalline silica. Call a poison control center for treatment advice.

Zinc St—For a zinc overdose or toxic exposure, seek medical care immediately at the nearest emergency room.

Chloride St—Poisoning can result from an overdose of mercuric chloride. Ammonium Chloride is a slight poison, skin irritant, lung irritant, and eye irritant. Polyvinyl Chloride (PVC) plastic, commonly known as "vinyl," has come to be known as the poison plastic and is being phased out. Benzyl chloride is a poison and corrosive.

Oxide St—For a zinc oxide overdose, call Poison Control. Silver Oxide: Poison. Mercuric oxide: vomiting; diarrhea (bloody). Nitric Oxide is a poison gas. Bis(tributyltin)oxide is a metabolic poison of very high toxicity. Contact with the skin, swallowing, or inhalation of spray may be fatal. Beryllium Oxide: Poison! May be fatal if ingested orally, absorbed through skin, or inhaled.

Sulphide St—Hydrogen sulphide is a broad-spectrum poison that can damage several different systems in the body. Barium sulphide is often used as a rat poison.

You might as well live in Toxi-City on the corner of Poison and Disease. Only Kaolin and Iodide Streets offer hope—kaolin serves as a general antidote, while potassium iodide acts as a thyroid-blocking agent in radiation poisoning. Residents of and visitors to Broken Hill, in the event of an emergency …

As the town expanded, less threatening names like Thomas, Williams, and Newton crept in. There's a Lane Street followed by the obligatory Lane Lane (surely named by the city of Townsville's

Department of Redundancy Department), as well as surnames of the greats in memory if not always deed, Australian explorers such as Burke, Wills, Sturt, and Eyre.

Heading north to Tibooburra on the Silver City Highway, we spot a number of emu herds on the run (perhaps "flocks" is the technical term, but these cartoon cattle of the bird world kick up dust rather than fly). Jon reckons the sole event in the lives of these insecure feather dusters is people in cars stopping to look at them. It takes about 30 seconds for our presence to sink into their brains, just the time it takes for Jon to get out the digital camera, turn it on, wait for the viewing screen to come up, aim, and—where are they?

The unyielding terrain looks as if it's normally covered with snow and ice. It's tundra-like, devoid of trees, less a landscape than a stingy lack of inspiration stretched out and extended over dull hills. In the distance, low mountains suggest purple pewter but stop short of a commitment. The odd remnant of a car wreck lies about.

I'm surprised it's not on the map—they have room, my navigator quips.

Back in 1985, you might have come across Jon pushing his Double-Piston, Triple-Neck Wheeling Violin on this very stretch of road.[43]

We pull off at Fowler's Gap, a desolate parking lot with a garbage bin, a utility fence, and, to our delight, an art fence: a Silver City Highway Sculpture Project by Alison Clouston. The artist describes on a plaque how:

> Fourteen thousand years ago Aboriginal people engraved the rock near here. Their descendants worked with European pastoralists to

---

[43] The Double-Piston, Triple-Neck Wheeling Violin was powered with a piston mechanism straight out of the era of the steam engine. Two bows were attached to the pistons, and as the wheel went around it pushed the bows up and down, sounding an arpeggio. The violin had three necks, two in the main playing part, with a bridge dividing down the middle, and a third with five resonating strings.

A vital environmental consideration determining the music was the condition of the road. Small bumps gave rise to significant spiccato affects. As I pushed it along, depending on the speed, I got the sense not of how long a piece of music is, but of how far it is. Of course, by walking backwards, the performer could hear what he had just played—in retrograde. Thus, with this instrument a new dimension was added to the parameters of musical structure, that of distance.

Image/sound at http://www.jonroseweb.com/d_picts_wheeling_violin.html.

establish stations and herd sheep. Fencing changed the management of sheep and landscape, symbolically marking a new order on the land. The oldest fences at Fowler's Gap Station date from around 1850. To fence the boundaries some 25,000 trees were cut from once prolific stands of mulga, laboriously drilled with brace and bit, postholes dug in hard and rocky ground.

Materials from the small, misshapen circle of a fence are largely local: a red gum trunk salvaged from the creek cutting, ochres exposed by road work, and gnarled mulga posts, former telephone poles. For her, the posts evoke "stockyards, fences and human struggle in a new land." Two rows of white metal slats bolted onto wooden posts serve as a frame. The immense gum trunk lies atop the serpentining fence, slicing right through the middle, crooking here and there, and finally dipping to earth in a point reminiscent of a waterwitch.

Nearby stands the utility fence, a new five-wire of unclear purpose. Despite a fierce wind, we record it, both as an aeolian instrument, then with us both bowing, a trio as it were. Humming, popping, rattling, tinkling—and that echo. In our judgment, the wind lacked sensitivity to the other two musicians and overplayed its part. We've been upstaged, but what can you do? Musicians know to never perform with children or animals, and now we must add aeolian fences to the list. We spend the night right here, enjoying flour tortillas stuffed with sautéed vegetables, green olives, and melted cheese with a 1999 Andrew Harris Cabernet from Mudgee.

The next morning's film set is decorated in orange, green, and purple—an unanticipated respite from the usual domination of red earth, yellow sun, and blue sky. There's been a bit of rain and grass shoots are showing up. We zip through Packsaddle, a roadhouse whose sole charm lies in its name and the half-mile of sealed road in front of it. We're anticipating Milparinka; the word is an Aboriginal one suggesting you could find a well or water here.[44]

Jon has arranged for us to play Milparinka's new graveyard fence on Easter Sunday. Since most of this near-ghost town's inhabitants reside there, it makes sense to perform to this built-in (dug-in, if you will) audience. The historic buildings are in various states of severe disrepair or nonexistence, although the Albert Hotel dating from 1881 again operates.

---

[44] In 1884 Charles Sturt and his 15 men were the first Europeans to visit Milparinka. As was so often the case in Australia, explorers sent out to find places of significance like the illusory great inland sea found themselves crossing endless deserts instead. Sure of finding the land's arteries and blood vessels, a boat was included in Sturt's baggage train. He and his men spent months entrapped here in the scorched and blistered bleakness, finding the earth's dry bones instead. His assistant, James Poole, died of scurvy and is buried nearby at Depôt Glen. The others miraculously survived.

We stop in to introduce ourselves, the musical centerpiece of their inaugural Once a Jolly Swagman festival, promising to return the next night to take our reserved room for the weekend. Then we head out, beginning with a side road. The area ranges from scrub-covered dunes to broad gibber (Aboriginal for a rock of throwing size) plains, with gum-lined creeks and rugged sandstone jump-ups.

The bristly grasses are memorable in name: in addition to Mitchell, there's never-fail, woolly-butt, and bottle-washer. Jon stumbles upon some aged fence posts, which he sets to photographing. They're weathered faces, characters with a story and anxious to speak. We see owls, parrots, a mother and child bound together, wise and evil spirits. On the ground is the carcass of a melted sheep, exposed thighbones pointing to a pile of seemingly plastic woolen curls. The New York downtown art scene needs look no further for a shocker.

The breast bounce-ometer is reading high as we continue along another viciously corrugated outback road.

Guess what those two hills over there are called on the map? Jon asks.

Two Hills?

Yes.

And a bit later we pass One Tree. It's brown mud and blowflies for a long stretch and only a liar or a poet would tell you more. You can't wax about it: cartons of mud, parades of flies, spills of—no, you just can't; there's nothing to spill but tears. "Serfers' Paradise," Jon calls it, having bought a local postcard showing ragged, unsmiling miners' kids in the early 20s when the talk if not the reality around here was all gold, gold, gold.

> So far so good, but where was the labour to replace the stockmen and the poor, rum-besotted shepherds who had rushed off at the first clarion call of gold? … The money [the landholder] made he must now put into fences, since it soon became obvious that shepherds would be from henceforth an extinct race in the land, while an ever-hungrier pack of small men clamoured about the borders of his run.[45]

Things pick up later as we dip into a floodway. To either side of us, silky grey gums bend toward the creek we're crossing, their high branches hooking fingers over brown water. The smooth bark of their trunks ends in sunken shadowy circles, as if they've sprung up from middle earth. Although giants in size, the trees evoke misshapen dwarves. We take another hypnotic dip into a wider floodway a few minutes later. This one mimics a seaweed-littered beach at low tide after a storm. Twisted bits of roots and branches and strips of tree tissue that never could specialize are wound round the gum trunks. The light's

---

[45] Durack, Mary (1959/1997) *Kings in Grass Castles*, Sydney: Bantam Books, 23.

reflection overshoots the water's surface, as if the mirrored branches were rising up several feet out of the stream. The optical illusion holds even in the photograph, although we fail to find the Madonna.

I am reminded of a Persian carpet exhibition in London. The color and light seemed to hover on a higher plane than the level of the rugs. They were flying carpets.

We reach the hottest place in the state, Tibooburra (from an Aboriginal word for a group of granite outcrops), its handful of pubs, gas stations, and hotels all competing for our attention. The town serves as a staging area for those heading elsewhere. For the average tourist, Tibooburra is positioned on the edge of Sturt National Park, but for us the salient point is it's 35 miles to Warri Warri Gate where the Dingo Fence runs along the Queensland/New South Wales border.

We stop just outside town to read that the Silver City Highway to Warri Warri is closed, but not to Jon. He's a natural pessimist, but "NO ..." signs encourage and inspire him. We go back to check with the ranger, having just a day to spare before we need to be back south for our concert.

Go ahead and try, he says. The signs are usually several days behind—just be careful.

The ranger didn't ask our names or estimated return time. I note it but defer, trying to overcome my need for insurance, trying to just go native. We head north. The area is in the midst of a severe drought, the worst in a hundred years. Most everything looks arid and forsaken, although there was rain several weeks back that must account for the road closure. Seven miles in, I hallucinate a large wave across the gravel road. No, I'm correct. A truck coming toward us just dipped into a creek.

I slow to survey my mission. The LandCruiser's snorkel tube can provide air to the engine if the car is submerged, but it needn't. I don't anticipate any heroics on my part. The six-foot high fathometer registers well under a yard of water. Without the measuring stick and the other truck's example, I would be intimidated by this wide, dark stretch. I'd stop, have Jon get out and eyeball it, he'd assure me it was fine, I'd counter that it was *not*, he'd then have to insist I go forward, I'd have a moment of panic and regret, then I'd just do it, devil-may-care, like looking both ways as a pedestrian on a Sydney street, still unsure which way the traffic flows, then just making a run for it. As we ford the stream, in my peripheral vision I see great gnarled trees with exposed root systems, but I keep my eyes on the task of getting us through.

We cross another couple of creeks, one with just an inch or two of water, no worries. Our arrival at the much-anticipated border fence is greeted with wind, flies, and heat, but then there's a price for everything. We record and film every which way, a growing rhythmic animation played out with bouncing bows, squeaking bows, bows between wires, and bows atop the fence—stormy notes on rough seas.

Then we drive along the fence, inventing a road, to a jump-up where echo upon echo of the fence scallop their way down along the border. Even a confirmed fence hater would fall for this vista, although I'm uneasy with the slip-sliding vehicle. Jon snaps his *Whore's Breakfast* diptych of items on the fence, first a pack of cigarettes and later a Coke can.[46]

We decide to take the scenic Jump-Up Loop Road back to cover new ground. It's devoid of the promised roos, emus, and eagles. The drought has wreaked havoc. Except for the flies, it's quiet. Too.

We stop at the park's Olive Downs Campground, registering and paying, although with the road closed no one will be checking. It's getting dark, but the flies are still massive in number and hyper in attitude, like a young child just before his unwanted bedtime. Jon goes out to record them while I cook dinner. When he comes in, I hand him the antibiotic hand cleanser.

It's a short drive the next morning to the jump-up where we look out over segregated sections of white, olive, brown, and beige rocks. Perhaps this is the very place where Charles Sturt observed in his journal:

> The stones were not, however, rounded by attrition, or mixed together, but laid on the plains in distinct patches, as if large masses of the different rocks had been placed at certain distances from each other, and then shivered into pieces.[47]

As we continue, we discover it's the *soil* of Olive Downs that's green, not a grass species or the rocks. We come across an abandoned couple, Mr. Saw and Mrs. Rake. Jon later decides to rescue these tools, but I nix going back. We're on a Road Closed adventure, and I'm concentrating, checking off dry creek beds as we cross them. I don't want to lose count. I figure we have crossed four or five already, but it's hard to tell because all but one have been dry for a long time as they gradually morph from creek beds to memory lines. The last one, number eight, will be the worst if we get that far.

---

[46] Another of Jon's fence photos from this shoot will become the cover art for the Corner Country brochure.
[47] Sturt, Charles (1849/2001) *Narrative of an Expedition into Central Australia*, North Adelaide: Corkwood Press, 117.

Just as we climb into our vehicle, I spot a deadly eastern brown snake taking his absolute time crossing the road. He alters his course and approaches us.

Snake! Snake! Snake! Camera! Camera! Camera! I shout to Jon, who obliges.

We get so close that he has to direct me; the six-foot venommeister is on Jon's side of the vehicle, and I can no longer see it. After he gets the photo, I carefully back up so as not to hurt the serpent, hoping one of his kind might return the favor some day.

Mount King Bore is our next pullover, an inoperative windmill with a full-tilt wind. Jon pokes around, but I limit my time outside. I know the physical snake is a half mile back, but the remembered snake is right here with me, threatening a venom cocktail enhanced by 60 million years of evolution and delivered by an intimate assassin. "Old fence posts here/previous stop, scattered curls rusting wire, snake on brain," I jot.

We see ahead an unthreatening inch or two of water with tire tracks in the ground leading up to it. I'm tentative on multiple levels, trying to disregard my gut instincts. Ignore snake, ignore water, ignore tracks, ignore boy pressure, ignore girl fear—just go. Down, down, down. Buried to our chassis in no time at all. In Jon's mind we weren't displaying the least amount of bravado.

We just look at each other; then Jon puts on his highest shoes to survey. It's not good. For just one moment our fences were down, and now we're caught in disgrace. I send him forward with a note: "Bogged at next creek, Friday, April 17." He returns with it still in hand, the land ahead of us presenting even swampier conditions. No one's coming from that direction; there's no immediate hope. The real creek, the serious one that the park service will check, if they check, certainly not this Easter weekend or Easter Monday, will be the one closest to them. Jon estimates we are number three in line.

We are stuck in a place not on our map as a potential problem, and we'll not see company for a while. We begin to make mental adjustments both large and small in nature, careful not to fight or blame. Jon spends an hour out in the muck putting stones and brush under the wheels, digging and swearing. It's soft and wet, sucking him in to his boot tops. Digging is a tedious process of filling the spade, then scraping it, then scraping the scraper, each effort yielding half of what it should. When I get out, I notice that even the seemingly dry bits collapse when I walk on them, then cake onto my shoes. Neither the surface of the ground nor of my shoes is stable. We make a few more attempts to back out, but the wheels don't even turn. It's hard to know how to proceed. There's no bottom to the muck and no way to get under the wheels.

Of course, this insurance lover has rented an EPIRB (emergency position indicating radio beacon), but it's a $15,000 fine to press the button in a nonemergency. Even then, they could take 48 hours to get here. Should we go out for a snakebite, finding a legit reason? We keep our heads. We lunch instead, pondering our options over a half bottle of 1998 Richmond Grove Coonawarra Cabernet as we dine on stuffed grapevine leaves and marinated vegetables. Cell phone—no reception. Patience—holding. I take another look at the trickle just ahead of us. To look at that, we just should not be stuck, but trees line both sides of the road for a fair distance, nature's warning sign that water is buried here.

We consider whom else to blame, like the park ranger who didn't ask our name and return time.

A woman would have, I declare. And by the time the Albert Hotel in Milparinka realizes we aren't there for our room or our gig, the park office in Tibooburra will be closed for the weekend, our ranger off on his own holiday. There's no way we'll make our concert on the Graveyard Fence. We're in mud jail.

Jon considers walking out, departing about 3 a.m. with as much water as he can carry.

It's 12 miles at least. The planet's second deadliest snake and its kin are loose out there. Never leave your vehicle, say all the books. I won't hear of it. Plus, I'm sure they will miss us and immediately alert someone.

Jon laughs at my naiveté.

Ruth, who hired us—does she know where we might go?

Not really.

Exactly what did we tell to whom? Everything is slow except our brains. Not-so-good Friday.

Digging, reading, writing—and always the mind begins again. We feel compelled to come up with a plan, and we can't get started. As I am washing up the dinner dishes, Jon says, come look at this! There's a light! Several in fact!

I climb into the front seat with him. We can just make out light through the trees. I imagine a bunch of hardy blokes setting up camp for the three-day Easter weekend. I start the car and go for the horn. They are just on the other side of the creek. - - - . . . - - - goes my horn, then I do it with the lights, bright dim bright, SOS patterns, a sound and light show they cannot miss. Horn, lights, confident, jubilant—we're home free, except why aren't they signaling back? Okay, they gotta finish their beers before they risk their rears.

It's huge, Jon observes, an entire boy scout camp or something.

The fragmented light through the trees rises a bit, intensifies, and suddenly disentangles itself from the tree branches; at the same moment we both realize we've been signaling to the moon. We howl with laughter; we're know-nothing neophytes, easy targets of the full moon disguising itself as the torchlights of half an army.

The next day, Jon pines for the rake and saw we bypassed. He sees them as an omen, the tools presaging our demise at Twelve Mile Creek. He tries to walk a bit to ease the tedium but is almost bogged just from his own weight. He settles for gathering more wood and stones close by.

I see him covered in flies, perhaps a thousand, a picture of absolute misery, filth, and fatigue, and yet he goes on for hours. Flies outline his right back pocket, a black patch on beige shorts. When he returns I find the garment gives up no evidence as to why the intense fly interest. His wallet?

We watch and listen. Every time the wind changes, it sounds like a car approaching. Jon heard 10 phantom cars on his brief morning walk. Cars half-heard, the sound of desire.

The galahs are big here, hosting a convention of Easter aerial maneuvers: we're grey-we're pink-we're grey. He reckons their count at over 3000. They are party animals that like how they look and sound. When they fill the air with their metallic "chirrink-chirrink," they smack of a Sydney art opening. With all parties, there's a few who won't leave. Ten percent stay up most of the night shrieking.

A week before a recording or important concert, knowing I have to produce, I begin hearing things I didn't under less stress. Our memories are like that now. Little details we didn't think we fully took in come front and center.

Remember, when we pulled up in Milparinka, that man leaving the hotel carrying a small burgundy simulated leather suitcase and a pillow tucked under his other arm?

Yeah, he walked across the gravel road to that makeshift hovel.

What was his story?

Who knows?

And then that other guy emerged from the hovel, varrrooming his motorcycle a whole hundred yards to the orange plastic fence. I mean, he could have walked—how bored was he?

Jon told the Albert Hotel folks we'd return in a day but didn't say where we were going. Still, we could only head north to the park since we had come from the south, wouldn't they realize? If someone really wanted to find us, this swamp would be the logical place. We remember seeing one car go up the main park road and two come down but none on this scenic loop. Since we paid at the campground last night, Jon's name on the envelope, at some point they'll know we were near here, but we could have taken the main road back.

Hallucination: 12 Mile Creek Theater—in front of the bogged car a stream crosses the road hidden on either side by bushes and trees. It has the makings of a bush theater with various actors appearing stage right and going with the flow so to speak, disappearing stage left. First come the kangaroos, then the odd croc saunters past, then onto hippos, giraffes, lions; then we reach the people/beast combos, figures of hate cross the stage stopping midway for a cheap leer at us, their captive audience.

While stranded, Jon takes the opportunity to rephoto a fence post like the one from the top end of the Rabbit-Proof Fence at Cape Keraudren. That one vanished into digital space the last time he edited the fence slide collection. He enters his trance-like ritual whereby, head down, he goes round and round the fence post chanting profanities at the horror of flies as he tries to see through the camera's viewfinder, the image of which is obliterated by the sun's total wipe-out rays.

When Jon returns, he sets to writing with a vengeance. Then he reads to me:

THE ORIGINS OF DANCE. Along with music, the origins of dance tend to be left in the mists of time. But we can surmise that dance punctuated the various critical parts of our ancestors' lives such as birth, death, marriage, the arrival of something good to eat, the return of the warriors, etc. I would like to add to this list of fundamentals that dancing is a time-honored method of keeping the flies at bay, hence the expression '"no flies on him" for someone who can dance fast enough. It seems clear to me that here in outback Australia the Aborigines have been dancing for over 40,000 years not only for religious ceremony or because it keeps you fit but because of the flies. Of course, this doesn't address the problem of why most dancing happens after dusk when the flies have all gone home to prepare for the following day's mayhem, but I do think The Fly Dance reflects man's long-standing and unwinnable battle against the little shits.

Bogged down as we are in our less than hermetically sealed four-wheel-drive, we pass the time killing as many flies as possible—mostly using the splat technique. Hollis prefers the paper hanky. I prefer the physical blood contact. But eventually one is forced outside our defensive ramparts to attend to the calls of nature (becoming more frequent, I'm afraid, the longer we stay here).

Leaving the car is not a major problem. The maneuver is carried out with precision and with an element of surprise. They are just not ready for that car door to suddenly swing open and a fly-netted warrior to leap forth with an angry cry. As the door slams shut, perhaps 10 flies in the front line get in, more by accident than battle campaign design. Getting back in, however, presents a formidable problem. After a matter of seconds beyond the keep, one is covered with hundreds of flies. Looking at my arm, I see there is no landing space left on my airport; the next wave circles above in a holding pattern, genetically programmed to know that wherever their mates are, there must they also be.

How to get back into the castle without bringing a battalion of them with me? Dance. I'm not at this stage suggesting a waltz or foxtrot—I'm recommending something post-Sarah Bernhardt, post-Martha Graham, post-Pina Bausch, post-contact improvisation, first-past-the-post dance. No, I'm indicating here total unrestrained free form, maximum waving around of arms, jumping up and down, running this way and that, and the occasional loud scream. Don't worry, the flies are fast learners, they pick up on your moves quickly. You have to invent new moves all the time, or it gets boring for them. However, flies are never bored to *death*—they like death, the smell of death, the smell we will all have one day when we are also dead. By creating total confusion you get one chance, when you are about two feet ahead of the pursuing army, to open the door and jump in. This must be done in one move; otherwise, all is lost, and you have a carful of flies.

The dance-and-in method works about 65-70 percent, which means you will spend the next two hours hunting down 200–300 flies. Oh, I nearly forgot the prisoners. The fly net is never 100 percent fly-proof, not if you want to breath and see without choking to death. So, carefully take off the net, sealing the hole quickly. You have perhaps 20 to 30 prisoners caught while infiltrating your perimeter. Slowly screw up the fly net and place it on the dashboard. A pleasure as old as life itself wells up inside you as the entrapped flies make their last little free-form gestures.

Unlike our history of warfare where we finally arrived through a process of club, bow and arrow, sword, and gunpowder to aerial bombardment of defenseless civilians, the flies have never bothered with warfare evolution; they have had it down from long before we were around. Islamic fundamentalist suicide approach is never far from their collective spirit. They know that there is that big shit heap in the sky.

He's not exaggerating. The flies are as unremitting as gateless fences. Our veils have saved us every day of this trip. Jon wears my backup, not being the type to have his own. Purchased in the Katherine sporting goods store, it looks properly masculine, hunter green netting topped with a camouflage circle to prevent sunburn. My newer purchase from the Alice Springs Telegraph Station is white with a hole on top that you slip over a hat. When the flies are not present, you elegantly fold the veil up over the brim. *À la mode* or *passé de mode*, wearing them immediately brings feelings of claustrophobia and cataracts, a premonition of how it will be in not so long. I read they now have metal-weighted suits and out-of-focus spectacles for people to experience the handicaps and deficits of old age. Skip the expensive goggles and put on a fly veil, I say.

The scene is stable at 12 Mile Creek Theater, save one tiny cloud drifting stage left to right. Our safety-net boasts ABC, BBC, aircon, fine wine in proper glasses, ample food-water-gas, and an emergency beeper we're too poor and too proud to push. We enjoy the leisurely lunch we never take, today a 2002 Buloke Reserve Petit Verdot and Japanese rice crackers for starters, then pasta with semi-dried tomatoes in olive oil with garlic and chilies, the crunch of pine nuts, hazel nuts, and pumpkin seeds, and a dusting of Parmesan cheese. Underneath it all, I'm apologetic that I've not gone native. An avid hiker in "friendly" country, *here* I sit in the car. I can imagine an Aboriginal mob out poking around, discovering all sorts of flora and fauna, sifting and comparing, reading tracks, picnicking on witchetty grubs and other delicacies in the midst of 100 different signs well read. Is it me who is resistant and reluctant, I ponder, or is it the land?

Jon decides to dig again after he writes a card to his youngest daughter.

Make it your last wise words of advice, I tease. Sign it with your enduring love.

We restudy our maps, park info, and four-wheel-drive instructions but find nothing new to learn or do. Our minds, like our car wheels, just spin without getting anywhere. I propose that 12 Mile Creek should be renamed 12 Mile Swamp, containing as of our latest estimate four impassable sections.

I practice the violin, beginning with the Texas-style tune "Billy in the Lowground" about a fiddler who tries to fiddle himself out of a sinkhole; then I rest in the afternoon heat. As I begin to drift off, I hear the sound of a fly, and only one, and it's okay. My lifelong attitude has shifted from oh-my-god-there's-a-fly-in-the-house-it's-dirty-now-kill-it! to one of almost comfort, the buzzing of one fly imparting the sense of a lazy summer's nap. (It is alleged that some Australians living in fly country get so used to flies getting stuck on their food that if enough don't get drowned by themselves, these hardened souls end up catching more to put on.) While I rest, Jon digs and digs, swears, drinks water, and digs some more. He's remaking the track, his Roman road, and we have all the time in the world.

Without notice a truck pulls up. A statuesque blonde woman with a smile of amusement and an air of utter confidence descends from the vehicle, followed by two blokes in seriously framed fly veils spreading out from their heads in improbable circles like hats only imaginable on a Paris catwalk.

Vell, dat serves you right, hmm, she teases.

White shirt with stripes, beige trousers—she's a ranger. She's here on her off-hours with some friends to check the water tank levels. The three walk around with Jon assessing the situation.

I'm madly putting things away, readying the car to be moved. I hear Jon try to justify our actions, explaining that the park ranger in the office left it to our discretion.

Oh him, she says dismissively. Vell, ve'll soon have you out of here, and with that she swallows a fly and spits furiously.

The blokes just stand around, mute. She's clearly in control of the scene, and they're prepared to do as told by this *Übermensch*. She and Jon do shorthand bios in German as they place a tow belt under the vehicle. She's been in Oz 10 years, she's from Hannover, she loves her adopted country. She approaches the passenger side of the LandCruiser, and I roll down the window.

My savior!

Ya, I hope, now put it in reverse, but keep the clutch in until you feel the veels connect, then let the clutch out.

Flies stream in with the window down, but who cares? She stays next to the car to direct me as the blokes begin to winch. Jon's half-completed road makes it easier than it might have been, and just as suddenly as we were stuck, we are free. When the vehicle is clearly out of the muck, I stop and get out.

Ja, ja. Hier geht alles endlich los.

They plan to go on through the swamp and ask us to wait to make sure they make it.

It's going to be worse the next bit over, Jon warns.

She wades through and agrees. They'll head back to town the long way, like us. We offer them a glass of wine, which they graciously decline. I blow them kisses as they head out.

It all happened so fast. We never even got their names. I drive full-tilt boogie to Milparinka, getting us there in two hours. To my shock but per Jon's prediction, no one at the Albert Hotel seems to notice we are 24 hours late. The pub's doing pretty good change, and Jon feels we should be friendly and hang out, not rush into a much-needed shower. We join the Flying Padre, the Rev. John C. Blair, and his wife Becky for dinner.

What's the special? I ask the waitress.

Tuna mornay.

Can you describe it?

Uh, not really. Let me check with the kitchen.

Half an hour later, it is *she* who has cooked our tuna mornay, or her idea of what it might be. She has the good sense to offer us abundant sauces—tomato (aka ketchup), tartar, and mustard. It is ruled that France may not collect royalties on this, an early 60s all-American meal, as "mornay" appears in word but not deed.

A young outback couple soon to be wed by the padre briefly joins us.

Groom: Yeah, we were bloody oath down there, and it took bloody oath all day to get the thing.

Bride: Yeah, I was totally buggered.

The sincere young couple obviously doesn't consider this to be swearing.

After dinner, I head for the women's bathroom for a long shower, employing every product in my arsenal. The unlockable and in all other ways Spartan guest rooms circle an indoor garden with pond that doubles as dining room. The walls and floor are stone, so it stays fairly cool in the heat and looks cool, which helps as well. A breezeway leads to the outside door, which is kept open. I can imagine one of Australia's finest snakes sashaying in some night.

They don't like people, Jon says to reassure me.

Becky told me at dinner that it's good I didn't run over the snake—if you hit their tail, they've been known to come up through the open window and strike, or they'll wrap themselves round the chassis and unleash their venom at an opportune, for them, moment.

Jon rolls his eyes.

We return to the dining room for the evening's entertainment and are seated next to John Traeger and his wife. He's up from Broken Hill to auction off bits of this and that for the Milparinka Heritage and Tourism Association (the organization in charge of writing the tourist-speak for Milparinka, searching for stock phrases analogous to other clichés and yet different enough to pull you in). Traeger's wife says he even auctions in his dreams. He has another virtue: a keen enthusiasm for the Dog Fence. Jon sets up an interview for the next day. Then we go to bed, exhausted. Just as we're drifting off, we hear the auction commence, and Jon piles out of bed to record it. It's music to his ears, just like a fence. On his return, he can't sleep. He's imagining a suite of compositions for string quartet plus auctioneer, the strings to play rhythms and counterpoints to the auctioneer's *Sprechgesang*.

After the auction comes the karaoke, the quality of the singing deteriorating with the quantity of the drinking in a predictable manner. We keep getting up to peek out from our nearby room. Most of the wannabe singers are young women. Finally, three drunk blokes take the stage to shout and mug through "Ring of Fire," beer cans welded to each right hand for moral support. "Achy, Breaky Heart" sends us back to bed, but we can't resist leaning out of our room in our underwear to join in every chorus of "Come on baby, do the locomotion." When we do, we see line—or rather wave—dancers. They are very drunk indeed.

W e rise early and poke around the long block that is town. Perhaps a thousand screeching sulphur-crested cockatoos are slowly making their way along the creek. We meet James, the district officer for the state arts council, who has assisted in funds for our concert here. He suggests a hike, and I'm attentively taking notes on how to find the place. He ends his description with a warning: Mind the silver snakes at the end—death adders. My enthusiasm plummets to zero.

The fashion here is boots, belts, blue jeans, and Wrangler shirts; it's the wild west, and real men walk bow-legged, lean back on verandahs smoking cigarettes, give a knuckle-cracking handshake, and ride their hand on their belt or jeans pocket with a Marlboro Man touch. Let the womenfolk gregariously spill the ink—the men communicate in their shorthand of postures, gestures, and silences. I hear on the radio that 40 percent of Australian men have some form of erectile dysfunction and wonder what's the body language for that.

Jon discovers that the medieval hovel across the road is a portable roo-butchering plant. It's a small operation, just some refrigerated trucks and a few fenced guard dogs roaming among several trailers where the be-hoveled live. I'm reminded of the dye pits of Morocco: men standing in chemicals to their waist, flies swarming, the heat and stench full-on.

The old sandstone courthouse dates from 1886 but closed in 1929. Like the hotel, it has been restored. The history of the town and region is recounted on its walls. In the 20s, every station had a dogger to fight the enemies of fences—roly-poly buildups, sand, and floods as well as wild animals. Native timber was devastated to build post-and-rail fences; once gone, mulga trees don't grow back. Since 1945 all posts except corner and strainer posts must be steel. I learn that solar panels now power some electric fences.

We have agreed to play music for the Easter service. In preparation, Jon stretches a wire across a wooden table in the courthouse and calls it an instrument. He also assembles some corrugated iron, a plastic bucket, a hubcap, clappers, a drumstick, and a musical saw. I'll be on fiddle and organ.

The Flying Padre must be pleased with his full house. He leads us through classic hymns. There's power in the music as the people sing together. From football stadiums to small churches, if our species gets to the point where singing has no significance, then society has unwound. We conclude with a Handel violin sonata, me on violin and Jon on his bush percussion kit. It sounds like folk music, and no wonder—the separation between high art and folk art was indistinct when the music was written.[48]

The only part of the sermon that sticks with me is when the Flying Padre describes his trip up, ending with: "I land the plane, taxi to the pub, and shoot a photo of the plane by the pub to send to my bishop." Laughter all around.

There's not many avant-garde musicians who can say they met a good contact after playing the Sunday morning service. The Sturt Meadows station owner is a fence enthusiast.

Church is followed by the reënactment of a gold heist and subsequent mock trial, which we punctuate with music. The antique horse-drawn Cobb & Co. coach appears from over the hill to the strains of the "William Tell Overture," the robbers display some impressive horsemanship, and the "local police" are indeed the local police.

The weak link in the proceedings is the actress. Just as she is sentenced to life in prison for her part in the heist, a baby cries out from the back of the courtroom. The father holds the baby up, but the amateur actress, the baby's mother in real life, is unable to rise to the occasion with an improvised plea for mercy in the name of her child. Jon and I have no choice but to transition to Chopin's "Funeral March," and the three actors are led to their tragic end.

---

[48] As Cornelius Cardew set out in his incisive but unfashionable tome *Stockhausen Serves Imperialism* (1974, London: Latimer New Dimensions Limited), the weight of the Western music canon lies heavily on the backs of European folk musicians. Even at the end of the Baroque era, the instrument and the musician were still the primary ingredient for music making—the composer's role was that of instigator, arranger, and fixer (the name "Bach" was interchangeable with the name and role of "town musician").

Being violinists, both of us notice the direct and immutable links in the instrument-based lines of Bach's string writing, the corresponding lines of anonymous fiddle music, the musical memes descending through the generations as dance forms, and the renewable notions of figured bass and improvisation in perhaps the twentieth century's greatest invention—jazz. And that's only from a violinist's viewpoint. After the composer took over as resident genius with a direct line to God, it didn't stop Mozart, Beethoven, Brahms, Liszt, Mahler, Bartók, Copland, Bernstein, and others from dipping into the vernacular pot whenever the Omnipotent put the struggling music scribe on hold.

Even the *bête noir* of modernism, Arnold Schoenberg, informed his *Pierrot Lunaire* from his regular gig, writing and playing music for the Berlin cabaret scene. These days, in the absence of almost any professional music work, you just buy in your "folk," delivering a world music purée such as Philip Glass's recent global smorgasbord or Australian composer Peter Sculthorpe's "Aboriginizing" by way of sticking a didgeridoo in the middle of a symphony orchestra.

We get lots of positive comments about our music afterwards. Americans will always come up and tell you what they think, even if they have nothing to say. Australians won't unless they are particularly moved or have really taken it in. Even then, they might choose to talk about some technical aspect.

Next, we drive up to the graveyard, which bears the names of many pioneers of the region, and set up our equipment: several contact microphones under wires, two battery-powered amplifiers, and a bass bow apiece. A couple approaches us with an open bottle of wine and invites us to have a glass. It's their friends' Hunter Valley Cabernet Sauvignon, but it's pre-concert so we decline. They just give us the bottle, as friendly and easygoing a couple as ever I did meet. We exchange small talk. He's an accountant; she's knowledgeable about wine. For us, the bogging is still uppermost in our minds.

I was bogged Friday, and I was bogged Saturday, the accountant responds.

We're ceasing to take it so personally, letting go of the thought that locals see us as darn fools from the big city. Ruth, our employer for this concert, joins in.

That family over there was bogged last night with a trailer full of pregnant ewes. We were up 'til late—we finally had to get the tractor.

When I ask Ruth about our bogging, she assures me that at some point she would have alerted the authorities that we'd gone missing.

After our graveyard fence concert, Jon proceeds to his interviews.

My name is John Blair, I'm the Uniting Church Flying Padre for West of the Darling Presbytery, it's an area of 42,000 square miles, it runs from the corner country, the northwestern boundary of South Australia and New South Wales, then east towards Hungerford, then it drops down west of Louth to the river again and diagonally runs with the river southwest back to just above Wentworth and Mildura, it's dry country.

When you're flying and you see these demarcation lines that are fences, do you have an emotional response to that?

When I was flying back from Alice Springs last week, I looked down and saw the fences, and I thought it was ironic that something could be so worked at by nameless men, put in the ground and run for such a distance, and here I was just flying over it at such a quick pace.

It's a wonder to me why they've built a brand new fence around the cemetery here—to keep the remains of people in or visitors out?

167

My wife and I have a running, loving quarrel about whether we should put a picket fence around our house or not—once you establish a fence, there's the maintenance factor, and being a lazy husband on Saturday afternoons, the last thing I want to do is go out and fix the fence, but she says there is a sense of orderliness that she relies upon, that she expects, enjoys about the world, putting and keeping things in order and showing respect for one's ancestors.

Order would make sense here, it's such an intense place to exist, you feel very fragile and paying respect to the dead by building a fence around them …

I guess it shows sacred or holy ground in the mind of the person who builds it, and I'm wondering how the descendents who are buried in that area would come and enjoy your music themselves.

It certainly changes how we perceive what we are going to do. A fence can be a very brutal structure, keeping out wild dogs from sheep, but here it has a reverence. I mentioned playing the fence to a guy at the bar and he said, Fair dinkum? He can't believe this is going to be serious music by serious musicians on a fence. In terms of the history, music and religion have been linked forever, but this is possibly the first time that anyone played a perimeter fence around a graveyard.

This is Easter Sunday, an appropriate day to make music in that place, part of my enthusiasm for the concert is knowing that before you touch the fence music comes from it based on air speed and wind on that wire.

There are barriers and boundaries no matter how adventurous the instrument might be. By working to those limits and within them, you create the expression, the meaning. Some people ask us to play a tune on it. Could you play "Waltzing Matilda" on the fence? You theoretically could, but if you want to play "Waltzing Matilda," you'd play it on the violin or piano because that's what they're made for. The fence has its own music, so we're trying to reveal and uncover what that fence does. Of course, the wind uncovers some, but there's more to it. To most people, with just some discreet amplification, it's going all out, it's the most complicated sound, like electronic music, and then you look at the landscape here, which is something like being on the moon.

I think it's perfect.

My father had been a stubborn ironbark corner post you could strain a fence with 8 taut lines and never see it budge but it didn't take a day to realise Uncle James were dug too shallow or placed in sandy soil.[49]

[49] Carey, Peter (2000) *True History of the Kelly Gang*, St. Lucia, Queensland: University of Queensland Press, 44.

I'm John Traeger, I'm a territory livestock sales manager for Wesfarmers Landmark in Broken Hill, the last 34 years I've had quite a bit to do with people who live on the Dog Fence, their involvement with maintaining it, and other issues relating to dogs attacking livestock.

You told me last night you'd done 12 years as a journalist and got into the politics of the Fence.

We had an editor at the Rural Press, Steve Swan, a very good newspaperman, and he said one day when we looked like we had nothing to do, "Go out and see what sort of trouble you can stir up," so I headed to some old friends of mine, George and Val Summers at Murnpeowi Station on the Strzelecki Track, it's a cattle station on the northern side of the Fence, probably 800-square miles, and I told George what it was about and there was a bit of a stir about the maintenance of the Fence and George took me out in an old Toyota one day, he said, "Take this one out, it's got some air conditioning," and when I got in it there were no windows in it, anyway we took a bottle of cold water and off we went to the Dog Fence, I took some nice black-and-white photographs of George along the Fence and wrote a little story, "Send the dogs south," he said, "They can eat bloody sheep, I'm sick of them eatin' the cattle, they can have roast lamb instead of beef burgers."

Doug Fuller from Rose Hill, he told me, "John, if you go to the zoo and you're looking at the lion, where are ya?" I said, "Well, I'm outside." "And if you go in with a keeper to feed it, where are ya?" "Well, I s'pose I'm inside with the lion." And he said, "Well I'm inside with the dogs and those silly bastards down south reckon I'm outside."

Did anybody work out the cost without a fence, for grain, sheep, cattle—could anything happen without it?

I suppose it could. A lot of people say dingoes won't attack cattle but I've had photographic evidence supplied to me and also firsthand I took photos of small cows that had been attacked by dogs, they will eat cattle occasionally but it's more a pack situation, I've seen sheep that haven't got a mark on them that are dead, they've just been scared to death, the main thing is to keep the dogs out of sheep country, and I don't have any sort of romantic view, the Fence is there for practical purposes, and I can only admire the people who have seen fit to look after it the last 100 years.

One of the problems in Moolawatana, and to a lesser extent Erudina, is the ground's very acidic and the fellows were forever buying miles and miles of foot netting, one day the inspector came along, and when he found a hole he'd tie a piece of yellow plastic ribbon so that told you to fix the hole up, and we're walkin' along with Mike Sheehan and this little bloke is kickin' holes in the foot netting and the bloke behind him would tie a ribbon on it, and after about a half an hour of this and two miles, Mike said, "If he kicks another hole in that bloody foot netting, I'm going to kick his ass," the people that look after it are still pioneers.

How'd you get into auctioneering?

When I was a small child, my father had a farm in the Adelaide Hills and I can remember two stock graders arrived to buy some lambs and they pulled up in a green Ford Customline and had double-breasted suits with fob chains and the whole bit, elastic-sided boots, and they bought the lambs and they went away and from that day on when people said what do ya want to be, I'd say, I wanna be a stock agent, they'd say, "Why in the hell would you wanna be a stock agent?" and I used to say, "So I can have a green Ford Customline."

You've got really good projection, apart from the microphone.

There's a normal tone in your voice and you think you sound the same as an auctioneer as you talk but in actual fact what you do, what you're taught is, "Sell out of your guts, boy, not out of your lungs," and you find pretty early, say you've got 20,000 sheep in front of you and 40, 50 60 maybe 100 lots, well that's a fair day's work, particularly in a dusty yard, and an auctioneer as a front man has a bit more respect and you as a front man have to present yourself, it's a presentation thing.

It's entertainment, in the oral tradition. In music we talk about chops.

I've had the privilege of selling the stud rams at the Adelaide Show, we were three auctioneers on the plank for four and a half or five hours, we'd do probably an hour each and rest, we were plying for big biquies [bucks] there, it's one thing selling a bit of gear for the Flying Doctor or the Milparinka Heritage Association, but if you stand in front of a crowd selling somebody's livestock, it's a full-on professional job.

What about style?

The tone in your voice should create a sense of urgency, you build up the crescendo, I'm gonna knock it down—this is your last chance. Compare Queensland auctioneering to Victoria or South Australia, it's like chalk and cheese, it's the same job within a few cents, but the way they sound, the different rhythms, the nasal thing, language is different too, they call it "the high bone" in Dubbo, but we say "between the pins" in Adelaide, yeah, it's an oral tradition alright, when Brian Leslie auctions dairy cattle in the eastern states, he is actually singing, it's like he has a melody.

We can't depart without bowing Milparinka's Dead Sheep Fence (as we name it). The plus: a great-sounding fence, God's own instrument; the price: there's a dead sheep here, its head wedged between two main posts right where we're bowing. We seem to specialize in playing for the dead of late. The sheep's final resting fence begins to groan and moan, whine and complain with the prompting of our bows. A frenzied saxophone/percussion duo you'd think to hear the recording, the all-hell-breaks-loose pandemonium of a spirit that cannot find rest. The sheep's eyes must be long gone but the illusion of their presence is fixed; they stare into eternity.

Off we go, into the wild blue yonder. Beware the cows crossing symbol, which has been adjusted with white paint to predict zebras instead.

We gas up in Tibooburra before heading on to Cameron Corner. I approach the handsome young policeman in the car across the pump aisle.

Great acting!
I wasn't acting.
Weren't you in Milparinka yesterday?
Yes, but I wasn't acting, he teases dryly.
Well, you were terrific.

It's a demanding drive, the unsealed road, although officially open, often in shocking condition. Still, there are no swampy bits—just uneven patches of potholes, wicked pointy rocks, and washboards that go for half an hour at a time. Our reward is a slowly modulating vista of stony tablelands and downs, desert sand dunefields, and floodplains and temporary lakes. Halfway to the Corner, with no indication on the map, we come over a hill to a 40–acre lake immediately below, the road running straight as an arrow through it. It must be a mirage, maybe we're supposed to drive through, I see signs in the middle, no, they're halfway underwater, another bogging for sure, but there's no other visible road. We're befuddled …normally the road does the thinking for us. It's noon, and I declare lunch. We ponder our alternatives over a chickpea, eggplant, and goat's cheese salad.

Another car arrives. We confer. The driver insists there must be an alternate route and turns back. Later we see him rounding the lake.

He gets out and waves. We go three miles back, and forth, and back, trying to find the track and finally spot it. Why no sign? In the dark would you even notice the lake, or would you just plow right into it? Okay, we see it on the map, Waka Claypan. It's a dot, not a circle outline of a lake. What is this, Aboriginal art or a proper map? I'm impatient, still a novice to the perverse fluctuations of seasons and years. In mapping these parts, a cartographer is not what's called for. Forget triangulation. Give me a philosopher and a statistician to debate and discharge the charting of extremes or averages, and throw in a climatologist and an oral historian to predict the future and recollect the past. The concept of an unmappable area appeals to me, but the reality does not. If I only had a songline, a comprehensive story from the beginning of the Dreamtime, I'd have all this information plus a song in my heart.

As usual, we're heading for the Dingo Fence but farther west this time, the Fortville Gate at Cameron Corner where New South Wales, Queensland, and South Australia meet. The Scottish surveyor John Brewer Cameron fixed the position in 1880. We arrive to not much, photograph the gate, then open and drive through it into Queensland. Aside from a plaque commemorating the meeting of three states, we find a small roadhouse run by a couple of older blokes and several teenagers. Two bathrooms next to the gas pumps are marked Drip Dry and Flip Dry. It's a lonely crossroads with every destination hundreds of miles away. The notice in the bar says, "Please be considerate of our neighbors when departing this establishment."

We order a drink, fair payment for the local information we are hoping to collect while here. And since my red wine is something even a Parisian clochard would turn up his nose at, soaking up info rather than vino is the order of the day. Johny G is the man in charge. Bill, who Jon had telephoned from Sydney in the hopes of doing an interview, is absent. Jon asks Johny G to stand in for his boss. Our man has to warm to the idea.

Come back in an hour, he says.

When we do, he quietly takes a beer from the fridge and goes out back before returning for his moment behind the mic.

My name's Johny G, I live at Cameron Corner where the three states meet, I work behind the bar and manage the place when Bill's not here, I came here 16 months ago from Omicron Station, which is the adjoining property, and I share my time between the two, goin' down there for the mustering season or if they need a hand to do the bull run or anything.

Which side of the fence is that?

North of the Dog Fence, in Queensland.

Theoretically, you're in the wild country up there, unprotected by the Fence.

I don't worry about that, we have the odd dingo pop up but they don't stay because there's no pickin's for 'em, they look for campsites since there aren't any sheep, cattle they don't bother, although they can get a young one down, but it doesn't happen much these days, they got it pretty much under control with the Fence.

So even on the other side of the Fence, it stops them from coming into the area. How long have you lived in this area?

About four years, before then I was in Dubbo, not as isolated as this, but I can handle the isolation fairly well, I like the area and what I do, I like to meet the people that come here, everyday's different, you meet different people doing different things, different nationalities, and everybody's on holidays and they're for a good time.

What about the weather?

The highest temperature this year in the shade out front was 117.5 Fahrenheit, it was 131 out in the flat, that's a big day, we sit in the bar for the day and don't dare go outside, I've gone for two days in the hot weather without seeing a car, it's a harsh environment, I choose to do it and am quite happy to do it.

Tell us about the communications tower you have here.

I think it helps with radio, it's pretty ...like nobody wants to talk much about it but as far as we know that's just a big Telecom tower, it could be anything, military, it's a really big tower for an area like this, only two of us live here permanently—if you take the surrounding properties into consideration, maybe 20, 25 people, every Friday night, everybody comes to town, we have a few drinks and a feed, a bit of a yarn, what happened this week, what's gonna happen next week, how many cattle are goin' where ...the next bar is 85 miles to Tibooburra, and almost 200 to Innamincka, that's the other option.

People coming in to eat and drink and buy a few souvenirs, that's the main income of the place?

We've just created accommodation in the back, I spend my time workin' around the place, we've got a dam down the back now with enough water in there for two years, before that we had to cart water from 20 miles away twice a week sometimes, and Bill goes down to Broken Hill for provisions one, maybe two times a week.

Do you ever go out there when you're by yourself and look at the Fence?

I sit every night and look to the Fence, I look at the stars—it's thick, it's thick, there's millions of stars there, which people in Sydney never ever see, that's all here, all you gotta do is park yourself out the front there overnight, turn all the lights off and bang, that's it.

We're heading out for the long Dingo Fence drive. Okay, I do need insurance. In my book, to be called circumspect is a compliment. At my pleading, Jon goes in to tell Johny G if we're not back by …call … I note the odometer reading, so if we bog we will know where we are and, for example, if it's possible to walk out. This leg of the trip is not my idea, this is a bad idea, driving down the basically unattended Dingo Fence for 62 miles, then cutting across other isolated and potentially swampy land back up to Corner Country, but here we go.

We don't get more than a mile when the road looks swampy, but it can't be—we're following our directions to a T. I'm steering in one direction, but the car heads in another. I try to wish us through; no sudden actions, I tell myself. Before I can turn a wish into a proper thought, we're stuck again, on the very road that Len, the district manager of the Fence, has instructed us to take.

Jon walks back for help, meaning Johny G or the teenagers. Not long after he departs, the fence runner shows up in the lightest, smallest golf-cart-of-
a-vehicle possible, driving almost on the Fence to avoid the water, whereas we were instructed to stay on the road 20 feet away from the Fence. My brief wave to him allows at least 50 flies to enter our car. He passes by, then stops when it's dry enough to dare and walks back in the muck.

Mark is his name. More flies stream in. He knew we were coming, Len told him about the possible interview with Jon, and he's on his way to Cameron Corner to turn around and come back. He wonders out loud if any vehicle can get close enough to pull us out. He wonders why Len told us to take this road since his boss was through here last night and took a different road. And now I wonder to myself why Len didn't tell Johny G to give us this message.

I occupy myself killing flies. Jon returns with two teenagers in a four-wheel-drive, followed by Mark. They dare not get close to the vehicle, and the tow belt is not long enough. Mark begins by digging, and immediately he sinks in over his boot tops. Muck collects on the shovel. People are at half speed, flies at double. Please, no one say the word "futile." They tie a rope to the tow belt to double its length, attach it to the other vehicle, and give a tug. The rope snaps. They set up the winch, but it doesn't work. Every time they confer, I think Mark will give up. The teenagers are sent for wood. Mark axes the wood to bits. More digging. Try again. We budge a bit, then are stuck again. It's quicksand for Mark and Jon, dicey even with a shovel for a third leg, and fly hell. More conferring. Finally, unbogged! I scrape mud off the tires, chassis, and mudflaps, while Jon records Mark inside his little truck.

I'm Mark Tillie, I'm 24, and I've been here three years, I look after 40 miles of the Dingo Fence on the border of South Australia/New South Wales.

What's an average day?

It all depends on what your day starts off with, you look for rust, if you see a bit of rust around the dirt, you put a bit of black on it, that's what the black's for, you might have wind, you gotta watch your sand building up, you lift your one fence up a bit higher and the one that lost the sand you move it a bit lower, you got the black netting down at the bottom, which is plastic-coasted, then you got your chook wire, then your marsupial, which is a lot bigger diameter, you separate that wire between the marsupial and the chook wire, and you raise it up and put in some more chook wire.

It's five, six feet high. The dogs can jump how high?

Four feet's the minimum for the Fence, anything gettin' near four feet's gotta be topped, it all depends on how much of a slope you've got into it, it might be twelve feet this side but five feet the other, you hardly ever get a dog to jump, wild dogs are not very good jumpers, they'll try to dig, kangaroos and emus run into it, cattle fight from either side, especially two bulls and one of the horns might get caught in the netting and they just walk along it and break the whole thing down.

How often are you here?

I do 20 miles a day, my house is in the center of my section, it comes with the job, Monday I usually go south, Tuesday I come this way, Wednesday south, I just do it that way, on a day like this we've ANZAC Day [Australia's national memorial day for those who have fought and died in wars] comin' up, I'll have to run both ways tomorrow because of the weekend.

Do you have any thoughts about the Fence apart from thinking it's something you've gotta fix all the time?

When I first come up, I knew it was the Dog Fence, I'd never seen it before, I told everyone it's up near Cameron's Corner, and everyone said, "What's Cameron's Corner?" I didn't know much about it, I was living in Broken Hill at the time, I know every part of it now, I quite like it, in me three years I've done over 50,000 miles just on this section.

You very kindly helped us get unbogged, unstuck. How many times have you been stuck?

One, two, three times in the white vehicle and one time in my car.

You had to ring the boss up?

I have to get out meself, you've gotta know all the tricks of the trade, you've gotta use everything around ya as a tool.

You have a little winch, but there's no trees to attach it to.

That's why the tracks in this section are right on the Fence there, you stay right on and if you get stuck you just go to the next strongest post. I got stuck on a section where I went out like you did, off the road, I sat there for four hours just winching, every time I'd hop in it would just sink.

We return to the roadhouse to give our thanks to the teenagers for helping us de-bog and get to talking to Luke.

Amazing things happen to me, but I'm not going to say, it's kinda far out.

[Kate elbows him.] Go on, tell 'em.

Aliens?

You're on the right track, should I say it?—no one believes it, but I talk to the dead, in my head, it's happening twenty-four hours a day right now, out here there's about three of them, they're weird.

You know their names?

Their names aren't important, they've given me a name, say their name is somethin', but you don't always believe a spirit even if it comes from your dead grandma, you can't trust everything that they say.

How long have you been dealing with the dead?

They understand the way I think and they know me backwards, I was thinking really terrible things, they really don't care but I was really shocked in how I think because I trained myself to hear meself think and when they talk with me I've basically got to think what they say as well, so I've got so many things flying through my head.

It's busy. Does coming to Cameron Corner, it's a strange place, a Mecca of fences and borders, all these theoretical lines are meeting, the world doesn't care if there are lines or not, the geography, the dogs, the cattle, but does that affect your talking to the dead? Is it quieter here?

Not really, I've basically been allocated by life about thirty or so spirits, wherever I am in Australia they all come through, it's pretty hard to distinguish between voices but you get their personalities.

So voices but no visual representation?

Yeah, they communicate through my eyesight, smells, impressions, feelings, like they hug you with these feelings that say five sentences in two seconds, you just understand what they mean.

I was talking to a guardian angel but they don't answer you back, it was just a big opening in my head, I knew something was there and he just listened to me, all the other spirits kinda stepped back.

If we went northwest from here to the Simpson Desert, would they still be with you in a place where few people if any have ever been?

The spirit world tends to be the busiest around where people have been because of the vibrations they leave. They are stronger in populated areas, but whether I hear them or not is a different story ... I'm itchin' to get into space and it wouldn't surprise me one bit if I could still hear them there.

What about hearing other species, like a dog?

I heard a spirit of a dog, but a soul can manifest its voice into anything, they can play a whole song in my head, drums and everything, they get a perfect sound, it could have been a real dog, spirits always saying the dogs are up here, but I tend not to trust everything they say because it's mixed me up and they play a lot of games.

What about the Fence having a spirit?

Only the spirit of God is on it.

We return to earth and take our leave, heading north, passing one car on our six-hour drive. Just before nightfall (it's useless to stop before the flies disappear), we pull off the track and park on the desert floor. We sit on two milk crates, while the third one is our table, and stare at the deep red sand with tiny white bits of stone atop it. The desert floor looks designed, like what they used to do to houses in the 30s, a spray-on mixture of concrete and stones. It's a full moon, a dingo howls, and Jon paces.

I don't want to go to bed, he says. I want to communicate with the dingo.

Enhanced fly gear is required for our trip to Cooper Creek. The Innaminka Trading Post sells us each a khaki green, wide-brim hat with attached veil. Against my all-natural inclination, I am instructed to also purchase fly spray. A mini-crisis ensues. Weighing killer stuff versus the kinder, gentler choice, personal health versus fly stealth, aerosol or pump—I just can't do it. Jon is disgusted. I go back in and buy The Killer.

A dingo cuts across our campsite at sunset, and we hear a pack of them howling several times through the night. I record some birds in the morning: raven *(Corvus coronoides)* with flies, sulphur-crested cockatoo *(Cacatua galerita)* with flies, and magpie *(Gymnorhina tibicen)* with flies and mosquito. Pelicans *(Pelecanus conspicillatus)* are flying up and "Cruising Down the River" on a Sunday afternoon—all right, Monday.

We set out over 65 miles of sand dunes, which make for a smooth and swift drive, to seek our bliss at Coongie Lake. Here, too, we sit with fly veils to a chorus of aggressive flies. Although we now have the fly spray, I don't use it. It's poison.

You can't have a rational argument with or about flies. I've just had months of chemotherapy and 19 doses of radiation therapy—the lot, so I really don't care if a bit of fly spray is going to poison me or not.

This is a cattle monoculture now (and thus the flies?), but formerly four major tribes of Aborigines inhabited the region, each with 400 to 500 members. They didn't use canoes but instead caught mussels, crayfish, and fish by swimming. This waterway made it one of the great trading centers of the continent. Embracing the cycle of detaching and reattaching names, Charles Sturt named it Cooper "Creek" in 1845 after a South Australian judge. "I would gladly have laid this great creek down as a river," Sturt later observed, "But as it had no current I did not feel myself justified in doing so."

I interrupt my reading on the area to ask Jon, Where do you think the python is spending the day? And the curl snake?

We cut short our bliss and head back yet again through Innaminka. On the bridge and in the creek coming into town, there's a black-and-white ball: Australian pelicans, pied cormorants *(Phalacrocorax varius)*, black darters *(Anhinga melanogaster)*, crows, and the distinctive royal spoonbills *(Platalea regia)*, white with fantastic black spoon-shaped beaks. At the roadhouse while we wait for our lunch of lobster, chips, and salad, we sip on a glass of Houghton 2002 White

Burgundy (I note citrus, passion fruit, and tropical fruit), then wander round the room taking in the various newspaper clippings. I'm taken with the reports of the mother with six children eight and under, five of them girls, who was found living at Cooper Creek under a tree without even a blanket. The father had disappeared months prior.

> They live under the tree in all sorts of weather, exposed to the ravages of the frequent dust storms that rake the country, exposed to rain and sun, victims of mosquitoes, flies, sandflies, and even snakes.—May 16, 1937, Brisbane.

A cattle thief herding a thousand stolen cattle over untracked country from central Queensland to Adelaide originally blazed the historic Strzelecki Track. He was caught in his crime; however, due to his heroic efforts in establishing a new stock route, he was let off and went on to become a rich cattleman. Crime pays.

Along the still remote Strzelecki Track today, we pass a truck under escort towing a quarter-mile-long pythonesque pipeline.

The most common fence design is the five-wire with the barb on top, but in the Strzelecki area you often see a plain wire on top and barbed wires below. Are these cows genetically inclined to walk into a fence with their head down? Do they prefer a nice little scratch on top of their heads as opposed to the more regular cow's desire for a little tickle under the chin, hence the barb on the top? Or rather than a cow's habit of walking head up or head down, maybe it's a human aesthetic at work here—but what?[50]

---

[50] For years I assumed that while it might be okay bowing standard fence wire, there was no way that I was going to start playing music on a barbed-wire fence. How wrong I was!

Barbed wire isn't just one thing. Simultaneously invented in France and the USA in the 1860s, patented barbed wire comes in nearly 600 different designs. In the first two decades of its existence, many legal battles were fought about who invented what and when.

Barbed wire has the advantage of two strands instead of one and automatically adjusts itself to changes of temperature. When heat expands the two wires, the twist simply loosens, and when cold contracts them, the twist tightens, while barely altering the overall length of the wire. Quite an idea, almost beautiful.

Then there's the barbs and hey presto, we are overwhelmed by the received images: the concentration camp, the WWI trenches, the defense of private property, the confused and interchangeable Christian crown of thorns. The image of barbed wire is now a sexy staple of the advertising industry, not to mention contemporary art.

In Australia, a country of immigrants, we use barbed wire to incarcerate those who have escaped oppression to reach our shores. We fence them in to stop them from coming here—so goes the logic of those in authority.

The next two days I merely write where we stop for the night, followed by the word "flies." I recall that poison was administered with less and less regret.

Farther down the track and this time no longer preoccupied with how to circumnavigate it, we pile out to admire the Waka Claypan. The water reflects pink and orange against eggplant, even black, edges. In the center are islands of lime green. This is the lake that's here but not on the map, as opposed to the earlier one that wasn't there but appeared on the map.

Are accurate maps old-fashioned in our postmodern times? I could cut and paste this chart and use it in a collage without severely disturbing its reliability. In fact, I believe it's already been done to the one at hand. (Note to self: write up artspeak rave for potential gallery opening on how my deconstructed maps are treatises intended to provoke and revisit each other through inscription, composition, building up, erasing, and the informing and masking of a complex cartography of marks, signs, and representations. Translation: I'm lost.)

As we head up a hill, my entire world goes blue with nothing in my straight-ahead or peripheral vision but an ultramarine sky. Later we see blue *clouds.* I'm a frenzied teenage driver stuck in a video game six hours straight. After each unbogging, adrenaline pushes me faster. No further ill luck could befall us now.

All day we pass through saltbush and mulga plains. We make it to Packsaddle by dark, pulling off at a primitive "campsite," a parking lot really, which we then pull further off of until a fence stops us. We overlook a ravine. Below us we hear cattle lowing and engines revving.

But what does it sound like? Barbed wire is certainly hard to control, laterally challenging you might say. If the barbs are loose, it's rather like having a tambourine attached to your violin—a sort of shake, rattle and roll. If the barbs are firmly embedded, then you are likely to get a complex set of modulating pitches, more bang for your bow.

Nonviolin-playing people have often suggested that the violin is a tough instrument to play because, unlike the piano, you can't see where the notes are. One aspect of the barbed-wire fence that appeals to me is that it becomes very clear where the notes are—if you miss 'em, it's quite painful.

Also, the scale articulated by the barbs is extremely unorthodox and about as far as you can get from the equal-tempered scale upon which most western music is played. But the tyranny of the equal-tempered scale is not a subject on which we should dwell in the middle of an Australian desert.

My partner and fellow violinist Hollis Taylor refuses absolutely to play an electrified fence. She has good reason. While the voltage is unlikely to kill a person, I have received some mighty shocks up my arm. That's the unhealthy side of it. On the other hand (the unelectrocuted one), the surging current can produce rhythmic clicks and pops, which become part of the fence mix. Don't tell your local DJ, or they'll all be wanting to sample it.

Motorbikes are the preferred method of mustering these days for man and beast (the dogs can climb on back for a rest).

Spaghetti with butter beans, sun-dried tomatoes, and olives serves as our fast food during diminishing light. We linger over a bottle of 2001 Willow Bridge Shiraz before approaching the evening's final task. The LandCruiser's upper sleeping loft features minimal clearance and challenges us no matter what activity we have in mind. Had we tested it prior to departing, we would have kept the lower bunk. Remember the bumper sticker, "If this trailer's rockin', don't bother knockin'?" Forget it. Heard the white trash motto, "Jump 'em, pump 'em, dump 'em?" We can't manage it. Even the missionary position is out of the question in our prone home. Perhaps if we took out the mattress and just slept on our cares … Our routine, the only one we can figure, is to drop trou, step onto the wooden bench, cross to the higher kitchen counter, then, like crabs, wrest our way up, flat as she goes. Head, meet Ceiling.

In the morning chill we take a walk down the ravine, expecting a small stream, but it's neither dry nor filled with water, just an ill-defined, sloppy mud bath of a bottom. We find the Packsaddle Creek Fence is a fine one for an early morning play and film.

When we reach the mailbox that marks the beginning of the Sturt Meadows station, we stop to drop our Sunday-morning-service fence contact a note. Jon opens the large metal barrel to be greeted by a pile of rust.

I guess if you put your hand into the pile, you might be able to pull out a letter, similar to a magician pulling a white rabbit out of a hat, he says. The whole thing keeps going on the fumes of an oily rag in the left corner.

Maybe the oily rag is to keep bugs out—or snakes.

I have no idea. There's also a brick, but no mail.

Another hard day of driving (the road rhythm alternates between rip the strip on a sealed surface and limp-bump-chug on an unsealed one; a guy passes us twice in the limp phase, humiliating me both times by driving twice our speed, but in the end the turtle overtakes to observe the hare changing his tire) puts us at Mutawintji National Park's Homestead Creek Campground amongst majestic river red gums. The area is blessed with one of the few reliable sources of water around, making flora and fauna abundant.

Their brochure suggests keeping an eye out for kangaroos, emus, goannas, snakes, and euros (hill kangaroos). No need to look far afield— the roos are poking about right here in the campground. The park is also home to a small colony of the endangered yellow-footed rock wallaby *(Petrogale xanthopus)*, rediscovered in 1972, the only known colony in the state. We spot corellas *(Cacatua sanguinea)*, zebra finches *(Taeniopygia guttata)*, budgerigars *(Melopsittacus undulatus)*, apostle birds *(Struthidea cinerea)*, and magpies *(Gymnorhina tibicen)* in the considerable bird chorus.

Pied Butcherbird

This is the kind of landscape I expect. This is what the word "wilderness" means to most Americans—a place teeming with life, breathtaking in beauty, consoling and restorative. Not only a place but a mood, wilderness comes loaded with positive connotation. Inferiority in the arts, including an absence of antiquities such as cathedrals and castles, led early Americans to assault and celebrate the grandness of what was on hand: soaring peaks, plunging waterfalls, and great river systems with verdant banks.[51] Forests were our cathedrals.

We've got it easy in America. Yes, there's the odd desert, snowfall, grizzly bear, and poisonous snake. We just don't think of the outdoors as inhospitable, although it can be. The national parks, the open range, the cowboy—it's a romance, Americans and their wildernesses, and in all such affairs you overlook a few things, even obvious ones.

Mother Nature or Man versus Nature—take your pick. In Sydney, I've spoken with people who have no such illusions and no inclination to go bush, although they may mentally prize it. While living off the land has been a major American fantasy for even those city born-and-bred, the message in Australia is it's an alien place filled with the antagonism of the wild. Nature in America attests to God's presence, while here it's more often an indication of God's absence. America's wild west meant freedom; Australia's space began as a jail.

I wonder if there might even be some shame attached to European settlement's inability to live in harmony with nature. Certainly, it's not an easy country: 70 percent of it is classified as desert, and all produce comes from a mere 0.5 percent of the land. Unless you are an Aboriginal person in touch with the knowledge of millennia, things can easily go very wrong for a hiker or camper. Like water. Not enough, too much—I've never seen such a mess. The complexities are

---

[51] Seddon: 21.

enormous, both droughts and floods exacting a heavy toll on people and animals.

Droughts and floods, these catastrophic words rush in to describe the water fluctuation of this erratic climate. White settlement treated this continent as if it were empty: just add people, or sheep. The irrigation developers, imbued with the task of completing God's landscape, saw outback Australia as a packet of freeze-dried peas: just add water. (One outback town's newspaper is called *The Irrigator.*) In their myopia, Europeans found the continent unmapped, unnamed, and unclaimed, and set about turning it into "a farm and a quarry." It's too late to close Pandora's box—we're all here. Droughts and floods won't go back in; these words are our past trailing behind us and our future before us. More to the point, they're cultural baggage, a dead giveaway for "but it rains dependably in England …"

For the moment, we have water. We hike through a gorge with occasional dark rock pools, and then take a late afternoon ranger-escorted tour with Gerald. We follow him across a maze of overhangs and rock faces to inspect Aboriginal rock art, evidence of 8000 years of occupation in the area. Many of the paintings are hand stencils created by blowing liquefied ochre out of the mouth. The natural resonating chambers of a cave enhance Gerald's voice of Aboriginal authority. Seated, he tells their story and fields questions. We save most of ours.

As we walk back to our vehicles, Gerald says, Here's a trap-door spider hole.

Let's make him come out, suggests a young boy.

No, advises Gerald. Then we'd have to call the Flying Doctor.

Driving to camp, we see a red and a grey roo together, an interracial couple I note in my ignorance. Later, I discover that the female red kangaroo *is* smoky blue-grey. Dust effects appear on the road for no apparent reason, swirling off to the side and disappearing back into the red sand. When we get back to camp, Jon meets up with Gerald.

I'm Gerald Quale, I've worked at Mutawintji National Park as a tour guide since 1983, that was when we had the blockade at the historic site out here to gain more say into the management of our ancestors' art sites.

Who owned it before white settlement?

There's a wide range of groups that used Mutawintji, it was a meeting place, a bit like Uluru up in the Northern Territory, various groups and tribes would have a gathering for initiation or wedding ceremonies, they all lived under one law, most of them were subdialects of the main group, we're all traditional caretakers, as I would like to put it, of that area.

There are only two words I could find in any Aboriginal language book that related to fences. Do you have one in your language?

I haven't heard of one yet, maybe they didn't think it appropriate for it to be part of our language because it was not a natural phenomenon when our ancestors were growing up, fences were put up in places like Mutawintji by settlers to keep the stock away from the hills, and I suppose to keep our ancestors from getting into certain areas of significance and also certain water holes.

What's the relationship between fences and songlines?

A lot of fences crisscross songlines or dreaming tracks, our ancestors would just climb them, the only significant part of the fence would be based on the Rabbit-Proof Fence story— they don't figure in our songlines.

There's so much fencing, it's the biggest thing in Australia, millions of miles of this stuff. I'm trying to understand what it's like to have all this stuff over your heartland.

I grew up with fences and learned it was a necessity if you are a property owner, I worked on stations and that, but lookin' from my ancestors' point of view if there's a fence in front of me, I'd find a way to knock it down, even today they are still using fencing to stop us from gettin' in to our traditional hunting and gathering areas, especially along the Darling River where we have certain favorite water holes and fishing spots, our grandparents have been takin' us there for years to catch fish, certain owners put a chain on the gate and lock it, legally he's reneging on his western lands lease because any access road from a public thoroughfare onto a river you aren't allowed to lock, you can shut the gate but it always has to be kept unlocked because the public have rightful access to that river, plus most of that area along the Darling River is on a stock route.

Is it a ludicrous situation for you, the idea of people carving up and owning land?

Settlers when they first came out, one person owned millions of acres of land, and on that you'd have three or four different Aboriginal groups utilizing it, or particularly with Mutawintji you got about seven or eight different groups that used it, and when they broke it up into pastoral leases and put up all their fences, then they only had one person who looked after that area, and it gradually deteriorated from the stock and introduced animals.

On the tour you said the population of this area was 25,000 to 30,000 people. Maybe now there are 250 here.

Yeah, the Aboriginal Protection Board played a big part in the relocation of Aboriginal people, my mother, for instance, she was born in Pooncarie on the Darling River and was relocated from there to Menindee, and she traveled around with a great-grandmother and was kept away from the long arms of the law that were looking for her, my wife is part of the Stolen Generation, I lived next door to her when she was taken, barricades and fences—that's what they lived behind, I always asked why are we put on missions and reserves, on a ten-acre block, 20 or 30 families living on that ten-acre block with a fence around it, what are they trying to protect you from, why were you put there in the first place?

Can you give me a sense of the relationship between you and the dingo? Do you have more than one word for it?

No, we just call it *gulli*, the name for a dog, dingoes were used by our ancestors for hunting purposes, also as companions, their pet, there are some stories relating to the dingo, I'll learn them in the not-too-distant future from my uncle, he'll only teach me certain things when I start showing that I'm ready to learn it and that I respect what I've been told, in my eyes he's an elder.

How old is he?

He's always changing his age, about 55 I think he is, his grandmother taught him, he did a lot of traveling with her with a horse and sulky up and down the Darling River from Bourke to Wentworth, he knows about the country, he's the senior sites officer for New South Wales for the National Parks and Wildlife Service.

In general, do you feel the future is looking positive?

We still retain our traditional links with the land, we still retain our language, we still firmly believe in our traditional laws, but unfortunately the younger generation are starting to think Sony Playstation and cinemas and that, whereas in the 60s and 70s I grew up out in the bush and TVs and that doesn't worry me ...during the school holidays, I try to get my sons out in the bush and teach them ...
but only if they behave, they aren't allowed to go walkabouts in town, but out in the bush they can go wherever they like, especially at Mutawintji except significant areas, I've pointed them to which areas they can go and which they can't.

Are there any songs about dingoes?

Not that I know, they probably exist, there's certain things people will tell you and others they won't, my mother would always say I could tell you a lot but I'll only tell you a little, so I leave it at that, the white man has the three Rs: readin', writin', and 'rithmetic, we got the three Ls—look, listen, and learn, that's what I do when I'm out there when he's workin' at certain sites and I don't know what the site's about, and he'll say if you just look for a minute, and sometimes he'll say if you listen to the wind, it'll tell ya.

Can you imagine the park having no fences?

We're getting rid of some of the fences, most but not all, some we'd like to leave there to keep the goats out so they don't destroy the cave paintings, we put an electric fence around an original fence to keep the goats and inquisitive people out, so it comes in handy both ways, around Broken Hill millions of mulga trees went to make fences, lookin' at certain areas now where they cut trees and where the stock deteriorated the land—there's a horticulturist who propagates his natural seeds that he collects from the bush, we're lookin' to get him in there to do certain areas that are bare and use some of the fencing as tree guards, to keep the introduced animals like the goats and rabbits out.

So there's an interesting contradiction. Fencing to keep the goats out, fencing to protect trees, which were originally cut down to make the fence …

Around the historic site, the fence was put up not only to keep the cattle and sheep from gettin' in certain water holes but also to keep my ancestors out from those significant areas where the initiation sites are, but we use them today to keep people whose ancestors probably built those fences, to keep them out.

As we press on, I'm trying to work it out, the signs and silences, the foreignness for me of things *not* talked about. I imagine the struggle to coerce an oral culture into a written one (or keep it from this process, or deposit it in the halfway house of code) when knowledge is taught by innuendo, when wisdom inhabits secret caves, paths, and rhythms.

My education was predicated on the duty and right to know as much as possible, now. Asking was precocious, not disrespectful. This "superior" knowledge was implicated in the right to possess; thus we justified the throwing up of barriers, which blocked a culture of walking STOP singing STOP mapping STOP remembering STOP chronicling STOP celebrating STOP. "Walking encyclopedia" is the phrase employed by European invaders and their descendants to describe the most triumphant of their learned, but certainly in the field of natural history the Aboriginal people are the walking encyclopedias. How confusing for these custodians of memory to be dispossessed of land that they long understood when ownership to their thinking equaled understanding, and to watch Europeans suddenly claim to own the land when they understood it not (all this while the education experience accomplished

186

in initiation rites for Aboriginal males was gradually being replaced by jail terms).

European settlement created its own lines and points. We drive on, connecting dots, passing fences without stopping to photograph them. We've seen their ilk before. There aren't too many we haven't snapped. Oh yeah, we've got that kind, and that. It's like hearing a jazz player and knowing all their licks, *that* Charlie Parker lick, *that* blues lick—play me something I haven't already heard. What gets our attention now has to be special, like the six-foot-high black plastic fence, a sort of Christo installation cutting through tall grasses. Its function? Maybe it's useless and therefore art. We've seen taut sheets of plastic surrounding an orchard, grey plastic cobbled together surrounding nothing much, a low length of thickly-woven, off-white plastic (like what certain religious practices might require you to wear to bed) surrounding a new home, and black and white moths fluttering between sheets of a white reinforced-plastic fence climbing a telephone pole. What do these plastic barriers keep in and out?

Back through Broken Hill on ANZAC Day, we're counting on a restaurant meal or at least refreshing our larder at a grocer's. Finding everything closed, we settle for pulling over on the outskirts of town. Jon and I are in the back piecing together a lunch when I see a shocked look in his eye. Then I feel it too. The emergency brake has snapped off, and the vehicle is rolling. He jumps out and manages to get in the front to brake before we head down an embankment, all in the time it takes me to bruise my leg getting out.

W e head west, crossing Dismal Bridge, second cousin to Mount Hopeless, then straight on to the dot of Yunta (it's not much bigger in 3-D) where we gas up. From here we'll turn north toward another part of the Dingo Fence.

The gas station manager quizzes us, Headin' off to see Frank, Jim, or John?

John.

Yeah, he was in here last month.

Okay, his point is well taken; only a few hardy souls live north of here. The road is long, and so is the sign warning of the dangers of travel on it. However, we find it in good condition, and I'm able to relate to the track as freedom, the "On the Road Again" that Willie sings about as opposed to the bondage of previous days' driving.

Do you think that's a joke word? I ask as we pass Winninninnie Creek.

Jon assures me it's an Aboriginal one.

We make it by sundown to the Dingo Fence at Frome Downs. I brake just over the grid and pull off for the night. Lake Frome borders the property of the homestead we just passed. We had hoped to see this immense salt lake whose
crust is reputed to be the brightest spot on earth when seen from space but were warned that the pastoralist doesn't look with enthusiasm upon curious trespassers. At least there's a free show with dinner. An electrical storm comes not in bolts or sheets of lightning but in chaotic waves, flashing pale yellow to cerise on the horizon. As we climb up to become our pancake selves for the night, I notice that I, like Jon, have gone feral. I'm slapping insects with the flat of my bare hands.

At sunrise, we inspect our iconic barrier. It's old, originally of three-foot high mulga posts later raised by adding higher posts to support more netting. It appears drunken and capricious, with oblique posts and bits of barbed wire woven in helter-skelter. A number of patches complete its knitted, netted, knotted weave. Three gaping holes are right in front of us. I rosin up my bow, grab a loose and rusted wire, and have a go. The seeming disorder works to our advantage. The Wild Card Hodgepodge Fence is a favorite both to look at and to play. We linger, contemplating sonorities in collision.

Only one car passes, late in the night, in the 15 hours we are here. On departing, we retrace the previous day's drive, stopping after just eight miles at a grid we had overlooked in the twilight. A dingo carcass hangs by its hind legs on the Fence, front limbs collapsed on the ground. Tan and golden hairs still cleave to its parched hide, but its head has shifted to more disturbing shades. Patches of the top layer of skin have been eaten away, revealing a shaved-looking transparent blue skin, while the hide that remains is dusted salmon pink by the soil on which the muzzle rests. Whiskers assert themselves, eyes long ago eaten retain presence, ears point, and broken teeth protrude from its snarl-unto-death. Matter unclaimed by insects clots the mouth. Death absolutely bustles; each specialist claims its part. When the feeding frenzy begins to die down, even what's left, of dingoes at least, is a trophy that must be displayed. Someone has placed crumbling sections of its spine on the fence post. Twelve feet from this spanking new fence we see a remnant of the old one.

Our auctioneer has put us on to John McEntee of Erudina Station. Blue heelers and border collies welcome us as we pull up to his large, well-kept homestead. Our host emerges in a checkered shirt and jeans; his face is soft and accommodating, belying his lifetime out-of-doors. We sit round the kitchen table.

We were just up at the Frome Downs property. There are three huge gaping holes on the Dog Fence there.

It doesn't take long to deteriorate, the kangaroo will start the damage and the bigger, stronger animals will enlarge that.

Does the tradition of hanging a dead dingo from the Fence actually work to put them off?

Oh no, that attracts more, it's a bit like fly spray, apply that and you get a bit more.

What's your feeling about the dingo? Most of the people we've spoken with have absolutely no bad feeling towards the animal

All life has equal value really, you just can't pick one out, but if the law says it's a nuisance, well then that's the law of the land.

Have we got any idea how many dingoes there are right now?

That would vary a lot on season, with rabbit or sheep population, if there's easy food, that allows them to build up fairly quickly, when you read explorers' journals traveling in the 1840s and 1860s, the number of reports they have of dingoes are "Saw a dog today" and then they go for weeks and then "Saw another dog," very scanty, by introducing livestock, creating feed for the dogs, they increased, so by the 1890s records show over a thousand killed, in our worst dingo year here we caught 60 dingoes, some years only five.

They strike me as a lonely animal.

Depends, they're like a domestic dog, nothing too different really, they were traded from the north of Australia back through the Malaysian islands, you can go to a lot of places in Southeast Asia and you'll see dingoes running around there, it hasn't been here for all time, the date is debatable.

Which Aboriginal languages have you studied?

It started in my school days in Adelaide, there weren't a lot of textbooks to draw on, just word lists drawn from various sources and quite old ones, and we didn't have knowledge of the phonetic system, so I went to the Aboriginals themselves and had very good teachers for 25 years.

How many white people were going to learn?

There were a few, but they were just using it to converse, I wanted the accuracy of the phonetics, that's what didn't seem to be there earlier on, some people could just learn and carry on a conversation with them, that's one thing I still can't really do, that's the other hemisphere of the brain, one side looks after vocab and sound, and the other will look after the grammar and put them together.

From an Aboriginal viewpoint, the history of the fence has happened extremely fast, suddenly they were there. Is there a word for "fence?"

They had their own type of fence, of brush though, not of wire, it was created to force animals into a pit trap or a net trap, we would call that just the wing, like in a cattle or sheep yard, that's a *yarroo*, with a rolled R.

Was it the same word for a "wire fence?"

I don't know, they seemed to cotton on to a lot of European ideas and some of them were really quite interesting, how they called European items, they'd construct that out of their own language rather than always copy an imitation of English, they went out of their way, it's a very flexible language.

What about the word for dingo? Does it vary?

Yes, a local around-the-camp sort of dog, that's *wilca*, but it varies language by language, usually the names are after an attribute of the animal, this is guesswork at the moment, but it would be nice to have some proof that it would have something to do with a verb, *willa*—to lick, the animal that licks, that's some people's impression, further north in Cooper's Creek, it's *gindala*.

How much are we still on the frontier here, how much knowledge is there?

The knowledge about the region is very scant, I haven't scratched the surface in terms of my research, diseases such as smallpox and the common cold arrived in this area before exploration, and that really decimated a lot of the population in this area before settlement, so they were down to 30 to 50 from a normal group of say 300 to 500, that made it very difficult to carry on their cultural ways so they had to amalgamate, find another group of 50, that intermixed those languages although some languages stayed strong and survived that amalgamation whereas others fell off on the side.

Let's talk about your musical interests.

I once made a string instrument from a tennis racket ...

Do you make up your own pieces?

I attempt, but I'm too much of a perfectionist, it has to add up right and if it doesn't fit mathematically, I can't get around to make it better, classical music from 1600 to 1900 interests me, but it doesn't matter where it comes from or by whom as long as it's dated 1700-1800, end of baroque and into rococo, that's my period.

Then I jump straight from there into the 1960s, the guitar, 50s, 60s—it could be anyone, I was never great on Elvis but definitely Buddy Holly and the Crickets, Roy Orbison, even Roy Orbison's backing group composed some very interesting music, the Art Movement, a bit of Bach and his sons, I prefer instrumental, very few instrumentals actually got to number one.

Before we depart, we request some music. McEntee leads us upstairs where we take a seat among his books and instruments, family heirlooms, and oversized brown leather furniture. The hush of a conservative club moderates the room.

First, he applies a spanner to his pianola to tune it. Then he sits down to what is normally a bland, dull-sounding instrument. His tall, upright pianola sounds instead like the brighter fortepiano of the mid to late 1700s (his preferred era), complete with grain, rattle, and buzz.[52]

On leaving his homestead, we see six wedge-tailed eagles feasting on a dead roo. The wildlife continues to come in sixes with an emu ballet: two shaggy partners rush onto the road then retreat, two more head out twirling batons and circle back, then a third pair perform their turntail dance, all in split-second precision sure to delight any stage manager. And the costume design—brilliant! Loved those feather tutus!

From McEntee's station it's not far to Flinders Ranges National Park, although the road is primitive and slow going. I'm exhausted by the drive, careful at every moment not to hit a large rock or even a small, sharp one. Avoiding a flat tire is a matter of pride for me.

At the park headquarters, I uncharacteristically send Jon in alone to make a reservation for us to camp while I sit in the car and recover. To expedite our arrival at the campground, I skip even washing my face in the luxuriousness of a public bathroom with running water.

Next to the Headquarters is a sign for the beginning of Wilpena Pound. I've never heard of it, and Jon doesn't burden me with this information. Later, I read that Wilpena Pound is the best-known feature of the Ranges, a 30-square-mile natural basin accessible only by a narrow gap through which a creek exits the pound.

You wouldn't really have wanted to go there, would you? he asks. [His idea is no fence, no sense going.]

What he failed to find out is that the Bunyeroo Gorge camping area has nothing but "bushcamping," meaning we have paid to drive on rocks and pull off onto bigger rocks and stop for the night, like we always do but normally free-of-charge. There's no shower, not even an outhouse. Once we park, I cannot walk enough to dispel my anger. How

---

[52] John McEntee can be heard playing his pianola at http://www.abc.net.au/arts/adlib

is it we can live without a shower in a bogging and never have a fight, but give me the hope of a shower and then take it away and I go postal?

I experience a collapse of psychological defenses. I can neither eat dinner nor speak. I've gone stark-raving, rabbit-proof mad. That night I dream that we are brushing our teeth outside in the dark, and I spread toothpaste all over Jon's face. When I wake up I wonder did I, or did I just want to? I'm sure I did not. Okay, I'll ask.

You did, he says matter-of-factly.

We make our way slower than slow through the Brachina Gorge. The rough and ruinous track is littered with sinister holes and punctuated by occasional creeks. (In America we drive by or over creeks, in Australia we drive in them.) When I can look up rather than down, I see a veritable geological trail, a spectacular sequence of exposed sedimentary rock by which geologists read history and to which they give serious names and dates. We read colors and shapes in the compressed and colliding layers and are content. When seen from a distance, part of the North Flinders Ranges resembles Islamic script.

"Fence recording Greenwell Creek on Old Ghan Track, creek dry, aggressive flies, dizzy in full sun, very hot + difficult," I jot in my notebook. I'm still rebuilding my psyche and awaiting a shower. The reality of outback travel is heat, wind, flies, filth, fatigue, and melancholy—but the show must go on. Fortunately, I can rely on Jon and habit.

twelve steps for bowing a fence—a woman's perspective

Prior to each fence performance, I run through my list:
1. Check hair and makeup.
2. Suit up in sun-proof hat and clothes, ant-proof stockings, and snake-proof high boots.
3. Roadie pops by to announce, "Five minutes, Miss Taylor."
4. Apply sunscreen to face and hands.
5. Take a long pull of water.
6. Tighten and rosin bows.
7. Attach fly veil (obscuring Step #1).
8. Apply more rosin as delay tactic to avoid time in direct sun.
9. Exit vehicle and join sweating, swearing male.
10. Return to vehicle for items above male forgot.
11. Direct all energy towards surveying immediate performance area for snakes, bulls, rams, spiders, biting bull ants, fresh cow pies, electrified fence wires, rusty barbs, landowners, or police.
12. Rosin fence wires and hand male his perfectly rosined bow.

Lights. Camera. Action.

${B}$reakfast Time Creek and Sundown Creek are about 15 miles apart, which we guess is how far the naming party walked that day. Tea Tree Creek is next, and just after that we encounter Deception Creek, indicating a bad start to the next day. The most southerly of creeks in the Lake Eyre Basin is Leigh Creek, but it's also a town, a company one, both pleasant and inviting

We arrive on a sleepy Sunday and take a free shower at the service station, then purchase some organic foods at a nearby shop. The bubbly attendant tells me that an American company now owns Leigh Creek.

It's a great place to live and raise children, she volunteers.

The original town was demolished when it was discovered to be sitting on huge coal reserves. A new Leigh Creek emerged not far away in 1980, landscaped, modern, and uniform, a victory of town planning.

Leigh Creek's mine supplies the Port Augusta power station, Jon reads as we head out of the new town toward the open-cut that was the old one.

It goes on forever, enormous squeezed cones of waste dominating the view to our right. On our left the soil is variously dotted yellow-green, dark green, and red-orange. It would be brown if it were a children's paint-the-dots color book, all the watercolors melting into mud when attacked with a wet paintbrush. We pass a willy-willy, Aboriginal for a column of rotating dust. An imaginary dancer kicks up the dirt, then in my mind's eye an entire square dance is circling back home and do-si-do-ing.

Just onto the neatly-graded Birdsville Track we see a huge sign—yes, another list of detailed warnings … what you should bring and what you will not find in this vast mineral wilderness. It's like something my mother would prepare, and as such it warms my heart rather than disturbs me. We spend the night at the base of a steep hill, clambering up it to a distant view of Harry Lake. "The ascent was steep and difficult, nor did the view from its summit reward our toil," observed Charles Sturt about a similar site.[53]

One car passes in the 14 hours we are here. An expert on the radio states it's the worst fly year in ages, a plague. This comes as no surprise. The fly veil is definitely this season's look. All our movies and photos have us in veils, and ours are getting so much wear that I've begun patching them. We turn around after reaching our goal, a new

---

[53] Sturt, Charles: 156.

but uninteresting stretch of the Dingo Fence, although it did have a hubcap on it, and head back south.[54]

---

[54] If there is a single fence post standing alone, people for some reason have a desire to decorate it, to honor it because it has survived, or to make it feel wanted. Sometimes there is a handy item lying nearby that can be used as a suitable *objet de gloire* such as a bucket with hole, a lone boot with hole, a tire or old bottle (always with hole), or a baby's jump suit with five holes (see Lindy Chamberlain's my-baby-was-eaten-by-a-dingo case, early 1980s). Plastic bags are aeronautically efficient objects. Is there anything more existentialist than an empty plastic bag caught up by the wind and left fluttering hopelessly on a barbed-wire fence?

We've photographed fences festooned with figurines, antique jars, crosses, horseshoes, wagon wheels, lamb skulls, shopping bags, flags, condoms, flowers, ribbons, underwear, and billy cans. Winton has an entire fence given over to kitsch, with redundant machine parts, helmets, and garden statuary stuck in it and a sewing machine on top. Then there are those who will place their rusted chains, highway diversion cones, and scarecrows on a fence. Triumphant killers hang dead dingoes and snakes on a fence. Why not attach fishhooks? When the rivers are up, it's an easy way to fish.

What sign-hanger can resist the ready-made ease of a fence—surely not a real estate agent or someone trying to sell $2 bags of pony poo? There are fences that clearly don't work so well, hence the tons of deadly 1080 poison liberally spread down the 3300 miles of the Dingo Fence. On the other hand, fences designed to stop enthusiastic tourists falling over the cliffs at The Great Australian Bight appear to have worked well—so far, anyway. Top-secret military bases tell you to TURN AROUND NOW! before you even reach their perimeter fences; signs across the Nullarbor warn of the dangerous UNFENCED ROAD; nothing short of an archaeological dig will let you uncover the remains of the No. 1 Rabbit-Proof Fence at its termination point on the northern coast of Western Australia.

Consider the cactus, tree, mushroom, and anthills we saw poking through fences. We saw fences pickily pass through other fences without touching, as if contact with a lowlier fence could violate the loftier. The corrugated iron fence in its various chronological shades of rust is ubiquitous; the primary-colored fences of the newly rich suburbs possess all the subtlety of a Legoland layout; the brilliant white salt lakes devour their fences within a few decades (significantly hardwood posts last much longer than steel wires); and the recently-made desert fences of once optimistic pastoralists often hang in midair after the topsoil to which they were attached has been blown away.

We found a painting of a fence on a wall. Fence posts without any wire look lonely. It's difficult to imagine horses running around a racecourse without a fence. Like guitars, there are electric fences; one finds chain fences, rope fences, rubber tube fences, fences made out of sacking, and ones made from hubcaps and tires. All swimming pools must have a fence by law. BEWARE OF DOG behind the fence is nearly passé; we've moved on to the ultramodern DOG CONTAINED BY INVISIBLE FENCE with sensors.

There are plastic temporary fences, there are flexi-fences, fences you can see through, and fences you can't see until it's too late. Graveyard fences keep the living from the dead or, depending on your point of view, the dead from the living. Railway lines, telegraph lines, pipelines, and butterflies often travel down the same route as

M arree, population 80, is situated at the southern end of both the Birdsville and Oodnadatta tracks. Things only liven up in odd years with the Marree Australian Camel Cup, held in memory of the Afghan camel trains that were centered here from the 1870s to the 1930s. The town later served as a staging post for the overland telegraph line and eventually as a major station for those traveling north by train. The legendary Ghan train commenced operation in 1926. It initially ran between Port Augusta and Oodnadatta and was extended further north to Alice Springs in 1929. A standard-gauge track served from Port Augusta to Marree. Everyone piled out in Marree to complete the rest of the journey on a narrow-gauge track. In 1980, Marree lost the train and most of its population.

We poke around, photographing the decaying reminders of a bygone era: one of the last narrow-gauge diesel-electric locomotives used on the old Ghan lies stranded and rusting on sidings, old rails outside the hotel serve as tethering posts, and a collection of houses that outlived the train's demise appear ready to cede to the harsh environment. Marree is today a sleepy service center for the enormous cattle stations in the area.

From here you can take scenic flights over Lake Eyre and Marree Man, the largest work of art in the world at two-and-a-half miles, an outline of an Aboriginal warrior etched into the sand in 1998 by unknown hands. We head for the Oodnadatta Track. Used by Aboriginal people for tens of thousands of years, the route spears into the outback, often following the old Ghan. Over the years, its tracks have warped and twisted in agony as the sun's blowtorch was applied. Jon's quite taken with the legendary Ghan, but when we get to the first sandhill with a fence on top, that's it—we're back on fences.

We head toward Lake Eyre. In 1964 Donald Campbell broke the world land-speed record here. It's really two lakes, North and South, connected by an eight-mile channel and surrounded by deserts. Known

---

fences. Some fences just fall over, and that's that. Sometimes they get a plaque on a wall if they were famous. There have been murders and suicides by fences.

Watch out for the fence with scarecrow; don't miss the scary Gothic fence; new trees planted for civic pride get a fence around them for protection against the menacing public; the socially sidelined like to write on fences— sometimes it becomes official art; birds, like politicians, are comfortable sitting on the fence; camels like to rub their necks on fences; snails cannot keep away from fence posts; spiders find them great places to build webs; unrelieved men, if they cannot find a bush, will use a fence; and where exactly does the Dingo Fence end in Queensland? We haven't found two locals who will agree on that.

in its entirety as Lake Eyre, it becomes full of water to its well-defined shoreline only several times a century but usually sees some water once a decade. Its more than 386,000-square-mile catchment area extends well into central Queensland and the Northern Territory. This massive salt lake is caught between the Simpson and Strzelecki deserts in a region where the annual evaporation rate is 30 times greater than the rainfall. Floods have filled the basin only four times since white settlement of the region. In 1974, it filled so high to qualify as a Great Filling, estimated to occur once in several centuries.[55]

How does it compare in size to Belgium? I ask.

Lake Eyre dwarfs that, Jon trumps. It drains an area the size of *all* of Western Europe.

Beep! I'm sorry, but I cannot accept that answer. I cling to the Belgium frame of reference as my gold standard. It works out to 32.75 Belgiums, I believe.

We lunch on the hill above Lake Eyre, taking in the emptiness of the harsh environment: salt crust, shiny gibber stones, clumps of cane grass, stunted samphire, saltbush, bluebush, and red dunes. Afterwards, Jon walks down in front of the car. I drive as far as I dare, then park, and we explore on foot. While we don't see standing water, it's mucky in the transitional mud/sand/salt area, and I note there have been boggings of late. In a freak occurrence, there's been a recent rain.

Once we arrive at the hypnotic, glaring salt crust, I say, Look at that fence post (like throwing a ball for a dog), and retreat to the car.

Jon ventures a quarter-mile out to investigate, but no—it's just a vertical stick pretending to be a fence post, so it doesn't count.

Your feet stick to the surface. The heat and light are disorienting, and the glare—you cannot focus. There is no color. When you look out very fast at something, you have black dots in front of your eyes. You look down and just see white, but not a white that implies passivity. This white attacks you. The hypnotically aggressive landscape eats into your eyes, giving no respite, and is more confrontational than looking out at the universe. The universe doesn't care, but Lake Eyre wants you to suffer.

Darkness blinds, but so can light. Lake Eyre proffers a mysterious, spiritual landscape where the lines of maps disappear into the imagination; ultimately, neither is able to fully confront space and time here. We head back up the hill toward sea level and a real town— oops, the road just turned pink. And now it's modulating to a soft mauve, the color of one of the Queen Mother's hats.

---

[55] Krieg, Terry (2002) *Walking on Eyre*, Adelaide: Terry Krieg.

Finally, we find an emu that can't escape the camera. He runs along a fence, bobbing awkwardly. Suddenly he's a tangle of flying feathers. I worry we've caused him to injure himself, but he's spilled through the fence and running off. Another emu got away! We reckon it's not the first time he disassembled and reassembled himself to get through a five-wire fence.

As the red sand dunes and native pine begin to disappear, a sealed road presents itself, announcing our proximity to the Olympic Dam mine, the largest mineral ore body in the world. Ten million tons of ore are mined annually, including copper (the world's sixth largest reserve), uranium (the world's largest reserve), gold (the world's tenth largest deposit), and silver (the world's—well, it doesn't say, but it's enough to keep Queenie in cutlery). The lode was only discovered in 1975. (So much of modern Australia has happened in our lifetimes; the place makes us feel geriatric. And most things that are not recent are ancient, like the rocks that date from some 4500 million years ago.)

A nearby town followed in 1987 to serve miners and their families. The guidebook nudges with words like "modern" and "oasis," and we concur that it's a fine place for a shower and a break. We check into the Roxby Downs Motor Inn, "the showpiece of South Australia's outback." Our room gives out onto a garden courtyard with a swimming pool, a hot tub, and inviting tables and chairs. The "stunning six-story high tent spire covers the complex, providing an unmistakable landmark in this remote desert region." We take out half a bottle of 1999 Summerfield Reserve Cabernet and sit down. Okay, we even look up at the Bedouin-like tent shape arching above us. Six stories high—well, it's just fine, although I can't say we are stunned.

What we notice is that this outdoorsy environment is poles asunder from everything we've experienced for three weeks. There are no insects. None. How? And while there are birds making a racket, there are no birds to be seen. Their canned songs in the key of B change occasionally to give the feel that they are cycling through the day.

It's got chirp factor, Jon says, as we try to imagine the number of settings on the electronic bird dial.

After a shower, it's dinnertime, and I dress up for my date. The muzak in the restaurant is all musicals and movie themes, like "Exodus." We sit along the window, looking out at the courtyard where a hen party gradually mounts to 20 women in their 30s. We can't decode their connection. They seem detached one from another. No gifts collect on the table. The event appears lacking in both business and pleasure. Two blokes sit smoking across the courtyard, empty beer bottles stacking up. We spend our meal trying to figure out everyone's story—have we become so unused to company that these people actually interest us?

Exactly how many different settings do you have for your electronic bird music? I ask as we check out.

What—uh, no Sir, we don't have electronic birds. Everything is natural here.

But where were they, then? There's nothing living in the minitropical jungle by the pool, not even a fly.

She's befuddled too.

> The wilderness was not in fact barren, and at least until whitefellas
> fenced off vast areas to serve as test sites and rocket ranges it was
> not blasted either.[56]

Woomera Prohibited Area is named after an Aboriginal aid to spear throwing: a stick fitted into the butt of a spear to extend it. The contemporary Woomera launches rockets and missiles. Australia was the fourth country in the world to launch its own satellite, after the United States, Russia, and France. Established in 1947 as a joint British/Australian project and declared under Australian Defence Force Regulation 35 as an area for the purposes of "the testing of war material," It covers approximately 49,000-square miles, or just over four Belgiums.

The official warning reads:

> There may be some items such as cylindrical rocket motor cases and
> nozzles, flat rectangular pieces of metal, spherical tanks or military
> projectiles encountered in the prohibited area. If any unusual item is
> encountered it must not be handled as it could cause serious injury or
> death.

Woomera is a particularly dangerous place for refugees. Australia's new system of "mandatory and non-reviewable detention" keeps asylum seekers, including pregnant women and their children, locked behind razor wire in desert camps, and one such camp is on the edge of the Woomera Prohibited Area. This freeze on processing applications has turned refugees into "detainees"—prisoners, really, incarcerated without charge, trial, or access to the legal system for years on end. Photos of the Woomera fence extravaganza show strips of galvanized steel forming a 20-foot-high fence topped by a spiral of shiny razor wire. Inside, a five-foot-high coil of razor wire stretches out on the dirt, with yet another metal fence rising behind that.

The Australian government does not directly run detention centers. Instead, from what I gather, it pays management fees to a

---

[56] Greer, Germaine (2003) *Whitefella Jump Up*, London: Profile Books, 10.

subsidiary of a US multinational corporation that manages tens of thousands of prisoners behind bars worldwide. This company can be fined $10,000 for each breakout that occurs, and recently there was a series of protests and escapes at the Woomera Detention Centre fence. (It looms large in our fence minds.)

In response, instead of heeding the refugees' pleas for more humane and bearable living conditions, we heard reports that the company introduced new security measures making Woomera even less hospitable. Things became so desperate that a number of detainees sewed their lips together in protest.

A five-day fact-finding mission conducted by the Human Rights and Equal Opportunities Commission produced a damning report, finding that the Australian government was in breach of the Convention on the Rights of the Child. It went on to state that there was no evidence for the government's assertion that parents had sewn children's lips together during the hunger strike. Amnesty International also issued a statement deploring the long-term detention of children. Since then, the Centre has been closed and the detainees moved.

We stop to play a tall communications tower and to bow the fence next to it. It stutters, then zooms off. It's slide central; we settle on the name Trombone Fence.

Trombone Fence

* Unheard fundamental D four octaves below?

When we arrive at the officially closed Detention Centre, (remember, anything forbidden is interpreted as YES, GO HERE, DO THIS by Jon), I make lunch just short of the sign while Jon pokes around, tape recorder in hand.

Get away from there! shouts a man from his fast-moving car as Jon records the sounds of the wrecked perimeter fence, downed by hundreds of protestors.

If Jon is breaking the law, the man should stop and arrest this fence-ologist, shouldn't he?

Unbelievably flat and uninteresting …Herbert Hoover is quoted as saying, not of his own personality but of the Kalgoorlie area of Western Australia. He could have been *here*. Looking out, it's bleak: flat, barren, isolated, and grey. Looking in, the fence borders a concrete floor the size of two football fields. The show has pulled out. Small canvas bags resembling pillows full of sand or dirt or hate are scattered about.

Hell for refugees who finally reach the lucky country. On closer inspection, the pillows seem to have been placed in some kind of formation. Prayer mats? That's it—a religious ceremony has taken place quite recently, and all the devotees have been snatched up into the Islamic equivalent of rapture just like that. No time to finish the prayer.

Woomera Fence Duo Refrain

We turn around now and drive to town where we come across a rocket museum surrounded by churches. Aging rockets, village churches—it all seems so '50s, but their combined theme is timeless: destroy human lives but save their souls.

Now, a decision. With a few days to spare, we must figure how to spend them. I lobby for Coober Pedy, the mostly underground town with a name I can't resist. Jon thinks we should head toward Port Augusta into salt lake country. I let him win but look for a way to unleash my displeasure at a surprise moment, like any good grudge-carrying goat. While I acknowledge that all our best salt lake images melted into the thin air of cyberspace during a computer glitch and we should replace them, I cling to Coober Pedy as a future destination.

The salt lakes are not just a frustration for *us*. Salinity is one of Australia's most pressing environmental problems. Farmland suffers from land clearing, overallocation, and inappropriate use of irrigation water, causing salinated wastelands. The continent is so flat that saline groundwater has not drained to the sea for millions of years. Even more insidious is dryland salinity, caused by the clearing of deep-rooted trees and shrubs and the grazing and hoof pounding of the introduced sheep and cattle. The soil of *terra australis* is a fossil.

We pass Red Hill, an Uluru without the tourists, followed by the splendid Horseshoe Hill. How'd they escape the maps and tourist texts? And how'd we miss them on our first trip through? In the town of Port Augusta, we come upon a crimson salt lake and then a prison with a fence as ugly as hell.

(No, this is the new detention center, Baxter, which replaced Woomera.)

The surrounding ranges have had their granite wrinkles botoxed—sharp lines and creases need not apply. We zip past Snowtown to our salt lakes, a series of them close together. No wonder you can't believe the guidebooks—we can't even write our own. Yes, we were here before, but we find it quite different, although nothing could have changed but our perception. At our favorite lake, we discover an aging fence we'd missed; we reshoot our lost photos and add some new takes.

Then it's back across Cockscomb Creek, Snakey Creek, and Racecourse Creek, and through Broken Hill to the scenic lookout at the Mundi Mundi plains. The road ends here according to the map, but we see it continues down somewhere, paved at least initially. It's already dark, but we can make out four cars slowly heading this way, lights flickering as they tuck in and out of curves in the hills below us. Jon surmises a party is in the works (and we do hear four cars in the very early morning, between 5:00 and 6:00 a.m., going back down the road).

Night on Bald Hill. The wind shakes the car unceasingly, the sound-effects knob turned fully up to ten. At the highest point around, we're unprotected, perfectly positioned to take the full brunt of the wind. It feels like a winter storm minus the rain. When we awake, from our pancake perch we see toasted golden hills leap-frogging in every direction. The sky hides behind a curtain of regal purple clouds floating upon a strip of blue horizon, and still the gusts jolt the car. It's the one morning I can't drag myself out of bed, reveling in the thought of winter after the heat and flies of summer.

We linger over our breakfast of peanut butter on nine-grain crackers plus a medley of dried apricot rounds, pear halves, and pineapple slices. On descending the paved road to see whence the night's four cars came, we immediately encounter a small dead roo, fresh roadkill; one of the party-going vehicles is suspect. We play the first fence at the bottom of the lookout. It begins hopefully but goes dull and dreary, losing nuance in the space of 15 minutes, so we pack up and return to historic Silverton. Camels, then horses, are just hanging around without fences.

For miles in every direction we've seen the rusting signs for MARIO'S PALACE HOTEL in Broken Hill. We check in to this impressive 1888 pub, which was featured in the film *Priscilla Queen of the Desert*. Upstairs we find one of the largest wraparound hotel balconies we've ever seen, an L-shaped affair ready to accommodate 300. Our musty room has extra-high ceilings wrapped in blue-flowered wallpaper with yellow trim on the upper half and cheap pale wood paneling below. Religious kitsch paintings hang high on the papered walls. A radio above the bed's headboard appears to predate radio. It cannot be tuned and is frozen in-between stations. Pink and white plastic flowers in a cup are perched above the radio, whether for us or as a memorial to the Virgin I cannot say.

If elegance is refusal, this decorator has never uttered a single negativity: YES to floral chintz curtains, crocheted covers for the toilet tissue, crocheted tablecloths and bits for the chair, pink satin pillows, pink sheets and pillowcases, a wine-red carpet, and a pale-green door. It's not so much eye candy as junk food. The lobby walls are covered in murals like Botticelli's *Birth of Venus*, and all manner of oddities hang on them and from the ceiling, like a deep sea fishing basket loaded with realistic lobsters—where would you find such a thing? Mario's Palace Hotel is Broken Hill's cabinet of curiosities.

It seems only appropriate that Jon take me to dinner at the Musician's Club. Guests must register as temporary members. There's a visual chart of the Club Dress Rules, and clearly Jon is wearing a disallowed T-shirt. The bloke at the front desk, without interrupting his phone call, sees us eyeing the chart and points to where to sign in. Bouncer-turned-greeter—they must want our money.

We order bubbles in the bar, expecting to hear musicians. There's everything but: the racket of patrons, pokies (Poker machines), beer dispensers, glasses, canned music, and five TVs bombards our ears. Neither can our eyes rest. Globs of primary color and flashing lights increase the pulse in the adjoining gaming center. A smoking couple sits at a blinking two-cherries-and-a-pineapple pokie screen, the woman passively watching her man play and very occasionally reaching in.

A couple in the bar alternate cell phone calls to kids, Did you do your homework? I love you.

Not the same family, we conclude.

There's an intense chain-smoker watching the four different TV channels above the bar and occasionally stealing a furtive glance at us. Is it me in black head to toe? Jon gets a beer chaser. I size up another bar patron—all hat and no cattle, I figure. The bandstand and dance floor lie empty. In two weeks' time, we could catch Chunky Custard, I read. Signs for responsible drinking compete with one flashing on a bar TV for responsible gambling and other posters on how to know if you're a problem gambler.[57] By the looks on their unhappy faces, it's a problem for them all.

The morning's assignment: find a good fence to play on a day trip toward the Twin Lakes at Wentworth. We do and stop to record. Jon can get the camera very low in a ditch right in front of the fence. One by one, six crows land near us, not black but the darkest emerald green. And okay, then …there's no food, so what are you doing here? Waiting for us to die? They pretend to pick at rusted metal to pass the time.

Twin Lakes 1

Farther on, we find another old fence; it sits low with wide wooden posts. The wires are close together, and the second from the top is barbed. I squeeze through with some difficulty. The goal is to take promotional shots, a series of a dozen or so, of the two of us. After pressing the camera button, Jon has 10 seconds to jump over, take up his

---

[57] The game Two-up was first recorded in Australia in 1854, and by WWI it was celebrated as Australia's national game. Two coins are placed tails up on a flat board called the kip; a ring-keeper calls "Come in spinner," and the spinner tosses the coins three feet above his head; bets are placed on a showing of two heads or two tails.

It's a simple game but mostly an illegal one. The lookout that warns players of police raids is called a "cockatoo." Two-up may be conducted only on ANZAC Day, the day commemorating the ill-fated 1915 Australia/New Zealand landing at Gallipoli. Broken Hill is an exception, where Two-up may be played year round under special license from the state Department of Gaming and Racing. How bizarre to outlaw gambling the old-fashioned, community-based way and instead permit corporate pokie parlors to rip off the populace!

This corporatization extends to state lotteries, casinos, and internet sports betting, and this pressure no doubt prefaces the complete legalization of most types of gaming and wagering. Spinmasters don't have to work too hard to make their case; phrases like "a vital and diverse industry and significant source of employment" and "a stable and growing source of government revenue" are all it takes to get the ear of a politician.

bow, and pose, landing his feet in the same spot each time. James, the arts councilor we met in Milparinka, drives up in the midst of this charade. Jon puffs, ready to explain and defend our actions to an irate landowner, not expecting to see anyone we know.

If I saw someone bowing a fence, it had to be you two, James chides.

We drive past a scene of carnage and reconstruct it in our minds: Car hits kangaroo with joey. Joey crawls out of dead mum and is hit by another car traveling in the opposite direction. Both vehicles were traveling too fast or at night.

We lunch above Lake Popiltah, a dry grey lake with equally grey fluffy birds with a black tail. You'd swear the photos are black and white; they merely register shades of grey. Not blue-grey, violet-grey, or green-grey—no, ashen. For miles we drive along a dying land with a paucity of detail. Even the fence posts are bleached and bloodless, their wire turned pewter (after a recent fire?).

We spend another night in Broken Hill, and then leave the hard-of-hearing but still quick-to-humor octogenarian Italian immigrant success story Mario in his palatial dining room awaiting breakfast clients. He sits alone amid his many grand, bizarre furnishings reminiscent of the Soviet East Bloc. You'd think the camera crew was still here filming. Surely when they leave, they'll take down all this overproduction. And speak to them about our bedroom.

Wilcannia to Cobar is thick with goats and roos. It's hard to slow down when we finally have a high-quality road, but I do and still need to remain at constant attention. We stop to film a few close-ups on what we expect to be the final fence on red, red earth. While holding the video camera, I'm aware I must sidestep a nearby dead roo. I can't afford to look around and jiggle the camera. At one point I back into it. The wire is a barbed one, all lines, points, and knives.

Now we're headed home, the country is friendly, and my notes reflect just a few creek names: Native Dog Creek and Stables Creek coming into Orange. Later, creeks named Broken Shaft, Sandy, Deep, Gosling, Rocks, Raglan, Frying Pan, and Ropes. And the tongue-twisting Bundlegumbie Road.

As we return to Sydney, we tally up Trip Two: The Dingo Fence. We've added 4000 miles to our total, which now stands at 14,000 miles. Our manager reports that contracts from Europe and Australia for Great Fences of Australia concerts are sitting on her desk. As promised, the Queensland Biennale has taken up our idea for a musical fence in Winton, right down to Jon's thought of making it a permanent part of the landscape. It's just a minor detail that they've handed the project to someone else (who sends us an email asking how to go about it). Our passion has become another's commerce, a jump-up we hadn't anticipated.

Grandes Cercados de Australia. We build a diminutive triangular fence inside the Academia de Bellas Artes in Madrid. Because of the building's historical status, no holes can go in the walls or floor; instead, the fence gets anchored to a windowsill giving out on a view of Madrid's skyline. In Barcelona, we set up at the Mercat de Flores, a flower market now by name only. This 60–foot musical fence cuts diagonally across the outdoor courtyard of the performing arts center. Surrounding us are five DVD players looping our various fence slide shows, while the outback movies are shown jumbo size on the white wall behind us.

The Serralves Museum of Contemporary Art in Porto, Portugal, features The Great Fences of Australia in its chic *pátio central:* one long white wall, one tree, and now one fence. All told in Europe, we perform 39 times to an audience of 13,000.

Ladies and Gentlemen, this is your pilot …once again we've managed to find the continent of Australia.

We erect a fence in the main foyer of the Art Gallery of New South Wales for the Sydney Festival and another on the Banks of the River Torrens in Adelaide. But Jon's still all over the map, planning our next outback tour de fence. His dream: filming an isolated fence stretching indefinitely across scalloping red sand dunes. He just knows it's out there somewhere, waiting for us. Our gig at the Darwin Festival gives us the excuse to stop off in Alice Springs beforehand in search of this fantasy fence.

THIRD FENCE TRIP.

It's so wet when we fly into Alice that we don't land on the first approach. The pilot announces he's never seen it so unseasonable. We circle very low, but from no angle do we get even a glimpse of Pine (TURN AROUND NOW!) Gap.

We're again in the "Red Centre" of Australia, the continent's private back yard (the front yard is the coast). As we discovered on our first trip here, Alice is the country's most remote outback town, beyond the inhabited fringe and beyond everyday experience. This suits us, and since we are not limited by a campervan, we can explore the desert landscapes in all four directions.

We have an appointment with Jim Cotterill at his roadhouse and caravan park, Jim's Place, an hour south of Alice. The explorer John McDouall Stuart desperately searched for water here in 1861 on his second attempt to cross the continent from south to north. With his continuation north in doubt, in desperation he dug a trench in the dry bed of the Hugh River. Overnight it filled, furnishing enough water for men and horses. Jim has named the village Stuart's Well in memory of him, although for the Arrernte people the distinctive feature is that it is the final resting place of the fierce gecko ancestor, Itirkawara.

We tell the barmaid that Jim is expecting us, and a few minutes later here they come: Jim, and on a chain next to him, Dinky.

Please don't approach him, let him approach you, keep your hands to your side, let him sniff around you, he'll breathe your breath and check your hair, but don't pet him.

I'm a dog person, but Dinky is special. He's a dingo, for starters.

Jim, tell us about Dinky.
I got Dinky through the local station owner, he was having a dingo baiting program, he found some puppies, they normally try to bait before the dingoes have their pups, a dingo only has one litter a year in the middle of the year, so if they can bait three or four months before that, they aren't going to have abandoned puppies, but in this case they were running a bit late for whatever reason, and there were puppies out there, that was nearly four years ago when he was discovered, I'd been around dingoes before and knew what they were like, you need to give them extra special care and attention, you must treat them like a family member because they're a pack animal.

He's very affectionate with me and my wife and daughters, very much like a cat, he doesn't take commands, you have to work around it, the first 12 months were very hectic, you sort of do what he wants to do, repetition's always very good, he travels with me on my front-end loader, and I remember a couple of times when the chain slipped over the side or whatever, and he learned that he had to be careful and wait for my command, so now whenever I get on the loader with him, he stands patiently when I get off, and I have to give him a command, and then he gets off.

My daughters both learned the piano. As Dinky was growing up (I got him at six- or eight-weeks old), I'd take him into Alice Springs to
see the family and do my errands, and if the girls were practicing, he'd sing along, some people would say he's only howling, but that's not true, is it? He holds tones, pitching notes, you play low, he sings low, you play high, he sings high, you play in between, he goes in between, he waits for people to start, and when they stop, he stops, he gives a little yawn at the end.

People took photos, he ended up in newspapers, then on ABC radio, then my wife heard that Hasbro® had a competition running to pay for $1000 for a question they would use in the twentieth anniversary edition of Trivial Pursuit, and my daughter sent in a question: "What is the name of the internationally acclaimed piano-playing singing dingo, and where does he live?"

We had sort of forgotten about it when they rang one day and said, "Dinky's a finalist."

In what? Oh, yes.

Then they rang back, "Well, he's not really a finalist— he's the winner. Can you fly him to Sydney for the press conference?"

Well, not really, I'm not going to put him in a dog box on a plane, it's bad enough for domestic dogs.

So they sent a photographer here from Sydney and in a couple of days Dinky was on TV. One announcer said, "The Northern Territory has a new singing sensation, Dinky the singing dingo."

Do you have a problem with the dingoes being baited?

I don't think they're trying to eliminate them, just bring their numbers down to a manageable level, they show some kind of respect by trying to bait before they have their pups, they do it in line with conservation requirements as well, over the years they've shot, they've trapped, they've used strychnine, and now they use 1080—it doesn't sound good, but they aren't trying to eliminate them totally, lost or dumped dogs are a more serious problem, because they might breed with dingoes, the dingo crosses are terrorizing people, and it's becoming a major issue, it's now hard to find purebred dingoes on the mainland because of the crosses, domestic dogs have two litters a year so the crosses will always outbreed the dingo, so I feel a culling program is necessary because it gets rid of a lot of those crossbred dingoes.

What about his security? He's on a very strong chain—is that because there is 1080 around here, or do you have to worry about what he might do?

It's a bit of all that, the other side of the yard here, I've got kangaroos and emus and ducks, I used to have chickens but you really can't have dingoes and chickens because somehow they'll always find their way in and kill 'em, there have been times when he has got off the chain, usually by someone not putting the clips on properly, and that's why I now use a double clip on the collar.

We are on a main road, when he was first found, it was across the road about two or three miles from here, there may be active baits out right now, plus if people saw a dingo out and about, they'd want to shoot it, if they had a rifle in the car, they'd want to take a shot at it, and dingoes are generally very easy shots, they'll just turn the whole body side on to you and just stand off the road, they're very easy to shoot, all right, and if they're domesticated, well they'll probably just walk up to the car, so it's for his sake too.

However, he does have areas where he can run, he gets a great deal of exercise, he runs from room to room in the house, he's got playthings up there, he does live in the house, they are by nature a pack animal, they live in groups, they have a dominant male and a dominant female, so in my case I have to be the top dog, he has to be subservient to me, but we live in the same den, in my house, he has an old divan that's his bed, and he gallops through the house, we've got a wooden floor, the house next door can hear him, he gallops up the walls, there's not a gecko left in the house, he just runs up the wall and grabs them off the ceiling, he just can't help himself.

Birds ...when he's free, he'll run up a tree, jumping from branch to branch to grab birds out of trees, even on a long chain, he'll jump up and grab a bird out of the air, doesn't eat it, just kills it, leaves it there for me, just like a cat, and he cleans himself like a cat, he will throw a mouse or lizard, more like a cat than a dog—up to 18 months of age, he imitated my other dog, a poor imitation of a barking dog, but his ears never go down, the aperture is always open.

What does he eat?

We feed him roo meat, I get it in large blocks from the butcher, and bones, and he's partial to dry food.

Dry food?

Yeah, turkey and rice dry food—he loves it, he delicately takes it out of your fingers, he is delicate and selective in his diet.

This uncertain link in the food chain climbs on my lap on his way up to the keyboard of Jim's 1884 Thürmer piano.[58] We exchange breaths from an inch away, Dinky making a thorough assessment with nose and eyes and God knows what else. The piano keys are dusty, not from lack of use but from the last paw performance.

Dinky takes his place on the keyboard, and I reach under him to thumb through the hymnal. He doesn't give me much room, but you don't really want to challenge him for territory 'til you know where you fit in the pack. I stake out the unclaimed keys, not my preferred octaves but I'll make do. I pound out four or five hymns, and Dinky delivers just as Jim promised. Hymns like "Men of Old" find Dinky in top form, pitching notes, going for tone, giving it his all, and he even does a little up-and-down paw cadenza, a very hip, downtown, concept-driven note cluster type of thing, in the middle of "Behold, A Rose Is Blooming."

(When I was a student—forestry, not music—and trying to learn to play a clarinet, a local dog used to join in, comments our friend and lyrebird expert Syd Curtis on hearing about Dinky. But I regarded it as justified criticism rather than singing along.)

---

[58] Comettant, Oscar (1890/1980) *In the Land of Kangaroos and Goldmines*, Adelaide: Rigby, 136-137:

"I do not believe there is a country in the world where music is more widespread than in Australia. Certainly there is none that has more grand pianos per head of population. 700,000 instruments have been sent from Europe to Australia since the vast territory became a centre of white settlement. Everywhere here the piano is considered to be a necessary piece of furniture. Rather than not have one of these sonorous instruments in the drawing room …they would go without a bed.

"…custom …demands that there be at least one piano in every Australian home; even in the most distant shacks, away from any centre of population, the humblest farmer will have the inescapable piano. Way out in the country they are not very expert in music, and the piano that adorns the humble dwellings will be cheap and nasty …constantly going wrong, but the main thing is that they look like a piano, with vulgar moulding and ostentatious double candle-brackets; they make a noise when you strike the keyboard, and often that is all that is required."

Next, Jon wants a go. Afterwards, he reaches up reflexively to pet Dinky. Nothing happens, but Jim politely reminds him not to.

We have to be careful, we're tourist-orientated, last year a man walked in here, saw Dinky, and immediately walked over and grabbed Dinky by the throat, silly as it sounds, that's exactly what the man did, Dinky pulled back and latched onto the man's hand, he hadn't sunk the teeth in, he just grabbed on to the man's hand, the problem started when the man ripped his hand away in shock, as I said Dinky didn't sink the teeth in, he had simply latched onto the hand, and it wasn't a snarl and growl and bark and bite, it was simply I've gotcha— the man realized he was in error and he apologized.

More recently, I've seen visitors come in, and they get down on hands and knees, or they bend over so their head's only inches away, and they sort of eyeball, stare at him right in the eyes, and then they make funny gestures with their hands or their face, and you know, it's all aggressive stuff, so I say to people, look, just leave him alone, he's not gonna hurt you, but the owner might.

I t's still raining, and Jon is sulking. Heavy rain makes for boggings even in a four-wheel-drive, and grasses grow quickly. He loves 100 percent red desert sand, none of that green stuff. I decide to take us for the day to Uluru (formerly Ayers Rock, and previous to that, had anyone asked, Uluru).

Early explorers pegged the interior the "ghastly blank" or the "dead heart," and even some contemporary writers continue to use this shorthand description. We take issue; historically, deserts seem to be a place where divine imagination is at work.[59]

---

[59] Consider the map of Aboriginal Australia. It's intense and varied, even in the deserts that are always empty on whitefella maps. What now constitutes the Northern Territory is positively busting with Belgiums—literally dozens of Aboriginal "countries" or language groups, and most of these can be subdivided into smaller clans and dialects. Aboriginal Australia is an extraordinary matrix of over 500 interlocking cultures. I can't think of any map that is more intense. How could we miss it—are whitefellas *that* stupid?

Yitha Yitha * Kureinji * Latje Latje * Madi Madi * Wiradjuri * Nari Nari * Wadi Wadi * Wemba Wemba * Wergaia * Djadjawurung * Baraba Baraba * Waveroo * Taungurong

That's just some of the Aboriginal nations in a small area north of Melbourne—a few Belgiums worth. These names go back to the roots of our

The traditional owners of Uluru are the Anangu people, finally recognized in 1985; they live in the nearby township of the Mutitjulu community, a population of about 130. Their ways are not our ways. The cover of the official visitor guide features the forthright smiles of two grandmothers and three granddaughters, all bare from the waist up except for red and white painted petals on their shoulders and upper chests. And inside, we read the history, the natural history, and a page entitled "Please Don't Climb the Rock." Uluru has great spiritual significance for them. They ask that we not climb it for safety and spiritual reasons. But for those who insist, and many do, there are pointers. A strenuous climb, it is best done first thing in the morning. It is closed on hot days and when it rains or winds are strong.

The surrounding park has a formality about it. The trees seem planted by the likes of Capability Brown (the eighteenth-century English landscape gardener known for his natural-looking parks, including Kew Gardens), and the shape of the trees is reminiscent of the pines of Rome. The rock itself rises 1140 feet from the desert and has a girth of nearly six miles. It's the world's most famous monolith, yet two-thirds of the rock lies beneath the surface. We've read all this; we're prepared—but we're not. Primeval mists (okay, clouds) swirl around its upper parts like the set for *The Lost World*. We watch it at sunset where its mood freewheels from purple to red, orange, and lilac. Although spectacular, the color is secondary to the shape, size, and mass.

The next morning we drive around it, and around again. A fly plague of copters buzzes over it. We see a giant heart muscle, with the impression of a spine in the middle. Then smaller details emerge: faces, eyes, mouths, incisions, skulls, swaths of fabulous fabric, contemporary art prints, vertical red, metaphor fails, alone standing at the base, the rock's summit masked by the clouds, and my head goes numb with the intensity of it.

---

humanity, the roots of our aurality, a time when all significant cultural transmission was by song. All ceremony, all artifacts, all stories, every vital rock, every geographical signpost had a song. To get from one of these countries to another, you had to know the relevant songs. The music had to be sung to bring the universe into a continuing state of existence; nothing existed without a song.

We are out here playing fences, which can be amusing, playful, even enjoyable. There was nothing prankish about the role of music in traditional Aboriginal culture—without the knowledge carried by that music, you would perish. Song was fundamental to survival.

In many nonwestern societies, there is no word for music—it's more important than that. Indispensible. Integral to life. In our rush to the twenty-first century, we seem to have lost the essence of music. The sound of music is everywhere, in a way that the inventors of muzak could never have imagined in their wildest dreams, but it has lost its value and power.

The *Aboriginal Australia* map is available at www.aiatsis.gov.au.

It's clearly *not* the dead heart of Australia; it's *the* pulsating singularity. How could the early explorers have got it so wrong?

We drive on to the 36 separate domes known collectively to the Anangu as Kata Tjuta (formerly The Olgas, and previous to that—well, you know). These top-heavy knobs resemble something you'd draw, not see in nature. Then we pass some roadwork, where desert sand is smoothly bulldozed so high that it's a red hug as we drive through.

We hear on the radio that some Aboriginal women near Katherine will be meeting about domestic violence: The men can have their own men-talk, men-camp, one woman says. We are concerned about our children who are witnessing men drinking and domestic violence.

Another speaks of a lack of cultural activities for the men, now that hardly any ceremonies are being taught. Next come the local news headlines from Tennent Creek: the chlorinated water vote was 80 percent for, the school nutrition program has been inaugurated, and dengue fever is on the rise ("Even with a slight rain, bleach your dog bowls weekly.")

We face a four-hour drive in the rain via King's Creek to Hermannsburg. I pass the time drive-by tree watching. There's the Three-branch Missile Tree *(Missilis tres branca)*, its entire branch department of three all thrusting horizontally to the right; the Conformist Tree *(Conformare uniformus unanimus)*, where all the branches begin normally but end up going straight up in a butch; the Cheerleader Tree *(Chantus cantus ignoramus)*, tossing up round tufts of foliage resembling pompoms; and the giant white-barked gum with two inexplicably blackened branches *(Pater dubius)*.

And then there's the Family Tree *(Regina et infantus regalis idiotus)*, which should have been cut down years ago.

Two hours in, the pavement ends and the gravel continuation of our road is marked closed. TURN AROUND, says the sign, and I always do. Two minor floodways and four puddles of water across the road are all we forded on the way in; on doubling back, we find the persistent rain has transformed that in short order into *twenty* or more stretches of water across the road, often murky and deep, and one carnival immersion flood. There was no warning that the road might be closed, we complain to each other. The following day, we see the road is well marked in the other direction and still closed.

Today's iconic artifact: one rusty car door propped up with a stick, the word "fuck" painted big on it. There's no sign of the rest of the car, as in "Fuck, the car fell off the door somewhere!"

German missionaries established Hermannsburg during the 1877 drought. Had these Lutheran zealots asked the indigenous people, they would have been told that a permanent supply of water could be found 50 miles away. The mission was abandoned in 1891, only to be turned around when Pastor Carl Strehlow arrived in 1894. An outstanding linguist and competent musician, he translated the Bible and hymns into the Arrernte language but discouraged the traditional Aboriginal beliefs and customs. Over the years, Christianity had its ups and downs.

The ownership of Hermannsburg Mission was transferred back to its traditional owners in 1982, although many of the families had left the Mission to move further out. The Outstation Movement has spurned about 35 small communities in the area. Hermannsburg serves as the hub of a cultural rejuvenation.

The mission is still here, its whitewashed church and various outbuildings shaded by tall river gums and date palms. It's an insistent bit of traditional German farmhouse architecture in stark contrast to the surrounding countryside. We tour the school, manse, church, mess hall, and gallery. Thiry-nine local artists are represented, including the painters of the famous Namatjira family.[60]

We meet up with the current pastor/choir director, David Roennfeldt, and his Aboriginal wife, Lily. Jon is interested in featuring the choir in one of his music projects, so we're here to record them as a preliminary step. David and Lily take us into the cool of the old stone church. Four rows of small picnic benches line each aisle; behind them are two more rows of crude board and cruder legs shaved to a point and stuck in the board. Up front, a crucifix and a plaque displaying hymn numbers hang above the pulpit, with a pump-style harmonium off to the right.

Getting the choir together is no straightforward task. First, the church bell is rung for five minutes. No response.

This can take a while, David mentions with resignation.

He resorts to his car, driving this way and that around the town, picking up singers as he goes.

Eight or ten women choristers gradually assemble, dressed in print skirts, sweaters, and sandals or sensible shoes. They tend not to go directly into a building; they sit outside until they have to enter. It's

---

[60] Albert Namatjira (1902-59) is perhaps Australia's most renowned Aboriginal artist. It's hard not to cringe when reading of his life and times. He used his income to support many of his people, was permitted to buy alcohol at a time when other Aborigines were not, was jailed in 1958 for supplying alcohol to his community (thus remaining true to his kinship responsibilities), and died a year after his release from prison.

A clipping hangs in the gallery: "First Native Artist! This painting was made in four weeks unaided."

worth our wait. With David on guitar, the Ntaria Ladies Choir sings "Rock of Ages" in their language, barely opening their mouths (two of the women manage to sing from the *side* of their mouth). A huge sound comes out. We are transfixed as they run through "When I Survey the Wondrous Cross" and "We Are Coming Together." For a final hymn, David plays clap-sticks while the women, seated with their legs straight out, beat rhythm on their laps with their hands as they sing.[61]

Afterwards, we go outside. From then on, we get it wrong. Jon and David, two tall white men, stand facing the women seated on the ground. Jon wants to explain his project but also to interview them about their choir and other aspects of their lives. Lily, the pastor's wife, is translating. For all the reasons that are obvious to us afterwards (positionally, culturally, men-women, secret-sacred), no one says much at all. We figure out too late that Jon might have left it to me; it was women's business.

We retire to David and Lily's house. He shows us the Lutheran Church of Australia's first hymnal, published in Hannover in 1891. It contains 53 hymns. Ted Strehlow, youngest child of Carl, was born here and spent 40 years speaking the language fluently and studying the Arrernte people. In his hymnal, he added diacritics such as accents and retroflex signs to capture sounds more accurately, but it was expensive and unwieldy and never got much use.

There's a campfire outside David and Lily's house where they often have lunch and dinner. As we depart, David walks us into the new church, which stands next to the old. It's bigger but without character, although the seats look solid.

Jon films a game of footie at the schoolyard; he's enchanted. I wait impatiently, noticing little but the recurring themes of kids with runny noses and the charred remains of campfires.

We head back to Alice Springs. The only thing going through this gap in the MacDonnell Ranges for most of the 1800s was the telegraph line—"the singing line," as the Aboriginal peoples called its aeolian characteristics. The sulphur-crested white cockatoos show off against red sand. Three smaller birds take off from the side of the road and fly straight into the car—those genes won't get replicated. A miniplague of suicidal "splatteroos" smears the windshield, making a helluva noise—like hailstones. Thirty seconds later, the bombardment stops as suddenly as it started.

Chicken ravioli with mushroom, onion, sun-dried tomato, and Parmesan cheese make for dinner, and our wine is appropriately Two Churches 2001, Barossa Shiraz.

---

[61] Jon's recordings of the choir can be found at http://www.abc.net.au/arts/adlib and http://www.jonroseweb.com/f_projects_pannikin.html

We get the weather report, and it's not good: still more rain. Alice is in a panic. Tourists are complaining. We pore over the map, trying to imagine a long drive out of this mess. I begin for the third time to make a case for Coober Pedy. This time, I've prepared my argument.

The Dog Fence is *right there*, I insist. It crosses the road in *three* places.

My words have been received, and we head south. I drive all day and by evening we are just 60 miles short of Jon's goal—The Dog Fence, that is, not the town of Coober Pedy. We camp next to the "Engraving Trees" (*Photogravurus uniformus*). Consistently 10 feet high, these perfect specimens are set against a fiery pink-orange and blue opalescent sky.

Jon wakes at 4:30 a.m., in absolute anticipation of the Fence. As is often the case, it's not accurately marked on the map, but we find it, aided by a small brown sign and a grid. He sets up the recording gear while I walk around.

A young dingo is roadkill on the grid, part of its body hanging down through the bars. No—it's a joey. I see its decaying mother underneath. The joey must have tried to crawl out after its mother's death, only to be struck by a car.

A vehicle pulls off the road toward us. I get back into the car. I'll let Jon explain what we're up to—or try--before I add the feminine touch.

Good morning.
Good morning.
Are you fence runners?
No, we're policemen.
So, before you ask me what I'm doing, let me first say I'm not blowing up the Fence. [Smiles] I'm playing it.
What are those things?
Contact microphones—we use them to record the fence. [Any formality initially detected now disappears.]
Oh, I see. Reckon you get a hot sound out of that when the wind is up.
Here, check it out with these headphones.
Crickey!

It's safe to get out, I reason.

Turns out Officers Bill Cunningham and Frank Abbott, who are fast becoming devotees of fence music, are heading to some off-limits reserves. We explain more about our project and are surprised to learn that they've already heard of it. They recommend a fence at a nearby secret (but decommissioned) military base that we should check out at Narrungar.

South Australia Police Department
Police Ancillary Report.[62]
NON-OFFENCE DETAILS

Occurred at 0705 hrs
on 07/06/2004
Stuart Hwy Coober Pedy SA 5723

* Cunningham/Abbott Coober Pedy CIB, while
proceeding in a southerly direction saw one Jonathan
Antony Rose acting suspiciously at the Dog Fence 30
miles north of Coober Pedy.

* Investigated and saw that Rose had electrical apparatus
attached to fence.

* Checked his bona fides and learned he is a professional
musician.

*He was engaged in recording the "sound of the wind on
the fence." Examples of his work produced.

*Was in company of Hollis Elizabeth Taylor, same
address.

*Rose stated he'll be doing similar recordings in remote
places in the area in the near future.

*Was in possession of a Toyota LandCruiser Reg. No.
_____.

---

[62] Officer Cunningham mailed this report to us several weeks later, along with a note
saying:

"We had a very busy week after we left you; we patrolled the Anangu
Pitjantjatjara Lands visiting some of the most scenically beautiful parts of Australia
you could wish to see. The Musgrave and Mann Ranges and Aboriginal communities
like Nyapari, Kanpi, Umuwa, Amata, Ernabella and so on.

"Not many of us 'whities' are privileged to see those places; they are especially
beautiful just before sundown. The silence is deafening, you especially would know
what I mean!

"Anyway, it was nice to speak to you and Hollis; you were the subject of
conversation for several days after. All the very best to you both. If you are passing
through Coober Pedy at any time, call in. Regards, Bill"

Coming in to Coober Pedy, the signs announce DANGER, KEEP OUT, DEEP MINE SHAFTS. Opal fields are being worked, evidenced by the humming, spitting, vibrating, dusting commotion coming from drilling shafts, tunneling machines, and blowers. The land is concrete to salmon to ochre in color and littered with piles of gravel, sand, and earth— testimony to the many holes dug in search of the opal.

It's popular for tourists to noodle for opal in the fields, hoping to find a missed gem. The tourist brochure warns that abandoned prospecting drill holes are up to 100 feet deep.

> Please beware and adhere to the following warnings. It is illegal to go on a pegged claim without the miner's permission. Beware of machinery in operation. Do not go onto the opal fields at night. Watch where you walk, and do not walk backwards, especially when taking photographs. Do not tamper with the warning signs, which also assist the Mine Rescue Squad.

The opal capital of the world (producing 90 percent of the world's supply), Coober Pedy has 30 different producing fields. Opals occur in four colors—blue, green, orange, and red, usually in combination. One lucky miner discovered a fully opalized backbone and tail of an extinct lizard (the bones numbered 35 pieces).

We see that some miners take refuge in small travel trailers parked helter-skelter. We round a bend to witness an entire tent village floating above red earth under a cerulean blue sky. Quite exceptionally, it's poured here too. We can't find a dry place. *Kupa piti* is Aboriginal, meaning boy's waterhole, which is crucial in an area that averages a mere six inches of rain per year. In 1967 a solar desalination plant produced fresh water from the saline water, which exists 330 feet below the surface. Today, after undergoing a complex process, water comes from a bore located north of town on the Oodnadatta Track.

Opals were discovered here in 1915 and miners began arriving immediately. By 1918, returning WWI soldiers-cum-miners introduced the idea of living underground in "dugouts," much as they had done in the French trenches. The temperature in dugouts varies only about 10 degrees, from 70 to 80 Fahrenheit. Above ground in summer, the thermometer has been known to fix itself well above the century Fahrenheit mark and not budge for days (this in a place that 120 million years ago was near the South Pole). Coober Pedian golfers carry a square of turf with them, and their club shirt has flies printed on the back. They claim to be the only golf club in the world to have reciprocal rights with Scotland's St. Andrews Links, the home of golf.

Augmenting the 3500 or so locals (from over 30 countries), many of whom live underground, are 100,000 tourists annually, who have their choice of accommodation variously entitled Mud Hut Motel, Desert Cave Hotel, Opal Cave, Look Out Cave, and Underground Motel. Should your stay be the spaceage Coober Pedy Hospital instead, rest assured that it also is mostly underground. Other attractions include the On the Level Snack bar, Underground Pottery, Underground Art Gallery, Underground Mine, and Underground Café & Didgeridoos (and Boomerangs).

They have their theme and they run with it. And we have ours, but we don't find fences *around* buildings here; rather, wire and corrugated iron fences go *over* the tops of the underground houses and businesses.

Intense heat is often a harbinger for religion, thus the Revival Underground Church, St. Peter and St. Paul's Underground Catholic Church, and the Anglican Catacomb Church, which is cut out of sandstone in the shape of a cross ("All of us are tourists in this life. Which way are you heading? Why stay in the pit?"). And don't forget the Greek Orthodox Church, nor the bounties of and reversals by the god of chance. Get rich or get religion is the town's cantus firmus.

We head out the Oodnadatta Track to the Dog Fence, marked by absolute flatness save the famous, and famously incorrect, sign: THE DOG FENCE: 9,600 KILOMETERS LONG; it's an error that many books and brochures copy. We record on the Fence at both sunset and sunrise. Jon snaps a photo of me in front of it with hundreds of silvery spider webs, one attached to each square in the wire, streaming horizontally in the wind. We're pressed into the flat earth by the weight of an unmediated sky; when we return to Coober Pedy, even a hill seems exotic.

It's time to follow up on the lead our police officers gave us. Headed south, we find quite a lively trailer culture on the roads, including "Liv 'N the Dream" on one motor home. We aren't trailer trash, we console ourselves. The universal road sign for a picnic area is a picnic table shaded by a tree, except in this country they are unable to deliver on the tree. And who would really want to picnic anyway? The sign to Glendambo tells it best:

> Welcome to Glendambo
> Elevation 150 m
> Population 22,500 Sheep
> Humans 30
> Flies 2,000,000 (approximately)

We drive past the town on our way to a salt lake, Lake Hart. Disappointingly, it's filled with water, but up the hill we find a perfect set for a fence performance. I bow long, slow notes while Jon staggers around taking video "moon shots" over red scalloped dunes and roo tracks in the soft sand. The next lake, a few miles later, is also filled. Turns out the police directed us to a prohibited area. Not much there, I write in my notebook and leave it at that. We can't enter or even take photos. I'm intimidated to even look. A fence is a warning I heed. Jon does not.

I find a brand new fence and gate still guarding some sort of military secrets, even though the nearby Woomera rocket test site has been closed for years. Fence—an indicator species. Indicator of value. Wouldn't it be cheaper to pull down the two little round bunkers (or weapons storage silos)? Still linked by single power cable. Searchlight at gate has no bulb. "Seven years prison for taking photos or flying over the area," insists the sign.

We retrace our steps and spend the night in Glendambo, tidier than any official Tidy Town. The gear junkies next to us echo this theme. They have a tent trailer with a fully furnished kitchen to the side: electric fry pan, electric kettle, even a mop and broom; then they're off in the morning to set it all up at the next place. There's a classic windmill in front of town, a circle of slats, a paddle off to one side, predictably circling until it's time for a short movie take, when it can be counted on to fall dead.

Back in Coober Pedy, I'm snagged by Riba's Caravan Park sign: "Founded 1996, world's first underground camping." I've gotta know. We camp outside in a parking space carved out of a rock, but the tent campers can set up in an underground mansion, with room after room of textured walls and spooky echo. Cocktail hour: Verse 1 Shiraz 2002, blueberry and earthy spices, to try to make sense of it all.

The dawn chorus is a rooster, a pigeon, and a drunk. Jon promises and promises an easy day, no extra projects, only the Dog Fence. But we turn around after 20 seconds to reëxamine a fence on a high hill—could it be an abandoned mine? We stop a few minutes later at an opal field to "just test" the perimeter fence. It's slack. I'm off the hook, I assume. But slack + wind = aeolian harp.[63] We record and film

---

[63] The alternative to the aeolian harp was the Eight-String Aeolian Violin. A sail on this violin caught the wind and excited the strings, making them sound. Pitch modulation was effected by continual use of the tuning pegs. It had twin necks, the second neck attached to the base of the instrument.

The strings had to be excited in just the right way, requiring technique quite different from bowing. If the strings were too tight, they'd just stop; there was little room to maneuver. The sail had to be somewhat slack, and it was difficult to get all the strings resonating, but when the wind conditions were right, it sounded great. (I had Mount Kosciusko in the windblown Snowy Mountains in my sights as a performance venue.) An option on windless days was to reverse a vacuum cleaner, employing its exhaust function. Nowadays, the experimental

the fence; then, he records a vibrating DEEP MINE SHAFTS sign. Vibrating is probably the wrong word, it's a wind-crazed, shaking metal spirit.

Red sand and gravel everywhere, sun in my eyes, driving blind on a bad road—if you're unsure of your age, go to a nightclub or rent a four-wheel-drive vehicle. At the Dog Fence, he suggests that she will pound a large rock on the fence post—not a musical technique taught or imagined when I was at school. Then Jon does a walkin' the fence routine with a stick bouncing along the wire. With the contact microphones in place and my headphones on, it's a *crescendo-descrescendo* any drummer would be proud of. Jon improvises on violin with the fence behind him, then turns to the camera and speaks:

The fence as a functional long-string instrument is a result of industrial mass production—something Stradivarius would have found hard to get his brain around. Despite the cultural Dark Ages that we now find ourselves in, new design for string instruments can still be found. This is a Vatilliotis tenor violin, made in Australia just three years ago. It sounds one octave lower than the standard model. Historically speaking, experimentation has always been a fundamental part of string instrument making. Within the Islamic tradition and its European offspring, there were rarely times when innovation wasn't the *modus operandi.*

The creative musician in this country is always being told by those who run our culture that the great Australian public is not interested in new music—they only want to hear the tried and tested, the copy. This patronizing attitude is one of the reasons why no identifiable genre such as bebop or reggae ever evolved in the modern state of Australia. Even Canada has its own fiddle tradition.

Where I'm standing now is right beside the Dingo, or Wild Dog, Fence. It's arguably the longest man-made anything on our little planet. It stretches through three states, and as its name suggests, it was constructed and is regularly maintained to keep the Australian beef and sheep industry south of the fence dog free. Now one thing's for sure: the guys who built this fence weren't concerned with the theory and practice of music as they labored away under a scorching sun. But we have to thank them, because they unwittingly designed and constructed the world's longest string instrument.

At the final lookout, I gesture and announce, Out there, a complete Belgium.

A couple of them, suggests Jon.

---

musician has "e-bows" that work magnetically, doing the same trick as the wind but with much less messing around.

Image/sound at http://www.jonroseweb.com/d_picts_aeolian_violin.html.

Still trying to make sense of the place, tonight with Preece Shiraz 2001, Victoria: morello cherries, vanilla bean, and coffee syrup on the nose; mulberry, plum, and spice on the palate. Now *that* makes sense. (And we drift off into senselessness.)

In the midst of an early morning dream, something goes plonk on the car roof.

Ahh! Uhh! Aaaaaaa!

Time for my lesson from the local raven.

Raven's Vowel Lesson

Ahhhhhhhhhhh! Uhhhhhhhhhhhh! Ehhhhhhhhhhhhhh!   Ahh   uhh   ehh   uhh!

Once more, this time with that strangled, drawn-out Doppler effect, instructs my mentor.

Aaa uhh aaa uhh aaaaaaoooooooouh!

By George, she's got it.

The morning winds bring a blast of white dust covering our vehicle and clothes and entering our noses, ears, eyes, and probably lungs. Oh, the mining life! Jon was against the place. Now I can't drag him away. He'd move here if I'd let him. As for me, I've had my fill.

From Coober Pedy to Marla, we see CATTLE CROSSING signs that have been modified by a local joker: CATTLE FUCKING, CATTLE JUMPING, CATTLE MOOING, CATTLE _____ING. Next up, playing and filming a fence on a red ridge with blue sky behind; it's barbed so I crawl under slowly, but I imagine how to limbo quickly if I see a snake. I play little swing rhythms with lots of silence between them.

We camp at Rainbow Valley. It's terrific, but …

Rainbow Valley has arguably the most extraordinary rock formations in Central Australia, rising sheer in front of a floodplain. It's also an intense sonic environment, destroyed by vacationers thanks to Queenie's birthday. Insecurity in such a place makes people share their inanities at an extremely loud volume. They carry their deserts in the center of themselves. A "telegraph" bird ra-ta-tats out his song, but nobody hears it. Super Hoon has brought his bass-boosted airport lounge muzak. I ask him to turn it off, *nicely* per Hollis' instructions.

You don't like music?

Yes, I'm here to listen to the music of this pristine environment, as I assume you are, too.

He is nonplussed, and as he switches off his sound system, he slams his door in anger. According to him, this place is *terra nullius*. There is no music here. He has done everybody a big favor by bringing along some nice, relaxing muzak to create an atmosphere. This stuff he is playing is cringe factor ten; it wouldn't even qualify as New Age. If you want to listen to airport lounge muzak, go sit in an airport lounge. Fifteen minutes later, the muzak is back on with a vengeance. Super Hoon wanders over to gloat.

You got outvoted—everyone wanted the music back.

I smile and respond, Democracy at work then. (Democracy as lowest common denominator. We realize "everyone" means his mates traveling with him.) Here's to Queenie.

The rock face at Rainbow Valley spreads out like a curtain. In the middle of the dramatic sunset, when the rocks turn scarlet, then purple, and all campers and cameras are focused on the changing view, a distant trio come shuffling into view over the saltpan, shouting at each other.

Take the photo!

Na, youse too far away, youse look like dots.

We are dots.

Agreed.

Thirty seconds of dingo howling erupts, then stops. Mr. Muzak and friends have circled the wagons round a campfire. We hear them vaguely: rutabaga rutabaga rutabaga rutabaga rutabaga bloody dingo rutabaga rutabaga rutabaga.

In the morning we hike. Everyone is gone but the Dots, leaving us in Paradise. I film Jon improvising on violin with bird counterpoint. Two "telegraph" birds hold forth a fifth apart. A third bird is riffing at a lower pitch. We estimate the reverb time at three seconds from one cliff to the other.

Fallen chunks are scattered at Jon's feet. Everything looks made and then broken, composed and then dispersed. It's the set for the shaping and forming and designing of the world. Behind him are rock walls—oh yes, I see The Anselm Kiefer Wall and another with weathered and pockmarked skulls, both human and animal, all from the distant past or the improbable future, nature's own memoirs. As we gingerly walk on the surface of this extravagant rock temple, our steps produce the hollow-sounding clatter of a Greek dance floor littered with broken plates.

We walk out still farther, sit down, and meditate on the place. Jon keeps to himself that there's a carpet python hole next to my feet 'til we get up to leave. Scraping blades and millstones have been found here, evidence of past Aboriginal presence. Emus, pigeons, goannas, and euros would have been their game. As many as 180 lizards per acre have been found in the spinifex grasslands southwest of Alice, with up to 42 species living side by side.

The claypan is a giant ice rink the size of downtown Brussels. Every movement of the sun makes a new picture in the orange, red, white, and purple rocks above it.[64] Whites come forward and reds recede, then vice versa. Fading hieroglyphics, abandoned printing plates. Jon sits in the middle of the claypan and looks into the camera:

Pioneers of the modern state of Australia made fences to last. It was a tough job. People died constructing the Rabbit-Proof Fences of Western Australia. Murders were committed. Fence runners have gone quite mad working on these structures. But these days, pastoralists can hardly afford the great expense of keeping all these fences in good repair. The task is overwhelming. Whatever your view on fences, necessity or folly, the geography will outlive the history.

Playing fences is not exactly rocket science, but this activity does correspond at least to one theory, that of the Uncertainty Principle. If you play a note on a fence, seven times out of ten when you come to play that note again, its position on the fence will have moved. This is frustrating as you can imagine. By playing the fence, you discover an often hidden sound world, an unfamiliar language, and structures that are more intuitive than reasoned.

Stop!

I grab the camera and put it under my shirt. Heads down, eyes closed, we sit it out, totally unprepared for the dust storm that envelopes us for 15 minutes. The camera survives, but our mucous membranes will remember this interlude for a week. Jon resumes.

The fence is probably our ultimate symbol for division, exploitation, and our compulsive view of life's experience in terms of duality. It's either them, or us.

For thousands of years Aboriginal groups were connected across these vast spaces by the aural knowledge base known as the songlines. And then, we turned up. Over the last 200 years, fences have clearly been used, knowingly or not, to destroy that culture. To make music ordinarily requires no justification; it has intrinsic beauty and value. In traveling 25,000 miles around Australia with this project, no one has ever

---

[64] The sand in the dune fields is red due to the grains having a veneer of iron oxide (rust), while the sandstone ranges are dark brown, purple, red orange, yellow, and even white. White sandstone has the least iron and is a relatively soft and fragile rock. These colors were formed between 80-20 million years ago when Central Australia had a warm, wet climate.

come up to us to complain; on the contrary, playing fences appeals to many. It seems a logical musical practice for this country.

But what does it mean to play a fence? Could it be seen as part of the current reconciliation and healing process? Is this a tribute to the tough frontier? Or is this the unexpected sonic consolation of a short and sometimes brutal history? So next time you're outback and you come across one of these, give it a go.

PLEASE SHUT THE GATE says the sign at the park exit, and we do, and undo, and do, back and forth until gate and chain have been preserved on video and audio. The film is of a slow, swinging motion set to its own eerie music.

On the road to the Henbury Meteorite Craters, a dark tree and several on-the-move camel humps silhouette the horizon. We lunch at the meteorite, a three-barb fence and a camel on the other side. Four thousand years ago, a large meteor traveling at 25,000 miles per hour broke up before impact and hit here. As it broke up, "it" became "them," and the four largest pieces formed craters. The pieces were only as large as a 50-gallon fuel drum, so the great speed was critical. We walk around the scalloping rim of the largest crater formed by two overlapping impacts. American astronauts once visited here in preparation for their moon landing.

W e don't need much of an excuse to pop in again to see Dinky and Jim. We're looking for a bit of local advice. Jim says the Finke Desert Race will keep us from going where we've planned and suggests we head straight to the town of Finke. Ninety-three miles of rough road gets us just shy of town. We park in an empty field and open a Wyndham Estate Bin 555 Shiraz 2001. It's been a long day, and it's a dry town, so we can't go in. A truck approaches, and an Aboriginal man steps out.

You're on business property. If you just move over to the other side of the crossroads, you can park wherever you like.

Yes, sir.

—except there's no place to park. We've arrived at twilight with no idea how the place looks or is laid out. We're up and down the back roads trying to get it right, but finally pull off into some understandably inhospitable bushes and make dinner.

Fireworks. Aboriginal voices, mostly kids screaming. Endless cars filled with people front and back coming and going from every point of the compass—although logically they can only be coming from three directions. Campfires we can't find our way to, a passing ambulance … A plane lands close, right in front of us like a UFO. It's all happening right here in Finke. Jon stands outside the car and dictates, while I write as fast as possible.

Streams of cars are crisscrossing right where we are, either one hundred of them, or five every 20 minutes. Where the hell do they go when they turn left up there? One car is indicating, but it's not turning, just the regular nighttime winter songline negotiation, I suppose. There's guys whizzing around out there where we were asked to leave. I can't imagine what it looks like in the daylight, that's the thing. There's at least one set of headlights slowly traversing our space at all times, and sometimes three or four, and we aren't even in town—we're one mile from It.

We might be parked by the town generator; there's a sort of minimalist industrial music whirring on. Meanwhile there's lights on the runway …or is it a car going down the track? I can see five cars at the moment. Six! And a motorbike, or is it a car with one light? Yes, it's a car with one light masquerading as a motorbike. This is pretty lethal, this guy. He's only got one light on an undefined road; he's going up that left-hand channel. That's definitely a scene up there. I'm trying to figure out exactly how many points of the compass are involved here. One, two, three, four, five, six, seven. I think there are seven possible directional options.

Oh, my God! Finke's going mad! It's a purple and white extravaganza.

Here's a taxi-looking vehicle, followed by another car. That is definitely an ambulance coming back. Finke has just used up their town budget for the next five years. We've got the Rapmobile going by and a plane on the runway at the end of the fireworks.

Woof!
Get in and close the door!

It's just a dog. Another plane's circling. Maybe it wasn't a dog. Maybe it was a person crawling around on all fours. Another plane, no I think he was just changing direction over Finke because of the magnetic field. Finke by night. The other taxi-like vehicle. And another campfire—there's eight directional possibilities. The plane lights are off.

Jon as sportscaster has warmed to his task.

That's an Aboriginal car. They don't indicate turns, and it's crapped out. I predict he'll turn left, and he does. Whatever the hell is in there? If I had to put a spin on the whole thing, I would say that on big race day all the Aboriginal families come into town. You're gonna turn left, too. No! He's a right. On business land! Here comes the dude with the lamp. He's been backwards and forwards. He's pretending to be more than one guy.

As a privacy measure, Jon moves Big Yellow, his trusty suitcase, to the driver's seat and draws a huge face on him with a felt tip pen—our own personal bouncer in case things go to another level.

We are right by the hang. It's One Light, drifting aimlessly. He doesn't even stop. This is a bit unusual, One Light—but *signaling.* I think you should seriously consider doing your ablutions from inside. I don't know if I can cover you from all angles. Here's One Light again, but which one? I've identified two—no, It's definitely the One Light with the rattle. Just when you thought one sector had closed down, there's action, pretty well where we tried to camp. He's doin' business, where? On the business land, of course. Now he's stopped. Seven cars on this small stretch of road. Listen to the sound of the car. I'm going to try to predict a moment of total closure when there's no car ...impossible, here's a car and a shooting star. A car with a radio is rare. If you want to have a conversation with someone, you just drive—some kind of equivalent to the mobile phone?

It's surely late enough for a quick clandestine shower. But just as I prepare to bare all, one or several guys or dogs walk by.

In the morning, we drive into town. "Welcome to Aputula" (it sounds much better than "Finke"). We see it, and it's a vision of nomadic life: campfires, garbage, piles of people in their swags sleeping outdoors, even at the police station. This is not camping as a lifestyle choice or a holiday option; this is a tribal meeting place—camping is the *modus operandi.* T-shirts dry, or keep watch, on six-foot poles stuck in the ground.

The houses embrace an open-style tropical living plan, and some are heavily into corrugated iron. Town is just a few blocks, and at the end of town is the race. "Finke Desert Race Start/Day 2" proclaims the banner. I park between the car with the bullet hole in the door and the Northern Territory Police car.

Huge! White tires mark the beginning of the race, hundreds of them. Four barefoot Aboriginal aunties in black coats stand on the road, leaning in various cars, while naked children lean out and unintentionally moon us. Campfires dot the area, and through the smoke are concentric circles of uncles and aunties looking like they've always been here.

It all looks biblical, Jon announces, but then he corrects himself. No, it would have to be pre-biblical.

The police paddy wagon pulls up and a dozen Aboriginal men get out to watch the race. Another car drives a hundred yards from town. Seven people get out to watch for a bit, then pile back in and ride the hundred yards back.

Every few minutes, a woman with a megaphone and clipboard at a card table behind the flagman shouts, Ten seconds 5 4 3 2 1! An orange flag signals the start for another entrant, provoking a hovering copter to set off in desert pursuit. The race vehicles are everything from converted pickups and SUV's to seriously sandworthy dune buggies. They have names like Night Stalker and are sponsored by the likes of the Birdsville Hotel and Centre Radiators.

After an hour, we drive in the other direction on a lonely track toward the million square-mile Simpson Desert. Jon films a windmill squeaking and slurping.

Two teenage dingoes run next to us, up and down over the massive sand dunes, apparently unnerved that we can keep up with them.

We pass a junkyard at Andado Station, a mess of pipes, barrels, travel trailers, cars, corrugated iron, and other rusting bits. Another windmill circles like a Ferris wheel on the way into Old Andado Station.

Fence & Windmill at Andado Station

Jon records a white gate able to groan at almost all of its 360 degrees, and a second gate, which is higher pitched and more subdued.

Back in Finke, the gas station attendant says the normal population of 250 has swelled to 1000, maybe 1250, for the *footie* weekend, not the race as we'd assumed. FAXes stream in, vouching for folks who arrived without enough gas money to get home. People in the store buy six cigarettes at a time.

We return to the race starting point. A few officials are still milling about. Jon asks the woman with the clipboard and megaphone if we can head up the road now.

Well, it's technically closed until tomorrow morning, but go ahead—just be careful. [That always sounds like trouble to me.]

There's the race road, *unmarked*, and just a few yards to the right of it, another road, *marked* to where we're headed; we set off on the unmarked one, obeying her instructions rather than the sign. Immediately, something's wrong. I've unwittingly become the last contestant in a ruined sandbox.

I can't steer. The deep ruts are deciding where the car goes, not the driver. I start pressing buttons and give an inadvertent salute of the windshield wipers. Contestant number 176 is on an extremely fast training program. I open my mouth to shout, but nothing comes out. After a couple of minutes of panic, Jon thinks we can jump the LandCruiser up to the parallel road on the right, plowing over some bumps and bushes.

No, I can't.

Yes, you can.

No, don't make me do this. We don't even know where that road goes. Please!

You can do it; okay, just there, go! Now!

Gravity is temporarily suspended as we fly over the bump. We leave the soft, mushy sand for a bone-jarring road, our teeth vibrating like crazy.

This can't be right. What if we get lost in this desert?

For once, my trusty TURN AROUND NOW seems ill-advised. We debate which road to commit to as we whiz past the upside-down car wrecks of unsuccessful racers. We slip-slide on the soft, mushy track until we think we'll get stuck, then bump over to the bone-jarring road. Jon puts it together: the sandy bit is the Old Ghan Railway service track, while the corduroy hell-bouncer is the Old Ghan railway line with the sleepers and rails removed. They *both* lead to Alice. Instead of reading a river, I'm reading a road, at MTV speed, winding through— no, that's too poetic—dodging rocks, holes, wrecks, spinifex, mulga, and desert oaks.

We hear on the radio that a woman was shot at her camp overnight, prompting a copter evacuation. Later, we hear they have a winner: Finke to Alice in a winning time of 4:22. Did we hear that right? If I had kept going, I might have had a shot at it (2:15 Finke to Maryvale). We also hear that The Finke is one of the most difficult courses in one of the most remote places in the world. What were we thinking?

On the morning news, they're still covering the Desert Race, although not my coda to it. I thought my tough driving was over, but today we climb up over a precipitous mountain, feeling like the car is going to fall over backwards, only to find: "One way up and down sand dunes, travel slowly and put a flag atop your vehicle." We don't have a flag and settle for a prayer and a honk as we near the crest of every hill.

An enchanting chunk of floating fence—there's a mere six inches of the post left, and it's the bit in the wire—makes a fine slide guitar. The sliding fence post acts as a built-in pitch shifter. We name and perform on The Ewerre Sliding Fence.

Chambers Pillar is made of orange, red, and white layers of sandstone stacking up some 167 feet tall.[65] "A chimney," say the polite whitefella books; "male organ of a supernatural being on earth as a knob-tailed gecko reminding us of the need to observe kinship laws," say the blackfellas. The site is "sacred" to Aboriginal people and "of historical interest" to Europeans. Can't we agree on anything?

The bulletin board points out the local fauna: the southern boobook *(Ninox boobook)*, a small owl with a falsetto double-hoot "boo-book" call; the sandy inland and spinifex-hopping mice *(Muridae)*, which feed the "large, venomous" mulga snakes *(Pseudechis australis)* who often hunt on warm nights; and scorpions *(Urodacus)* ("Check bedding and clothing; they come out and wander the ground at night."). As we walk around, a feral camel heads toward us, having successfully thwarted the Camel Fence designed to protect this historic site from the likes of him.

Hi there, Jon says.

The camel responds by drawing closer still. I didn't really want a camel visitation and retreat some distance.

As many as one million feral camels are estimated to roam Australia's deserts. I know, I know—these ships of the desert are amazing. In a dust storm, they can close their nostrils. They have hair in their ears, a split upper lip for pulling leaves from the prickliest trees and shrubs, and a double row of eyelashes. They store fat in their hump, which insulates them from the sun. They can go without water for 17 days and can lose up to 25 percent of their body weight without ill effect. Their padded leathery feet do less damage than the hoofs of animals such as cattle, sheep, horses, donkeys, and goats, and their habit

---

[65] Until the coming of the railway in the 1920s, Chambers Pillar was a key landmark in the desert on the long overland journey from Adelaide to Alice Springs. John McDouall Stuart first came here in 1860 and named Chambers Pillar in honor of his friend and financial supporter, James Chambers. John Ross led the exploration party for the Overland Telegraph Line constructed in 1870-71. Many of these early travelers left a record of their visit on the soft white sandstone, but the use of graffiti to register your movements through the land is now discouraged.

of browsing on the move means that they do not generally feed intensively in any one area.

All very well, but I still don't want a wild camel in my life. According to the Department of the Environment and Heritage, the main agricultural damage caused by feral camels is to fences, which they lean on and knock down. Say hello to our case in point.

On departing, the road is variously sandy, corrugated, powdery, and slippery; it has chunks broken away, sudden holes, sudden ledges, and broken ridges; it's *in* creekbeds where we barely fit and along riverbeds, over boulders and smaller sharp rocks, on cap rock and through standing water. I'm often choosing the lesser of two or three evils. Jon plays a gate on leaving and gets both sides harmonizing.

Past a broken-down car. I try to imagine the scene. Open the hood. Shoot holes in the doors. Throw on a little gasoline. Throw your lit cigi in. And leave.

Alice is river red gum country.[66] East of Alice, we find the more rare ghost gum *(Eucalyptus papuana)*, found in tropical and arid regions of northern Australia and Papua New Guinea. Its pure white trunk and limbs contrast starkly with the rich red landscape. The largest known from the Eastern MacDonnell Ranges is 108 feet high and estimated at 300 years old. We pay it a visit and a compliment. Then we are hushed by Trephina Gorge's rock library.

Five camels are loose on the road to Ross River, wearing comfy slippers; when one runs, he goes cartoony, his upper lip flip-flopping and hoofs splaying.

Out last day in Alice we visit the Araluen Centre for Arts and Entertainment,[67] then the Alice Springs Reptile Centre, I learn that

---

[66] The river red gum (*Eucalyptus camalduleusis* or *apere* in Arrernte) is an absolute supermarket and pharmacy to the Eastern Arrernte people. The hollows are stocked with meat: galahs, budgerigars, perenties, tasty grubs, and 'til the 1930s, also bushtail possums. *Apere* ash mixed with other ingredients makes a chewing tobacco. Tiny sucking psyillids on the gum leaves produce sweet, white secretions called lerps. Leaves are used to flavor roasting meat. The hollow branches may contain sugarbag. The bark soaked in water makes an eye drop. This liquid is also effective as a wash for sores or swallowed to cure diarrhea. The yellow caps covering buds are used in necklaces, the branches are firewood, and the leaves serve as a tablecloth.

[67] The Centre is situated on a site culturally significant to Aboriginal people, with trees of significance and seven registered sacred sites. Outside, we stop to listen to taped traditional music and encounter Maggie, an artist. "That's a man come down on woman song (laughs). Do you want to buy a painting of it? Only $70."

The Strehlow Research Centre acts as a repository for material relating to Aboriginal peoples, housing the late Ted Strehlow's collection dating from 1932 to 1978. At the Memorial Cemetery next door, we find Olive Pink's grave (characteristically facing opposite from most others) and those of the artist Albert Namatjira and the explorer Harold Bell Lasseter, who died trying to find a lost gold

snakes are basically blind and deaf, and that their tongue receives this information instead. A python is passed around; or rather he passes himself around. I don't enter the love-fest, but do force myself to touch him. He's soft yet muscular. We gawk at thorny devils, frill neck lizards, perentie goannas, and some of the world's most venomous snakes— inland taipans, brown snakes, death adders, and mulga snakes.

Alice to Darwin: the airport scanner doesn't like the rusted barbed wire in our CD box package, but they load us on anyway. Established in 1869, bombed by the Japanese in 1942, ravaged by Cyclone Tracy in 1974, isolated Darwin and the Top End have a large Aboriginal population and a strong Asian presence that goes back to the pearling and gold mining days. Darwin was a multi-culti place before it was in vogue.

We're 12 degrees from the E-quator, I observe.

No, e-QUA-tor, Jon corrects.

Due to this proximity, however one pronounces it, Darwin's year-round weather averages 86 Fahrenheit in the daytime.

But it's no tropical paradise. I pick up a little brochure entitled "Living with Box Jellyfish *(Chironex fleckeri)*." The most venomous animal known to science, it can kill a person in two to three minutes. It has caused 60 deaths in the last hundred years. It is common along the beaches and mangroves around Darwin, as indicated by the warning notice: "October – May, DO NOT SWIM. June – September, Take care swimming. Severe stings have been recorded during this period." So the carefree months are …I can't quite work it out. "Millions of cells, one thousand would fit on the head of a pin …savage pain …muscles of the heart …"

"Crocodylus!" tempts another brochure, referring to a wildlife park with saltwater crocs *(Crocodilus porosus)* as well as lions and tigers and—well, not bears but cassowaries, dingoes, and wallabies.[68]

"Killer Sex Art On Display" reads the tabloid headline about the annual art show by local prison inmates. I head to the exhibition, where a handwritten note on the door warns: "Some works may offend." The

---

reef. There is a special section devoted to the early Afghan cameleers and their descendants, who are buried facing Mecca.

[68] "Salties" live in tidal rivers, fresh water lagoons, and swamps. They need eat only once a week, mainly small crabs and prawns when they are young, and later, larger fish, mammals, and birds, especially magpie geese. A mature croc can exceed 20 feet. They are predators to man; their potential prey is not limited to swimmers but includes anyone near the water's edge. They are known to take horses, buffalos, and cattle, and are cunning, patient, and extremely fast. They lie in wait just below the water with only a pair of eyes discreetly peering above the surface.

"killer" must be the inmate who has drawn a plane dropping bombs on defenseless civilians, a man with a Wall Street briefcase waving to an Aboriginal woman and child, and another work entitled "Which way to turn with no money, time or help," while his "sex art" must refer to "Inferno," a depiction of a prison rape. In the end, I'm only offended by the tabloid headline (and the news bursting through on the car radio that a former staff member of the now Chief Minister had sex with his girlfriend in the Speaker's chair in the debating chamber of The Northern Territory Parliament).

The Darwin Festival has commissioned a musical fence in its Botanical Gardens. I'm taken with the Aboriginal singing and dancing before our act. It's full on and, although totally within the tradition, there are new songs—one is about noisy airplanes. Much contemporary Aboriginal music lacks power, consisting mostly of imported models of country and western, reggae, and more recently hip hop with homemade lyrics dumped hopefully on top. What we witness is convincing, plus the group is egged on by dozens of family relations. Quite an atmosphere. I comment to the stage manager on how they were creating a real festival spirit.

Yeah, but we'll chuck 'em out of the park when they're done; don't want 'em hangin' around 'n' drinkin'.

His terse statement brings us down with a bump.

For three nights we perform on a fence stretched across the front of the stage, then it's off to the Nauiyu Aboriginal Community for one more musical fence. Lock your gas tank, advises the car rental agency rep. Don't know if they sniff it on that reserve, but no use takin' a chance.

Jon tunes in the radio. Big news: the introduced cane toad *(Bufo marinus)* now numbers in the billions.[69] They poison most of the native animals that eat them, including fish, crocs, snakes, goannas, mammals, and birds, and manage to be toxic at every stage from egg to tadpole to

---

[69] An amphibian with warty skin on its back, a high bony ridge over its eyes, circular pupils, and raised poison glands on both shoulders, the cane toad is now a pest in Australia after 102 were introduced to Queensland in 1935 to control cane grubs, the larvae of a beetle pest of sugar cane. Turns out, cane toads didn't jump high enough to reach the upper stalks where the cane grubs hunkered down. The cane toads dined elsewhere, and they bred.

In the face of one of Australia's worst environmental disasters, federal and state governments are looking for a biological control (here we go again) such as a parasite, disease, or virus. The northern quoll *(Dasyurus hallucatus)* is approaching extinction, and some have been enrolled in an island ark program, sent to various islands where the cane toad is still unknown. Even freshwater crocs are alarmingly affected. The Northern Territory has inaugurated a Cane Toad Trap Competition—not how *many* can you trap, but can you *design* a trap?

toadlets to adult toad. Life is complicated, and a number of situations short of actually eating a cane toad (yes, humans will die) come to mind.

The government has advice:

> Cats are too cautious to attack a cane toad. Some pet dogs attempt to eat cane toads, but they can be successfully treated if taken to a vet quickly. They will eat pet food but do not poison food or water by coming into contact with it, but should they drown in your pool or well, the water can become contaminated. The most humane way to kill a cane toad is to freeze it. Plastic shopping bags or something similar are useful to pick up the toad. Double bag it and tie tightly. Place in the freezer overnight. It has also been suggested that toad-proof perimeter fencing would help exclude cane toads from your property. Fine mesh to one metre would probably be adequate as they are poor climbers.

Now that's just fascinating, says Jon. A *toad* fence!

You can fence them, you can freeze them—but don't try to bet on them. Most anything goes in the Northern Territory, but illegal bets on cane toad races in a holiday park were punished.

We drive by a lazy nine-foot python, a goanna, and a bunch of termite mounds, future tennis courts of Australia. In addition to the standard Gothic buttresses, gills of fish, whole shelled walnuts, one of a set of bookends furiously shoving a tree, and stalactite/stalagmite conglomerations, the worst of these anthills masquerades as rotting East German concrete.

When we get to Nauiyu, we're the only whitefellas around; we feel like we've suddenly arrived in a foreign country—and we have. The locals are intent on cheering a number of concurrent football games. There is an immediate sense of community. Small, naked children are on the loose, as are serious, sturdy mid-sized dogs. We look up David Shoobridge, the white town clerk, who loads us in his rig for a drive round.

The small community of Nauiyu is located on the banks of the Daly River, 140 miles southwest of Darwin. Our population normally averages 450 but can swell to over 700 in the Wet season or when ceremony or other special events act as a drawing card. It was begun by the Catholic Church in the mid-1950s as a result of requests by local Aboriginal people for a health center and school, and operated as a Catholic mission until 1988 when the community incorporated.

Our airstrip is the only one capable of night operation for at least 60 miles in any direction. The night tarmac lighting comprises lights powered by solar charged batteries activated by radio signal from approaching aircraft. This signal will turn on the runway lights when the plane is about 12 miles away.

David is a former tour guide and has a ready answer to all my questions.

What's that bird circling overhead?
It's a whistling kite *(Haliastur sphenurus)*. Australia has 34 raptors ...
I see campfires are allowed.
Yes. Well, they'd just do it anyway.
We have a women's shelter where women can go if they feel threatened, and our own power plant, sewage and water treatment plant, carpentry shops, store, school, TV broadcast, auto mechanic ... We're a model community; the government brings people here when they need to show off a success story. The community is at the behest of the Daly River, a major conduit to the sea for various major rivers including the Katherine, the King, the Flora, and others all pouring down from the rugged Arnhemland escarpment.
The annual rising creates a small inland sea for several miles in all directions, leaving Nauiyu an island community. Five to six weeks a year, we are only accessible by boat. The community owns a property on high ground to store the cars.
During the '98 floods, we evacuated the whole place in 24 hours. The base of all buildings is above all but the most extreme flood situations. The annual inundation also necessitates constant irrigation of all grounds in the Dry to ensure a grass cover so floodwaters do not damage by eroding topsoil.
Here's the men's lagoon, and over there's the women's, their dreaming place. During the floods, this is where the crocs cross. I keep trying to get a CROCS CROSS HERE sign. It'd be just great for tourism, but the shop always has an excuse— like there's no international sign for crocs. They don't get it.
Have people been attacked by crocs here?
One guy tried to cross the river five years ago and didn't make it. We found his half-eaten body several days later. It wasn't a pretty sight.

We arrive at the river, still in a partial stage of flood, and watch a vehicle very carefully making its way through deep water. The water is a fence. The crocs potentially lurking in the water are its guardians. You wouldn't open the door and climb out if things went wrong.

Twilight approaches, and campfires begin to light up along the river's banks. We drive on.

About 3500 people live in various outposts across the river here. They're cut off for five months of the year. Aboriginal people have been gathering at this crossing, trading and making ceremonies, for millennia. It's been bounteous enough to allow people who lived more or less hand to mouth to gather in a large group. They arrived from distant places, speaking a multitude of tongues.

Nauiyu (pronounced Now-You or Nigh-You) is 10 clan groups; the main one, and the name of the main language, is Milikmilik. Nauiyu Nambiyu is the real name, which means "together" or "here we are together." In speeches, first we always acknowledge the traditional owners (in cities, they try to invite one to do the welcoming). It implies tolerance on our part, and for the invitee, I'm a guest so I can't muck up. Our main language is English, and then Creole (a mix of a number) plus pidgin. It's disrespectful to speak in pidgin unless you know the person well.[70]

That's Jimmy Numbatu, N-U-M-B-A-T-U (we don't know who Number One was). He's one of our seven councilors. He's illiterate. I put an agenda out for the meeting. He may be reading it upside down, or we'll be three subjects down when something occurs to him, so we back up.

Miriam, one of our most respected elders and nationally known as an educator, is known also as Anga. Our councilors were up at the Gold Coast. Miriam's room was on the fourteenth floor. Jimmy Numbatu decided to look for her. He was knocking on every door on every floor and was half the way through—"Do you know Anga?" he was asking. The switchboard lit up from all the intimidated guests.

Every three months we go around and check all the stoves. Jimmy couldn't understand why his smoked. If you just took that wallaby leg out, I told him. Another time he complained of his stove, "It shoot me!" It turns out he was hosing it out. Then there was the time he complained that his phone didn't work, and the cord was hanging by its side.

---

[70] On the radio we often hear about the Aboriginal "problem." The other day we heard a guy complaining that Aborigines speak English badly, making for misunderstandings. Many Aborigines speak two to four languages, with English placed perhaps number three on their list; the average whitefella can only manage English—sort of.

Sometimes our world confuses him, I see, but not nearly as much as his world does me. Send me out hunting. Watch me die in week numba-one.

There were no fat people when they lived on bush tucker, and it's got all their vitamins in there. My wife was the nurse here when we first came. She died four years ago of cancer. The women asked if I would like a burial shroud. I said yes, that she liked turtles. So overnight 40 women made the shroud. We buried it with her.

We arrive at the pub a mile off the community's property. I wonder if the word "pub" will be extended to a dry restaurant—no, beer and wine are in evidence. We order a glass of Château Cardboard and a meal. We sit below a metal roof, rain splatting, fans spinning, wind coming through the walls, the odd dog barking outside, while a Neil Diamond CD does its best to intrude on our conversation.

Mozzies, anyone? [The barman is making the rounds, passing around a spray can of mosquito repellent.]

Driving home in the dark, David takes a detour.

See that? It's reflecting tape tied to Coke cans. We put it high up in the trees to mark the way for boats during the Wet when we don't have cars. Everything looks different then, especially if you've had a drinking session at the pub

We pass a few folks staggering along the dark road for which things look different tonight. Police with flashlights are checking all cars in both directions to stop booze and boozers from entering Nauiyu.

The next morning we poke around town. I survey the store, which displays life's essentials and not much more: axes, traps, lanterns, a sleeping bag known as a Ghan Swag, dome tents, bright cotton print dresses, flashlights, VCRs, TVs, candles, insect repellent, and various groceries like 10 kilos of flour in a red plastic tub. The fruit-and-veg section is wilted and uninspiring. A bulletin board displays a photo of huge barramundi half-eaten by a croc and a clipping entitled "Monster Croc Fights 3 Hour Landing."

Molly Yawalminy is in charge of leaves at Nauiyu, along with her sister, Maureen. They rake the leaves, then scoop them up with their hands in an impossibly doubled over position while maintaining straight knees.

This make me healthy, we do leaves, not like the young girls.

Molly poses regally with her rake as her scepter. Her long, flowing hair is grey, brown, and black, and each of her white teeth has a brown patch squarely on it. There's a great distance between the completion of her nose and the beginning of her upper lip. It's extreme enough to make her a sensation as a model. The nobility of her face draws you in—back generations and generations. She's thin with spindly legs, a chest made flat by breasts that hang, and a slight bulge at her stomach. Her husband was very powerful. She had her first child when she was 14. She has four artist daughters and one son.

Maureen, she drinks sometime, she get drunk and sing song, "I'm drunk" [laughs]. My son no good, at pub, he drinks.

Molly was born in 1944. She came as a child from her homeland to work on one of the farms close to Daly River. She is still very much a traditional person, a great hunter and fisherwoman, and will walk for miles gathering food or plants for weaving.

Her husband was strictly a man of code, reports one of her sons-in-law, Much older than her. He used to knock off people when hunting if they got out of line, once fed a guy to crocs, axing him bit by bit.

Jon spends some time with Miriam-Rose Ungunmerr-Baumann, the school principal, discussing matters of education and culture—storytelling, ceremonies, dreaming, and music making. The school teaches bilingually, juggling up to 10 Aboriginal languages. They cover all the normal subjects plus skills like finding turtle eggs in a billabong (a pool of water) with your toes while keeping watch for crocs.

According to Miriam, the transition to a different lifestyle has been easier for the women, who are more open and outgoing, responsible and reliable. Miriam was the first painter in Nauiyu but was initially forbidden by the men to paint. She carefully and delicately walked the men through her case and after a time succeeded. Nauiyu now has a thriving community of painters, including about half the women and a handful of men. Their subject matter is invariably the Dreaming, country, and seasons. Collectors are already arriving from Darwin for the highlight of this year's arts festival, the annual auction of paintings.

Captain Cook was puzzled by the apparent indifference of the Aboriginal peoples of Australia toward the presence of his men and his ship, a reaction he received nowhere else in his voyages. Even more surprising was the Aboriginal indifference to gifts and to barter.[71]

From what I have said of the Natives of New-Holland they may appear to some to be the most wretched people upon Earth, but in

---

[71] Thomas, Nicholas (2003) *Discoveries: The Voyages of Captain Cook*, London: Penguin Books, 128.

reality they are far more happy than we Europeans; being wholly unacquainted not only with the superfluous but the necessary Conveniencies so much sought after in Europe, they are happy in not knowing the use of them. They live in a Tranquillity which is not disturb'd by the Inequality of Condition: The Earth and sea of their own accord furnished them with all things necessary for life, they covet not Magnificent Houses, Houshold-stuff & etc., they live in a warm and fine Climate and enjoy a very wholesome Air, so that they have very little need of Clothing and this they seem to be fully sencible of, for many to whome we gave Cloth & etc. to, left it carelessly upon the Sea beach and in the woods as a thing they had no manner of use for. In short they seem'd to set no value on any thing we gave them, nor would they ever part with any thing of their own for any one article we could offer them; this in my opinion argues that they think themselves provided with all the necessarys of Life and that they have no superfluities.

The longest continual cultural history in the world (variously estimated at 50,000 to 120,000 years old, in contrast with, say, the Old Testament, which describes events up to 6000 years ago) endured two ice ages and all the dramatic changes in between, only to be nearly obliterated in just a few hundred years by white Europeans.[72]

The Aboriginal sense of culture was linked to their profound ceremonial life and never intended to be a product for popular consumption. Theirs was a performative tradition; they more often *did* things than *made* things. Aboriginal painting has managed to bridge this gap, but music …I try to imagine false fronts to secret songs, but songs get lost when they are about increase, healing, and education—lost when replaced by stores, hospitals, and schools, lost when about traveling through country when fences block that travel.

We watch a traditional dance. The young men dancing in scarlet "diapers" are embarrassed and without power. They begin in two huddles, accompanied by old men on didgeridoo and clap-sticks, but the huddle with power belongs across the field to the football teams. Seventeen communities are fielding teams. They believe in what they're doing.

---

[72] Germaine Greer (2003) suggests that white Australians will never truly inhabit the land until they get in touch with their Aboriginality, while Paul Carter proposes that mere interest in their traditional wisdom will never be enough. We must swap something, something other than the latest scientific or high-tech wonders. "We cannot expect those across the table to furnish us with these concepts; we need to locate them within the neglected counter-traditions of our own culture," argues Carter (1996, *The Lie of the Land*, London: Faber and Faber, London: 365.)

Of course, no one has yet invited anyone to the table, but I find it an enchanting concept that we might trade something. Could that something be wisdom rather than knowledge? What wisdom of ours would be worth a trade? Might poems, music, and other art be a starting point?

I'm sitting on the bank watching one of the tournament games. It's a magic game and, although invented by whites, the Aborigines have made it their own. It's full of hard running, sudden weaving, quick changes of tempo, strategic positioning, and athletic jumping—hunting skills, you might say. At any moment I expect a boomerang to go whizzing past, defying gravity, and not a football.

The game's not going well for the local team judging by the screams from the teenage fans. One of the boys goes down; one of those fine fleeting legs has been broken. This will be the second medevac by plane in four hours.

Suddenly, Jimmy Numbalu is striding around the field shouting at the top of his voice. He stops just in front of me and launches into a diatribe, looking straight into my eyes. I understand nothing, of course. My neighbor explains that Jimmy Numbatu is pointing out to me how the opposition team is always cheating and that every time they come here one of their boys get hurt. I'm relieved it wasn't me that he was having a go at.

Curious Aboriginal children flock to us as we design the where and how of our musical fence. Jon unpacks his bass bow.

He's gonna use that stick to play the fence, says David.

You *liar* one, Kirin retorts.

The musical fence is three treated posts and several lengths of piano wire. The kids hang around the edges, just waiting to give the stretched wire a tug. Other than having to guard our instrument, it's all going well—but then several women approach Jon with a concern.

You can't play music with these. Them posts dead ones. We gotta bring 'em back to life. We paint 'em up.

Really? Yes, please.

Bernadette Tjingiling, Marita Sambono-Diyini, and Christina Yambeing have never painted together before. Sharing a pie plate of yellow, red, green, blue, white, black, and magenta acrylics, they sit on the ground around a post and communally cover one at a time. The first has turtles, fish, snakes, and other animals climbing a pale blue post. The second features the bush yam with soft brushwork. The third is cram-full of bright flowers and dragonflies. It's the time of year that dragonflies come out; they herald the beginning of the Dry, although they are late this year due to the weather.

There's magic with 'em, we're told.

The three women work late into the night. The next day, after we perform on the fence, the kids can hardly wait to give it a good thrashing; then the painted posts get auctioned off along with the year's best crop of paintings. Every available space on the vibrant posts celebrates some living thing.

It sets me reflecting on how it might have been here when every feature of the landscape was woven into song. This land was a giant travel book …a history book …a natural science book. The great Australian songbook stretched back and forward in time. And then it snapped.

Fence says, Backward/forward …inside/outside …mine/yours …high art/low art …beginning/end.

postscript

Jon's on tour in Israel. I call to tell him the fence book's finished.

What are you up to?

Well, this filmmaker's picking me up in an hour. There're some Israeli activists and some Palestinian activists who'll join us. We're driving to the security fence in Ramallah …

further reading

Blackburn, Julia (1994) *Daisy Bates in the Desert: A Woman's Life Among the Aborigines*, New York: Pantheon.

Burchett, George and Shimmin, Nick, Eds. (2005) *Memoirs of a Rebel Journalist: The Autobiography of Wilfred Burchett*, Sydney: University of New South Wales Press.

Chatwin, Bruce (1987) *The Songlines*, New York: Penguin Books.

Clendinnen, Inga (2003) *Dancing with Strangers*, Melbourne: Text Publishing.

Dark, Eleanor (1941/1960) *The Timeless Land*, London: Collins.

Diamond, Jared (1998) *Guns, Germs and Steel: A Short History of Everybody for the Last 13,000 Years*, London: Vintage.

Flanagan, Richard (2001) *Gould's Book of Fish*, Sydney: Picador.

Flannery, Tim (1994) *The Future Eaters*, Sydney: Reed New Holland.

Flannery, Tim (1998) *The Explorers*, Melbourne: Text Publishing.

Flannery, Tim (2004) *Country*, Melbourne: Text Publishing.

Harney, W.E. (1943) *Taboo*, Sydney: Australasian Publishing Co..

Hay, Ashley (2002) *Gum: The Story of Eucalypts and Their Champions*, Sydney: Duffy & Snellgrove.

Herbert, Xavier (1938/1996) *Capricornia*, Sydney: Angus and Robertson.

Hill, Barry (2002) *Broken Song: T.G.H. Strehlow and Aboriginal Possession*, Sydney: Knopf.

Hough, Richard (1994) *Captain James Cook*, London: Coronet Books.

Hughes, Robert (1986/1996) *The Fatal Shore*, London: The Harvil Press.

Krell, Alan (2002) *The Devil's Rope*, London: Reaktion Books.

Lindsay, Joan (1967/1998) *Picnic at Hanging Rock*, London: Vintage.

Madigan, Cecil (1946/2001) *Crossing the Dead Heart*, Marleston, South
     Australia: J.B. Books.

Marcus, Julie (2001) *The Indomitable Miss Pink: A Life in Anthropology*,
     Sydney: University of New South Wales Press.

Moorehead, Alan (1953) *Rum Jungle*, London: Hamish Hamilton.

Murgatroyd, Sarah (2002) *The Dig Tree: The Story of Burke and Wills*,
     Melbourne: Text Publishing.

Pilkington, Doris and Garimara, Nugi (1996) *Rabbit-Proof Fence*, St.
     Lucia, Queensland: University of Queensland Press.

Scott, Kim (1999) *Benang*, North Freemantle, Western Australia:
     Freemantle Arts Centre Press.

Toft, Klaus (2002) *The Navigators: The Great Race Between Matthew
     Flinders and Nicolas Baudin for the North-South Passage through
     Australia*, Sydney: Duffy & Snellgrove.

www.abc.net.au/arts/adlib

www.hollistaylor.com

www.jonroseweb.com

243